D0809730

Prefactoring

Extreme Abstraction • Extreme Separation • Extreme Readability

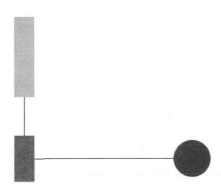

Ken Pugh

O'REILLY®

Beijing • Cambridge • Farnham • Köln • Paris • Sebastopol • Taipei • Tokyo

Prefactoring
Extreme Abstraction, Extreme Separation, Extreme Readability
by Ken Pugh

Published by O'Reilly Media, Inc.
1005 Gravenstein Highway North
Sebastopol, CA 95472.

O'Reilly books may be purchased for educational, business, or sales promotional
use. Online editions are also available for most titles (*safari.oreilly.com*). For more
information, contact our corporate/institutional sales department: (800) 998-9938
or *corporate@oreilly.com*.

Editor:	Jonathan Gennick
Production Editor:	Sarah Sherman
Cover Designer:	MendeDesign
Interior Designer:	Marcia Friedman
Creative Director:	Michele Wetherbee
Printing History:	September 2005: First Edition.

 This book uses RepKover™, a durable
and flexible lay-flat binding.
ISBN: 0-596-00874-0
[M]

This book is dedicated to Denny Bunn, a
longtime friend, teacher, and Ironman. He
lost his last race against cancer.

TABLE OF CONTENTS

	PREFACE	ix
1	INTRODUCTION TO PREFACTORING	1
	What Is Prefactoring?	1
	The Three Extremes	2
	The Guidelines Explored	3
	The Context for This Book	5
2	THE SYSTEM IN SO MANY WORDS	7
	Meet Sam	7
	Reinvention Avoidance	11
	What's in a Name?	11
	Splitters Versus Lumpers	13
	Clumping	15
	Abstracting	16
	Prototypes Are Worth a Thousand Words	20
3	GENERAL DEVELOPMENT ISSUES	23
	Start with the Big Picture	23
	Interface Contracts	24
	Validation	26
	Code Communicates	27
	Consistency Is Simplicity	31
	A Prefactoring Attitude	32
	Don't Repeat Yourself	33
	Documentation of Assumptions and Decisions	34
	Dealing with Deviations and Errors	34
	Speeding	39
	The Spreadsheet Conundrum	41
	Tools Are Tools—Use Them Wisely	43
4	GETTING THE BIG PICTURE	45
	The Rest of the Story	45
	Process	46
	The Initial Design	48
	Global Planning, Local Designing	51
	Testing Functionality	52
	Testing Quality	56
	Security	57

5	GOT CLASS?	59
	Categories and Classes	59
	Declaration Versus Execution	62
	Appropriate Inheritance	63
	Communicate with Text	65
	More Than One	67

6	A FEW WORDS ON CLASSES	69
	Honor the Class Maxims	69
	Three Laws of Objects	71
	Need Determines Class	73
	Polymorphism	75
	One Little Job	78
	Policy Versus Implementation	80
	Extreme Naming	81
	Overloading Functions	81

7	GETTING THERE	83
	Where We Are	83
	Separating Concerns	86
	Migrating to the New System	91

8	THE FIRST RELEASE	95
	The Proof Is in the Pudding	95
	Retrospective Time	96
	The System as It Stands Now	97
	Operations Interface	97
	Abstract Data Types	98
	Configuration	98
	Testing	98
	Dealing with Deviations and Errors	101
	A Little Prefactoring	102
	The First Released Iteration	103
	Sometimes Practice Does Not Match Theory	103
	The Rest of the Classes	106

9	ASSOCIATIONS AND STATES	107
	Sam's New Requirement	107
	Who's in Charge?	108
	The State of an Object	110

10	INTERFACES AND ADAPTATION	115
	The Catalog Search Use Case	115
	Designing the Interface	117
	Interface Development	119
	Interface Testing	120
	Interface Splitting	121
	Something Working	122

11	ZIP CODES AND INTERFACES	125
	Adaptation	125
	Pass the Buck	129
	Unwritten Code	130
	Indirection	132
	Logging	135
	Paradigm Mismatch	136
12	MORE REPORTS	137
	Fancy Reports	137
	Change Happens	139
	Exports	142
13	INVOICES, CREDIT CARDS, AND DISCOUNTS	145
	The Next Step	145
	The Language of the Client	149
	Security and Privacy	152
14	SAM IS EXPANDING	155
	The Second Store	155
	A New Development	157
	The Third Store	159
	Goodbye Sam	162
	Generality	162
15	A PRINTSERVER EXAMPLE	163
	Introduction	163
	The System	164
	The Message	165
	Testing	170
	Logging	171
	Still More Separation	172
	Epilogue	173
16	ANTISPAM EXAMPLE	175
	The Context	175
	Spam Checking	179
	The ReceivingMailServer	179
	ReceivedMailExaminer	186
	The Full Flow	191
17	EPILOGUE	193
A	GUIDELINES AND PRINCIPLES	195
B	SOURCE CODE	203
	INDEX	215

Preface

THE ART OF PREFACTORING APPLIES TO NEW PROJECTS THE INSIGHTS INTO DEVELOPING SOFTWARE YOU HAVE GLEANED FROM YOUR EXPERIENCE, as well as the experience of others, in developing software to new projects. The name of this book plays upon the term *refactoring*, popularized in Martin Fowler's book, *Refactoring: Improving the Design of Existing Code* (Addison-Wesley Professional, 1999). Refactoring is the practice of altering code to improve its internal structure without changing its external behavior.

This book delineates prefactoring guidelines in design, code, and testing. Applying the guidelines in this book does not guarantee that you will never need to refactor your design or code. However, you might decrease the amount of refactoring that is required.

Many of these guidelines are derived from the experiences of numerous developers over several years. Analyzing how code might have been initially developed to alleviate the need for refactoring produced other guidelines. Like Extreme Programming, some of the guidelines might seem extreme. Many revolve around the concepts of Extreme Abstraction, Extreme Separation of Concerns, and Extreme Readability.

Some guidelines contain references to *design patterns*. Design patterns are standard solutions to common problems in software design. The concept of software design patterns was popularized in *Design Patterns: Elements of Reusable Object-Oriented Software* by Erich

Gamma, Richard Helm, Ralph Johnson, and John Vlissides (Addison-Wesley Professional, 1995). That book discusses patterns of objects and classes that form the basis for the solutions to many common problems.*

A few of the guidelines actually might be called design patterns in pattern circles. According to *Design Patterns*, "Some people's patterns are another's design principle." In this book, I call them guidelines, because they include concepts that reoccur in numerous situations, not just as design patterns. These guidelines have not been put into a pattern format, since they are just suggested practices to follow when developing a program.

During my 35-year career, I have worked with computer languages ranging from IBM 360 assembler to C, C++, Java™, C#, HTML, and XML. I have also worked with frameworks including J2EE, Struts, and MFC. Along the way, I have had the opportunity to meet and interact with hundreds of developers. These developers have provided me with experiences related to many of the guidelines I discuss in this book.

During that same time, I have had the opportunity to learn from numerous well-known practitioners in the software development field. This book coalesces many of the themes they discussed in their writings, talks, and conversations with the practices I developed during my career. These people include Scott Ambler, Chuck Allison, James Bach, Kent Beck, Grady Booch, Alister Cockburn, Larry Constantine, Jim Coplien, Ward Cunningham, Gary Evans, Bruce Eckel, Martin Fowler, James Grenning, Payson Hall, Allen Holub, Andy Hunt, Jason Hunter, Eric Jackson, Ivar Jacobsen, Ron Jeffries, Cem Kaner, Joshua Kerievsky, Robert Martin, Bret Pettichord, P. J. Plauger, James Rumbaugh, Dan Saks, Jim Short, Joel Spolsky, Bjarne Stroustrup, Dave Thomas, Bill Venner, Gerry Weinberg, Karl Wiegers, and Rebecca Wirfs-Brock.

I have attempted to attribute the original proponent of each guideline I cover in the book; however, the source of many of the guidelines is unclear. If you know who originated any of the unattributed guidelines, please let me know. Some of them are listed in the book *201 Principles of Software Development* by Alan M. Davis (McGraw-Hill, 1995), in the book *Code Complete, Second Edition* by Steve McConnell (Microsoft Press, 2004), and on the Web at *http://c2.com/cgi/wiki*.

Enumerating guidelines without a context for them is like talking about curling without referring to hair or ice. Therefore, in this book, I present the guidelines in the context of the development of a CD rental system. To my knowledge, such a store does not exist. The video store example in Martin Fowler's refactoring book inspired this choice.

I love outdoor recreation. In particular, I enjoy windsurfing, backpacking, snowboarding, and biking. *Bitter Java* by Bruce A. Tate (Manning, 2002) gave me the idea to use sports analogies when describing programming. Scattered throughout the book are a few outdoor stories relevant to the topic under discussion.

---

* See *Head First Design Patterns* by Elisabeth Freeman, Eric Freeman, Bert Bates, and Kathy Sierra (O'Reilly, 2004) for another look at patterns.

Everybody Is Different

Different people view things slightly differently. The paper clip that shows up in a common word processor can be annoying or entertaining. A seemingly great idea for a user interface can turn out to be not so great since the system's users might have vastly different viewpoints than the system's developers.

People look at problems and solutions differently. I prefer to get an overview of a solution so that I can appreciate how the problem has been addressed. Examining a rough diagram of the major classes and a few sequence diagrams provides me information more quickly than wading through code.

Not everyone feels the way I do. Some people prefer to read the code. Viewing a class diagram provides no benefit to them. It is just noise. Neither approach is necessarily better or worse than the other is. The only time you will run into trouble is if you do not appreciate both approaches when you encounter a person who does it the other way.

Likewise, developers have a spectrum of preferences that run the gamut from strongly typed languages to nontyped languages and from big design up front to no design up front. Those on one end of the spectrum should appreciate the tradeoffs and context issues of those on the other end.

In addition, the guidelines presented in this book might be radically different from your current development paradigm. Comparing them to your own guidelines can help you to understand the tradeoffs made in your paradigm and may spur changes in your guidelines.

The Design Example

This book describes the development of a system that incorporates many features of some of the systems that have been created in the past. The experience of creating those systems forms some of the guidelines for developing new systems. Developers are not perfect. We cannot read our client's mind, and his mind might change. The development story outlined in this book shows where decisions were made that had unanticipated ramifications.

This book presents one of many possible designs that can solve your clients' requirements. There is no absolute measurement method for evaluating the "goodness" of a design. There are obviously good designs and bad designs, but there are many gray areas as well. Counting the number of methods, lines of code, or number of classes seems like a very objective way of measuring, but often the resulting number is not necessarily meaningful, except for the extremes. I measure designs with a gut feeling. This parallels the "code smells" of refactoring. A system's overall design gives me a gut feeling ranging from "warm tummy" to "upset stomach."

Audience

This book will appeal to readers who understand the basic concepts of object-oriented design. It gives them suggested guidelines to create more readable and maintainable code.

The book assumes that the reader has some familiarity with the basic Unified Modeling Language (UML) diagrams (class, sequence, and state), as well as some knowledge of an object-oriented language, such as Java, C++, C#, Ruby, or Python.

Contents of This Book

This book in organized into 17 chapters. The organization of the chapters follows the development of the sample system. It diverts in Chapter 3 to discuss general development issues and in Chapter 6 to examine object-oriented design. The sample system development ends in Chapter 14. Chapter 15 describes a real-life system designed using prefactoring guidelines, and Chapter 16 talks about the design of an antispam system.

Here is a detailed description of the chapter contents:

Chapter 1, *Introduction to Prefactoring*
  This is an introduction to the facets of prefactoring.

Chapter 2, *The System in So Many Words*
  We meet Sam, the client, to get an overall view of the desired system. We discuss creating a shared vocabulary for communication, and we use some extreme abstraction.

Chapter 3, *General Development Issues*
  We look at some general issues in developing a system. This includes the big picture, interface contracts, communicating with code, simplicity, dealing with errors, and the spreadsheet conundrum.

Chapter 4, *Getting the Big Picture*
  We continue talking with Sam to get a clearer understanding of the overall requirements—the big picture. Then we start to create a design for a system.

Chapter 5, *Got Class?*
  We take our system outline and develop the implementation classes. We explore how single or multiple classes can represent concepts.

Chapter 6, *A Few Words on Classes*
  We look at object-oriented design in general. The class maxims of cohesion and coupling are reviewed, along with the three laws of objects. Polymorphic behavior is demonstrated with both inheritance and interfaces.

Chapter 7, *Getting There*
  We address using separation of concerns to create reports. Planning for migration brings up some additional design issues.

Chapter 8, *The First Release*

We perform a retrospective on how well our design approach worked. We explore issues that were addressed during development and the additional classes that were created during coding.

Chapter 9, *Associations and States*

Sam presents us with new requirements. We explore using association classes in the system to implement the requirements. We examine how the state of objects in the system can be represented.

Chapter 10, *Interfaces and Adaptation*

We create interfaces for Sam's catalog-search use case. We explore how to test these interfaces and how to adapt implementations to meet these interfaces.

Chapter 11, *Zip Codes and Interfaces*

Sam asks that the system keeps track of customer addresses. We determine how to verify the Zip Codes in addresses using interfaces.

Chapter 12, *More Reports*

Sam decides he needs fancier reports and different reports. We implement his requests using some of the guidelines already introduced.

Chapter 13, *Invoices, Credit Cards, and Discounts*

Sam decides it is time to add the ability to invoice customers and charge those invoices to credit cards. We explore interfaces to external credit card processors. We add computation of customer discounts in terms that Sam can understand.

Chapter 14, *Sam Is Expanding*

Sam is expanding his operations. He is opening more stores, both locally and globally. His store is being featured on the Web. We use many of the previously presented guidelines to develop our approach to this expansion.

Chapter 15, *A Printserver Example*

This chapter presents a case study involving a real-world system used by libraries to charge for printouts of documents from personal computers. This chapter delineates where guidelines were employed.

Chapter 16, *Antispam Example*

This chapter examines how email is transmitted and received. It presents a proposed design for an email receiver and spam detector.

Chapter 17, *Epilogue*

We wrap up with some closing thoughts.

The Cover

The cover picture is a 1/72 scale model of an Azur NAA-57 airplane. The NAA-57 was based on the North American T-6 Texan, which was licensed to European manufacturers. Jeremy Mende of MendeDesign designed the cover. His design choice is appropriate to my hobbies. I am a private pilot, although I have not flown much in recent years, except for an expedition to Alaska a few years back.

Conventions Used in This Book

Pseudocode examples explain many of the guidelines in a concrete manner. I try to make the examples as generic as possible, as this is not a language guide. The code uses a combination of conventions from a number of languages. Class names use uppercase separation (e.g., `ClassName`). Attributes, variables, and method names use lowercase with underscores (e.g., `method_name( )`), à la the C++ Standard Template Library and Python.

For classes for which you must access an object's attributes, I show assignment to and from the attributes, as if they were properties of Eiffel or C#. In other languages or with other conventions, you probably will use get and set methods.

The following typographical conventions are used in this book:

Italic

Indicates new terms, URLs, email addresses, filenames, file extensions, pathnames, directories, and Unix utilities.

`Constant width`

Indicates commands, options, switches, variables, attributes, keys, functions, types, classes, namespaces, methods, modules, properties, parameters, values, objects, events, event handlers, XML tags, HTML tags, macros, the contents of files, and the output from commands. It also indicates class outlines in pseudocode.

User input

Shows user input or message transactions.

Boldface

Indicates states or enumerated values.

> NOTE
>
> This design element signifies a tip, suggestion, or general note.

This icon identifies a guideline.

Using Code Examples

This book is here to help you get your job done. In general, you may use the code in this book in your programs and documentation. You do not need to contact us for permission unless you are reproducing a significant portion of the code. For example, writing a program that uses several chunks of code from this book does not require permission. Selling or distributing a CD-ROM of examples from O'Reilly books does require permission. Answering a question by citing this book and quoting example code does not require permission. Incorporating a significant amount of example code from this book into your product's documentation does require permission.

We appreciate, but do not require, attribution. An attribution usually includes the title, author, publisher, and ISBN. For example: *"Prefactoring* by Ken Pugh. Copyright 2005 O'Reilly Media, Inc., 0-596-00874-0."

If you feel your use of code examples falls outside fair use or the permission given here, feel free to contact us at *permissions@oreilly.com*.

Comments and Questions

Please address comments and questions concerning this book to the publisher:

O'Reilly Media, Inc.
1005 Gravenstein Highway North
Sebastopol, CA 95472
(800) 998-9938 (in the United States or Canada)
(707) 829-0515 (international or local)
(707) 829-0104 (fax)

We have a web page for this book, where we list errata, examples, and any additional information. You can access this page at:

http://www.oreilly.com/catalog/prefactoring

To comment or ask technical questions about this book, send email to:

bookquestions@oreilly.com

For more information about our books, conferences, Resource Centers, and the O'Reilly Network, see our web site at:

http://www.oreilly.com

Safari Enabled

 When you see a Safari® Enabled icon on the cover of your favorite technology book, that means the book is available online through the O'Reilly Network Safari Bookshelf.

Safari offers a solution that's better than e-books. It's a virtual library that lets you easily search thousands of top technology books, cut and paste code samples, download chapters, and find quick answers when you need the most accurate, current information. Try it for free at *http://safari.oreilly.com*.

Acknowledgments

I thank my wife, Leslie Killeen, for putting up with my talking about this book for hours on end. She also read my drafts and suggested changes. She is a weaver, not a programmer, so the material was not in her field. For that reason, I doubly thank her.

I appreciate Jim Batterson, Pam Brown, Eric M. Burke, Gary K. Evans, Michael Green, Jason Hunter, Mark Kozel, Nitin Narayan, Graham Oakes, David Rasch, Ronald E. Thompson III, and many others, for reviewing the book and making numerous suggestions. I thank Rob Walsh, the co-founder of EnvisionWare, for permission to use his system as an example in Chapter 15. I thank John R Levine and Pete McNeil for reviewing Chapter 16. I thank Lisa Pulignani and McCabe and Associates for providing analysis reports on the sample program.

I thank Scott Ambler, Larry Constantine, Ken Estes, Danny Faught, Don Gray, Payson Hall, Gary McGraw, Ken Ritchie, Paul Strack, Dan Saks, and many others for attribution of many of the guidelines. I thank Gerry Weinberg for his suggestions.

Finally, I thank Jonathan Gennick, my editor at O'Reilly, Audrey Doyle, my copyeditor, and Sarah Sherman, my production editor, for helping me to produce this book.

CHAPTER ONE

Introduction to Prefactoring

WE START WITH AN INTRODUCTION TO THE FACETS OF PREFACTORING AND DISCUSS HOW IT RELATES TO ITS NAMESAKE, REFACTORING. We explain that what you get out of prefactoring depends upon your point of view and the context in which you develop. We introduce guidelines that represent suggestions of good practices appropriate to the development context.

What Is Prefactoring?

Refactoring is the practice of altering code to improve its internal structure without changing its external behavior. *Prefactoring* uses the insights you have gleaned from your experience, as well as the experience of others, in developing software. The expertise gained in refactoring is part of that experience.

I have condensed my ideas and the ideas I have heard from many developers over many years into the prefactoring guidelines we will explore in this book. Take them as a starting point to developing your own guidelines. Many guidelines relate to basic design principles, but they are expressed in different fashions. Other guidelines revolve around the concepts of Extreme Abstraction, Extreme Separation, and Extreme Readability. I will talk about those concepts later in this chapter.

Another facet of prefactoring is a concentration on interfaces. By considering interfaces—what components can do for you, instead of how they work—you further the goal of abstraction. Refactoring is also concerned with interfaces; the ones for which you do not change the external behavior, while you are altering the internal implementation.

Applying the guidelines in this book does not guarantee that you will never need to refactor your design or code. You might decrease the amount of refactoring that is required. Can you foresee everything? No. Are the decisions you make today final? No. It is practically impossible to think of everything or know everything in the beginning of a project. You will learn more things as a project goes along. However, you can use your experience and the experiences of others to guide you in a certain direction. You can make decisions today that might minimize changes tomorrow.

The Three Extremes

Abstraction, separation of concerns, and readability underlie many of the guidelines. These notions parallel some of the ideas in Extreme Programming. If abstraction is good, Extreme Abstraction is better; if separation of concerns is good, Extreme Separation is better; and if readability is good, Extreme Readability is better. Many of the guidelines present an extreme position, so you can differentiate it from your current practices. You might wind up finding your own in-between position that balances the tradeoffs in a manner appropriate to your situation.

Abstraction

Abstraction is one of the key principles in an object-oriented system. You specify operations without specifying the details of how those operations will be implemented—the "what" and not the "how." On one level, a system can be described with enough abstraction that either a manual, computer-aided, or automated procedure could implement it. However, sometimes a system is described so abstractly that you cannot imagine how it will operate until you can see a concrete realization, such as a prototype.

The flow of this book parallels abstraction. Operations and interfaces are stated in a language-insensitive manner, using only those facets such as classes, interfaces, and exceptions that are common to all object-oriented languages. Pseudocode is used to present the sequence and logic that an implementation might encompass. To demonstrate that the abstractions can become reality, code is shown after the interfaces have been defined on an abstract level.

As an example of Extreme Abstraction, one guideline suggests that concepts never be described with primitives (e.g., int or double).

Separation of Concerns

Separation of concerns deals with splitting responsibilities between different classes, different methods, and different variables. As we will see in the sample system, a typical class is the Customer class. One can assign to this class any method that deals with the Customer class.

Alternatively, one can create several classes that deal with the customer. These classes could include a `CustomerData` class for just holding the data; a `CustomerPersistence` class responsible for making the data persistent; a `CustomerGUIDisplay` class containing the widgets for displaying and inputting a `Customer` from a graphical user interface (GUI); a `CustomerImportExport` class that reads and writes textual representations of the data; a `CustomerModel` class that contains the behavior; and a `CustomerBusinessRule` class that contains the alterable rules for that behavior.

By separating a class into multiple classes, you allow for changes in one of the classes not to affect the other classes. If you change the GUI, for example, you do not have to change the business rules class. You might not necessarily want to split every one of your classes into as many classes as we do in the example system, but at least you should recognize that this is a possibility.

Readability

Code communicates to the computer and to the reader. Code should be written in a style that is understandable to all developers. The closer that code is to the requirements statement, the easier it is to match those requirements. As an example of Extreme Readability, one guideline suggests that your client or customer be able to read your code.

The Guidelines Explored

Our goal as developers is to make understandable, readable, and maintainable code. The guidelines in this book are designed to help you reach this goal. The guidelines presented in this book do not represent best practices. "Best" can be determined only in the context in which you are currently developing a system. However, the guidelines do represent suggestions for creating good practices appropriate to your context.

EXCEPTIONAL GUIDELINE

There are exceptions to every guideline, except this one.

Many of the guidelines are different manifestations of the same basic principles. The underlying principles have tradeoffs in their application, which also appear in the derived guidelines. For example, applying the principle of separation of concerns usually creates more classes and more methods. Consistency, even though it might increase the amount of code, also makes systems that do similar things have the same structure, thus decreasing learning. A concentration on interfaces and delegation increases the number of delegating methods.

Context Is Everything

One rule exists: nothing works everywhere, and hence, you must be the judge if a particular practice is appropriate for your application. You need to apply principles in context. The decision whether to use a particular principle or practice depends on the situation in which it is employed. When you try to apply the same principle or style to everything, you can create waste or confusion. To require vast documentation on a program that is to be used only as a transition to another program is wasteful. Failure to document fully the program in a cardiac pacemaker might be fatal. Similarly, some programs, such as pacemakers and avionics, need to deal with lots of error handling. Other programs can have simpler error processing, such as a browser that needs to display an error message only if it does not get a reply from the server.

The number of people involved in a system affects how you develop the system. I spend much less time worrying about prefactoring on simple scripts that only I use. If someone else is going to run the scripts, I spend more time dealing with issues such as input validation and meaningful error messages.

If a system involves architecture or technology that is new to you, an initial exploration of the solution space is valuable. You can create an end-to-end model of the system to try out all the technologies involved. This model can yield clues as to how these guidelines can be adapted to the new environment.

This book outlines abstract guidelines and examples of guidelines in action. Sometimes recognizing the situations in which a guideline is appropriate and applying the guideline appropriately is the biggest issue. Experience and discussion with others can help determine the appropriate use of a particular guideline.

BACKPACKING CONTEXT

I have to plan more before I embark on a weeklong backpacking trip than I do before I go out for a one-hour stroll. For a daylong event, I will probably put on hiking boots and take along a few items, such as snacks and water. For a one-hour stroll, I might wear just the shoes that I have on. The context of the hike influences my approach to it.

Adapt to Your Own Style

No one has the perfect way of creating software. It is still an art. Does one style fit all? What kind of car do you drive? Are other people wrong to drive a car that is different from yours? They have different needs, desires, value systems, and budgets. Their car might meet their values. In my opinion, only one car on the road is pretty close to being absolutely wrong: the Hummer.

The guidelines and themes presented in this book are suggestions. Treat them as starting points for examining your own software development process. By analyzing your approaches to different problems, you can create your own set of prefactoring guidelines that are applicable to your own experiences within your problem space.

Retrospect on Your Experiences

The guidelines in this book come from experience. You have experience in program development. You might have created a design from scratch or borrowed one from a previous system, or from an article or book. The design might have worked well or might have had serious flaws if it did not fit well with the problem it was intended to solve.

At the end of a project, you might have had a retrospective (read *Project Retrospectives: A Handbook for Team Reviews* by Norman L. Kerth [Dorset House, 2001]). In a retrospective, the project team evaluates the development process and preserves the lessons learned from its successes and failures. While many retrospectives concentrate on interpersonal issues, you should also examine the technical solution. "If you do not appreciate history, then you are doomed to repeat it" (George Santayana).

In a technical retrospective, you evaluate the design of the system you just finished building. How well did the architecture suit the problem space? What would you have done differently? What questions should you have asked in the beginning? What requirement changes forced you to alter the design dramatically? What prewritten components would you look for the next time?

You might have encountered a bug in your program. Instead of just solving the immediate bug, you might have analyzed it to determine why the bug occurred. For example, it might have been caused by failure to validate the input. Therefore, you add input validation to the list of guidelines to use when creating future code.

Experience of others is also applicable to your project. Much of what is being created today was accomplished in some way in the past. The books on patterns (such as *Design Patterns*, discussed in brief in the Preface) are an accumulation of that experience. What you develop today will be somewhat different from the past solution (or else you would simply use the past solution). Therefore, it is a matter of deciding what past practices to apply to the work you do today. However, if you impose a pattern that is not applicable to the circumstances of your project, you might create an antipattern.

The retrospective process need not occur just at the end of a project. Continual retrospectives can aid in refining the development process.

The Context for This Book

As I mentioned in the Preface, the guidelines in this book are presented in the context of the development of a system for a CD rental store. This development follows an agile process, which is a composite of iterative and incremental processes. Along the way, we encounter situations that are typical in the creation of a system, especially interactions with clients. We start with a set of requirements that are expressed in use cases. Complete details of each use case are not filled in until each use case is being implemented.

WHAT SAIL AND BOARD TO USE TODAY

I am standing on the shore with a few other windsurfers. No one has been out so far today. We are discussing the size of sail to rig and the size of board to sail. They are important decisions. If the sail is too big, you will be overpowered; the wind will pull you over. If it is too small, you will just plod along. If the board is too big, the waves will batter you. If it is too small, you will sink.

You guess and try to reach a common consensus with the other sailors. Local experience helps you to make the right decision. You see whitecaps, but the locals know that ones from a Northeast wind form in much less speed than those created by a wind from the Southeast.

Without any experience, you might often choose the wrong sail and board. The more experience you have, especially in terms of local conditions, the more often you will be right.

A preliminary analysis of the entire system is performed and an overall architecture is formed. The overall architecture is the big picture. It does not contain every detail of every class. After filling in the details for the first set of requirements, the solution is designed in detail and implemented. For waterfall programmers, it might seem as though we are coding too early. For extreme programmers, this might seem like overanalysis. I prefer such an intermediate approach. It is important to deliver a working system to the user early in the development cycle, but the system should fit into the overall solution to the problem.

AGILE DEVELOPMENT

Agile development is like lightweight backpacking. Lightweight backpackers carry much less equipment than regular backpackers do. Therefore, they can travel quicker and expend less energy.

Lightweight backpackers also are more experienced than regular backpackers. They carry only the essential items—the ones they absolutely need to complete the trip. Skill, knowledge, and experience complete the picture. They know how to camp to keep warm with the least amount of shelter. They know where water is located so that they can carry less water with them.

It takes a good deal more skill and experience to be an extreme lightweight backpacker. One needs to be able to fashion essential items from the materials found in nature.

On the other hand, heavyweight backpackers tend to feel they need to carry all the equipment necessary for any situations they might encounter. Their equipment gives them security. However, it also slows them down.

CHAPTER TWO

The System in So Many Words

WE MEET SAM, THE CLIENT, FOR WHOM WE ARE DEVELOPING A SYSTEM. Tim, a co-developer, and I interact with Sam to get an overall view of what he wants the system to do through use cases and prototypes. We work together to determine a common vocabulary to describe the system's requirements.

Meet Sam

Systems are not developed in a vacuum. They are created to meet an organization's needs. The client for whom a system is developed is the source of the requirements for the system and is the final decider of whether a system meets those requirements. Sam, the client, represents a composite of clients for whom I have developed systems over the years.

Sam owns the business CD Rental and Lawn Mower Repair. He started out with lawn mower repair and discovered that people who use lawn mowers like to listen to CDs and they prefer listening to a different CD each time they mow. Therefore, Sam came up with the idea of renting CDs. The service started out as a whim, but it has grown dramatically.

Sam contacted me about creating a system for keeping track of rentals in his store. His current system of using cards similar to library cards works, but it is unable to provide him the reports he feels his growing business requires.

Currently Sam has only one store. Since business is booming, he is considering opening several more stores. He wants us to design the system not only so it works in his store today, but so he can change it easily to accommodate multiple stores tomorrow.

Tim the Developer

Tim introduced me to Sam. Tim studied computer science in college and worked summers at Sam's CD Rental and Lawn Mower Repair. He has been working as a programmer for five years, the last couple of years with me. He is back in school getting a master's degree. We still work together, but mostly remotely. He takes courses and does some teaching, so he is often unavailable during the day, when I am talking with Sam.

Tim represents an amalgamation of programmers with whom I have worked. We work together on approaches to solutions, but usually work separately on code due to the remoteness factor. Because of our physical separation, code readability is extremely important.

Sam's Request

Sam came up with some features that he wants to incorporate into his system. They are based on what he already does with his index cards, as well as additional ideas that he developed in his head. He listed them on a sheet of paper:

- I want to be able to keep track of where each CD is, both when it is in the store and when someone has rented it (including who has rented it).

- I want the system to report when CDs are overdue.

- I want a catalog so that customers can see what CDs are available and what songs are on them.

- When I have multiple stores, the system should show which stores have a particular CD.

- I want to be able to offer discounts to frequent renters.

- I want a charge system that enables me to bill customers per month rather than per rental.

Sam's Use Cases

Sam, Tim, and I will develop the system with this list as the informal requirements for the system. We will transform these requirements into use cases.* I have found that writing use cases helps both me and the customer understand what the system needs to do. The cases are specified in sufficient detail so that we can appreciate the problem's scope and magnitude. Additional detail can be added later so that when it comes time to design or code, the necessary detail is available. Working through a system's use cases also helps to identify the users who should be consulted when their parts of the system undergo detailed specification and design.

---

* For further information on use cases, see *Writing Effective Use Cases* by Alistair Cockburn (Addison-Wesley Professional, 2000).

Sam and I explore, in more detail, the first item on his list:

"Sam, who do you want to keep track of CDs?" I asked.

Sam replied, "What do you mean?"

I continued, "Do you want the customers to be able to check out their own CDs?"

"No," he answered, "only the clerk should perform checkout."

"Then let's go through the steps of checking out a CD, since that sounds like a primary use case," I suggested.

"How about returning a CD?" Sam queried.

"That sounds like another one, so why don't you tell me about both of them," I requested.

Sam explained the checkout and return procedures. After some discussion, I put his narration into the following informal use case descriptions. These use cases describe how the new system should work and are based on how the current manual process operates:

Checkout_a_CD

    a. The customer brings a CD case to the clerk.

    b. The clerk retrieves the actual CD corresponding to the case.

    c. The customer presents his CD Store Customer Card. (The customer already has one of these for the manual system.) The clerk types the customer ID into the system.

    d. The clerk types the CD ID into the system.

    e. The system records that the CD is rented to that particular customer. It prints a rental contract.

    f. The customer signs the rental contract.

    g. The clerk files the rental contract in a file box named "Signed Rental Contracts."

Return_a_CD

    a. The clerk types the CD ID into the system.

    b. The system records that the CD has been returned.

    c. The system determines whether late fees apply and informs the clerk if that is the case.

An informal use case description can lead to enlightenment, especially when combined with an examination of what can go wrong at each step. I asked Sam what the clerk did in their current system if a customer did not have his CD Store Customer Card. He said that the clerk looks for the corresponding card in the customer file. We captured this information in another informal case.

Checkout_a_CD (extension if no customer ID)

a. The customer identifies himself using a photo ID.

b. The clerk enters information from the ID into the system.

c. The system searches for the customer ID using the information from the photo ID. If no matching customer is found, the system indicates an error.

The use cases presented so far are informal. They mix user actions with system actions. Some authors (e.g., Larry L. Constantine and Lucy A.D. Lockwood in *Software for Use: A Practical Guide to the Models and Methods of Usage Centered Design* [Addison-Wesley Professional, 1999]) suggest that the use cases be written in a more technology-independent manner. Actions that are unrelated to system processing will drop out of the flow and appear as comments. For example, the Checkout_a_CD use case might look like this:

Checkout_a_CD

a. The user enters the customer ID and the CD ID into the system.

b. The system records the entry. It responds by creating a rental contract for the customer to sign.

Notice that the actual way in which the IDs are entered into the system is not specified. The IDs could be scanned in using a bar code reader, typed in, or spoken and translated by a speech recognition program.

Initial use case descriptions might state exactly how customers expect the system to work. Before implementing the use cases, you can rework them into a more abstract, less-technology-dependent description. Removing the implementation details can help focus on the business policies and procedures that need to be programmed.

The Ilities

The purpose of requirements is not only to validate what the user wants, but also to verify that the implemented systems meet those wants. Requirements include more than just functional specifications as supplied by use cases. These other requirements relate to the software's quality. They are often called the *ilities*, since many of the terms end in *ility*. These quality specifications include reliability, testability, deployability, and performance.

Often these quality requirements are not documented for a system. They are implicit, such as in the case of Sam's system. It is assumed that the system will meet reasonable requirements. For example, its performance should ensure that users do not notice a delay.

For larger, more complex systems, documenting these quality requirements is essential. You can find further information on eliciting and documenting requirements in *Software Requirements*, Second Edition, by Karl E. Wiegers (Microsoft Press, 2003).

Reinvention Avoidance

Once Tim and I understand Sam's system requirements, our first step is to determine whether an existing program provides the features that we need. There is no sense in recreating the wheel if an existing wheel works the way we want. Our goal as developers is to solve the client's problem, not to just write code.

Sam had searched for a commercial program and did not find anything. It appears that he is in a unique business, so nothing has been written, which is not surprising.*

We suggested to him that the process of renting a CD is similar to the process of renting a videotape or DVD. He could purchase one of those programs and it would already have many of the features that he wanted. He decided that he would rather have his own custom program instead of dealing with the terminology and handling differences among CDs and DVDs. We recommended that if he decides to expand into selling CDs, we should investigate retail sales systems. A lot of functionality already exists in those systems that should not be re-created. If a preexisting solution fits into the overall system, at least that part of the wheel need not be recreated.†

DON'T REINVENT THE WHEEL

Look for existing solutions to problems before creating new solutions.

Since Sam wants us to develop a custom system, Tim and I start to analyze the problem. We need to outline the concepts involved in the problem and clarify our understanding of what needs to be solved.

What's in a Name?

Names are important, not just for the code but also for requirements and analysis. If you don't know what you're talking about, it's hard to design for it.

Sam described how he wants to keep track of the CDs. He also desired a catalog of all the CDs that he has for rent.

"So, what is a CD?" I asked Sam.

---

* Finding existing solutions can be problematic. Sometimes it can be hard to describe the solution you seek in such a way that Google™ can find a match.

† See *Software Tools* by Brian W. Kernighan (Addison-Wesley Professional, 1976) for the earliest discussion I have found on the issue of using tools to create solutions.

He paused for a moment and looked at me with a questioning expression on his face. He must have thought I was crazy. "You know, one of those round things you put in a CD player," he said.

"So, when you said you want a CD catalog, do you mean you want an entry in it for every round thing you have in your store?" I asked.

He paused again. "No, I want only one for each title, regardless of how many copies I have in the store."

I suggested, "So, let's decide to use two terms, one for the CD title and one for the CD copy. This way we minimize the opportunity for misunderstanding. What do you want to call each thing?"

"Now I see what you mean," he replied. "What do you suggest?"

I replied, "Let's call the title a CDRelease, and the other a CDDisc. We could use the name CDTitle, but that would start to get confusing when we talk about the title of a CDTitle. To clarify what we mean even further, we can describe each term with a sentence:

A *CDRelease* is a CD identified by its Universal Product Code (UPC).
A *CDDisc* is a physical copy of a CDRelease. CDDiscs, not CDReleases, are what are rented.

"Now is it possible that a CD which a customer would be looking for would be related to two different UPCs?" I asked.

"It's possible," he said. "But I don't think we need to worry about that. One would usually have the term *rerelease* in its title."

"We can always revisit this question if things change," I said. "Let's alter your requirements and the use cases to utilize these terms."

At this point, Sam and I came up with the following list of modified requirements:

- Keep track of where each CDDisc is, both when it is in the store and when someone has rented it (including who has rented it).

- Report when a CDDisc is overdue.

- Have a catalog so that customers can see which CDReleases are stocked, what songs are on each CDRelease, and which corresponding CDDiscs are available in the store.

Here is a modified use case:

Checkout_a_CDDisc

a. The user enters the customer ID and the CDDisc ID into the system.

b. The system records the entry. It responds by printing a rental contract for the customer to sign.

Names are subjective. As long as you and the client agree on a name, it does not matter if the name makes sense to the outside world. Here are some other possibilities for names of these two concepts:

CDUPC
> A CD identified by a UPC

CDPhysical
> A physical CD of a particular CDUPC

CDCatalogItem
> A CD identified by a UPC

CDRentalItem
> A physical CD copy of a particular CDCatalogItem

Attributes of these classes should use the same names as the customer uses. If the customer uses a full name, avoid making up an abbreviation for it. If the customer uses an abbreviation or acronym, use that. If you have a hard time recalling what the short form means, ask the customer to supply a longer name.

A ROSE BY ANY OTHER NAME IS NOT A ROSE

Create a clearly defined name for each concept in a system.[*]

Splitters Versus Lumpers

If the world were perfect, you would have exactly one unique name for each concept in a system. In this imperfect world, having two concepts with the same name leads to confusion. In Sam's case, the term *CD* was applied to both a CDRelease and a CDDisc. Separating the two concepts with two names clarified the requirements.

Using two different names for a single idea can also be confusing, albeit less so than two ideas with a single name. Referring to a physical CD as both a CDDisc and a CDPhysical might be justified by political measures. ("This department calls it this and that department calls it that.") Sam referred to the act of renting a CD as both renting a CD and checking out a CD. If these two terms really encompass the same operation, the duality of reference can be annoying, but might not be confusing.

Sometimes it is hard to determine whether you have two independent concepts or one. Try making up a one-line definition for a name. If it is difficult to create a simple definition, go ahead and use two names. Later on, if you find that the distinction was meaningless, you

[*] See *http://www.literateprogramming.com/* for a discussion of names.

can always declare the two names to be synonyms. Suppose that Sam and I came up with the terms *CDAlbum* and *CDRelease*. We might distinguish them by stating that a CDAlbum is a collection of songs with a title given to the set, and a CDRelease is a collection of songs that was released on a single CDDisc.

The conversion from one style of architecture, design, or coding to another is not necessarily symmetrical. Suppose that a single name has been used to denote two ideas. Later you decide that you need to replace that name with appropriate names for each idea. You need to examine each usage of the term carefully to determine which of the two concepts it represents. On the other hand, suppose that you have used two different names for a single concept. If you want to combine those into a single name, you can do a simple global replacement.

For example, suppose we have a class called Message, which represents messages displayed to the user. We think at the beginning that these messages are going to behave differently, so we divide them into WarningMessages, ErrorMessages, SevereErrorMessages, and ReallySevereErrorMessages. We make every message an object of one of these four classes. Later on, we realize that SevereErrorMessages and ReallySevereErrorMessages really do not behave differently. We can eliminate the distinction using a simple search and replace. Conversely, if we had not distinguished the two and later found that there should be a difference, we would have to look closely at each object of SevereErrorMessage to determine whether it should be categorized as ReallySevereErrorMessage.

SPLITTERS CAN BE LUMPED MORE EASILY THAN LUMPERS CAN BE SPLIT

It is easier to combine two concepts than it is to separate them.

Clumping

When Sam described his customers in detail, he mentioned that he needed to keep track of each customer's home address, including street, city, state, and Zip Code, as well as credit card billing address, including street, city, state, and Zip Code.

I asked him, "Do both of those addresses contain the same information?"

He replied affirmatively.

I said, "Then let's just describe the combination as an Address. That way, you don't have to keep mentioning all the parts unless there is something different about them."

"OK," he answered.

We clumped the data into a class, as follows:

```
class Address
    {
    String line1;
    String line2;
    String city;
    String state;
    String zip;
    }
```

At this point, we simply clump the related data, even though we have not assigned any behavior to the class. This data object helps in abstraction and in cutting down parameter lists. Even though the class contains only data at this point, we might be able to assign responsibility to it later on.*

Clumping and lumping look similar, but they have distinctly different meanings. *Clumping* involves combining a set of attributes into a single named concept. The attributes should form a cohesive whole. *Lumping* involves using a single name for two different concepts. Clumping is an abstraction technique, which makes for an efficient description of a set of data. Lumping can hide relevant distinctions between concepts.†

CLUMP DATA SO THAT THERE IS LESS TO THINK ABOUT

**Clumping data cuts down on the number of concepts
that have to be kept in mind.**

Abstracting

In creating a description of a use case or a model of a possible class, avoid using primitive data types. Pretend that `ints` or `doubles` do not exist. Almost every type of number can be described with an *abstract data type* (ADT). Items are priced in `Dollars` (or `CurrencyUnits`, if you are globally oriented). The number of physical copies of an item in an inventory is a `Count`. The discount that a good customer receives is denoted with a `Percentage`. The size of a `CDDisc` is expressed as a `Length` (or `LengthInMeters` or `LengthInInches` if you are going to be sending a satellite into space). The time for a single song on a `CDRelease` could be stored in a `TimePeriod`.

Using an ADT places the focus on what can be done with the type, not on how the type is represented. An ADT shows what you intend to do with the variable. You can declare the variable as a primitive data type and name the variable to reflect that intent. However, a variable declared as an abstract data type can have built-in validation, whereas a variable declared as a primitive cannot.

Each ADT needs a related description. For example, a `Count` represents a number of items. A `Count` can be zero or positive. If a `Count` is negative, it represents an invalid count. Declaring a variable as a `Count` conveys this information. You can create variations of `Count`. You may have a `CountWithLimit` data type with a maximum count that, if exceeded, would signal an error.

---

* Not all objects have behavior. Objects that contain just data (sometimes called *data transfer objects*) are useful in interfacing with GUI classes and passing as objects between networked systems. Data transfer objects are covered in Chapter 7.

† One reviewer notes that clumping without a responsibility definition for the class can lead to data-polluted classes. Clumping should also involve assigning operations to the clumped concept.

You can place limits on many different data types. For example, Ages (of humans) can range between 0 and 150 years, SpeedLimits (for automobiles) between 5 and 80 mph, and Elevations (for normal flying) between 0 and 60,000 feet.* All these types can be represented by an int or a double, but that is an implementation issue, not an abstraction issue.

Abstract types can contain more than just validation. A price can be represented in Dollars. The string representation of a Dollar differs from the string representation of a double. A string for Dollar has at least a currency symbol and perhaps some thousands separators (e.g., commas). Multiplying a Dollar by a number can result in a Dollar with cents, but not fractions of a cent. Here is a possible Dollar class:

```
class Dollar
    {
    Dollar multiply_with_rounding(double multiplier);
    Dollar add(Dollar another_dollar);
    Dollar subtract(Dollar another_dollar);
    String to_string();  //
    };
```

If your language provides the ability to define operators for a class (such as + and -), you can use arithmetic symbols for the corresponding operations. You can also use the appropriate method name to have a Dollar be converted automatically to a String if it appears in an appropriate context. How you represent the abstract data type that you use for a value is an implementation detail. You can make up a class for each type. If you work with C++, you can make up typedefs for each simple type for which there is no additional functionality. For other languages, you can convert some simple types into primitive types. In that case, you might want to use variable names that include the type (e.g., double price_in_dollars).

WHEN YOU'RE ABSTRACT, BE ABSTRACT ALL THE WAY
Do not describe data items using primitive data types.

This guideline suggests using explicit typing in describing the problem and the solution. By using abstract data types in the beginning, you are, in effect, more abstract. If you explicitly type all your attributes and parameters, you can always switch to implicit typing if the explicit typing gets in the way. It is much harder to go in reverse.†

---

* Once upon a time, Montana had no speed limit other than "reasonable speed." The upper limit still could be a reasonable number (e.g., 200).

† For an article on strong testing with languages that have implicit typing, see *http://www.artima.com/weblogs/viewpost.jsp?thread=4639*.

Not Just a String

A more descriptive data type can represent many data types represented typically by a String. For example, although a name can be declared as a String, you could declare it as a clumped data object:

```
class Name
    {
    String first_name;
    String last_name;
    String title;          // e.g. Mr. Mrs.
    String suffix;      // e.g. Jr. III
    };
```

To avoid the "everything is a String" syndrome, come up with a different type name to describe a variable that holds a set of characters that does not have any validation, formatting, or other meta-information associated with it. Suppose you decide on CommonString. Use that name in place of String to declare the data types of attributes, and reserve String as an implementation type. Then ask the question "Is that attribute really a CommonString?"

Let us revisit the Address class. Using CommonString, we can describe the class as follows:

```
class Address
    {
    CommonString line1;
    CommonString line2;
    CommonString city;
    CommonString state;
    CommonString zipcode;
    }
```

CommonStrings can contain any characters, just like an int can contain any integer values (within hardware limits). In Address, some fields are definitely not CommonStrings. A state is not a CommonString. Only certain values represent a valid state. For U.S. postal addresses, if we use abbreviations to represent the state, the abbreviation must appear on the U.S.

Postal Service's official list of abbreviations. So the state should be declared as a data type called State. This data type can provide an appropriate validation mechanism. That mechanism can check to see that a string is in the official list, or it can supply a set of strings of all official abbreviations for use in a drop-down display box.

A U.S. Zip Code is not just a CommonString either. You can describe it as a NumericString data type (e.g., one with all digits), as a FormattedString data type (one with five digits plus a dash plus four digits), or as a ZipCode data type. If any combination of digits was valid, using NumericString or FormattedString might be appropriate. However, declaring the attribute as a ZipCode type allows us to abstract away its actual representation.

Do not combine classes simply for implementation purposes. You can define both SocialSecurityNumbers and PhoneNumbers as strings of digits with two dashes. That does not make them equivalent—that is just accidental cohesion. They are two distinctly different classes with different validation. A phone number in the U.S. cannot begin with a 1 or a 0. Certain ranges of Social Security numbers are not used. These numbers can use the same type of formatted string for input or display purposes, but the semantics of each class are entirely different. You would never send a Social Security number to be dialed, nor would you attempt to record payroll taxes against a phone number. (All right, someone at some time will come up with a counterexample, so perhaps I should never say "never.")

Much data that might be a CommonString can be assigned its own data type. For example, filenames are usually typed as strings, but they cannot contain certain characters. In the Windows world, you cannot have any of the following characters in a filename: \, /, :, *, ", ?, <, >, or |. A FileName data type can represent a filename and enforce this limitation. An advantage of using a data type becomes apparent in graphical user interface (GUI) development. For instance, the user interface code could recognize the FileName data type and automatically insert a browse button next to a text field.

On the Web, parameter values for the Hypertext Transfer Protocol (HTTP) commands **GET** and **PUT** use encoded strings. Characters that are not alphabetic or numeric are encoded using their hexadecimal values. The encoded string is sent to the web server. Although the unencoded string and the encoded string are both implemented with strings, they are different. You can have invalid encoded strings—ones with unencoded punctuation, such as a hacker might send to a server. You could use an EncodedWebString class to represent strings on a server. If an input were not validated as an EncodedWebString, it would be rejected.

MOST STRINGS ARE MORE THAN JUST A STRING

Treat String **as a primitive data type. Describe attributes with abstract data types, instead of as** Strings.

Constant Avoidance

Similar to the way in which most strings are more than strings, most constant values are more than just constants. A constant value can usually be assigned a name that denotes the meaning of that constant. Avoid using the explicit value in a specification or executable code.* Declare the value as a constant and use the name of that constant in the document or the code.

If Sam mentions that the late fee for a rental is $3, I create a constant:

```
Dollar RENTAL_LATE_FEE = 3.00;
```

When reading the relevant documents later on, I need not concentrate on the actual value, only on the assigned name. Suppose this value was not transformed into a constant and the value of 3.00 was used frequently in the documents for other purposes. If I went searching for it, I would have to examine each appearance carefully to see if it was a reference to the rental late fee or to some other value.

You might not get rid of every constant value. The value 0 often appears in initializing variables or setting the initial index for an array. There is little to be gained by creating a named constant for zero.

If the value that a name represents is subject to change, the value should be kept with a configuration mechanism. In that case, the code would use the symbolic name to look up the configured value. The configuration mechanism could use an XML configuration file, a database table, or another form of persistence to store the values. For example, RENTAL_LATE_FEE is probably something that should exist in a configuration file rather than a con-

---

NEVER LET A CONSTANT SLIP INTO CODE

Use a symbolic name for all values.

Prototypes Are Worth a Thousand Words

It is often said that a picture is worth a thousand words. A prototype is like a picture. A user interface described in text is often harder for the customer to visualize than the same interface described with a diagram or picture. Use cases can provide excellent textual descriptions. A prototype (or screen mockup) gives a more concrete perspective on a program's intended operation. The prototype can spark feedback from the client in both the program's operation and in missing requirements.

---

* Michael Green, a reviewer, called this principle "No magic numbers!" after having to deal with numbers that could not be changed or removed (without negative side effects in apparently unrelated code). He could find no one who knew what they were for or why they were there.

DON'T THROW AWAY INFORMATION

When I was presenting these prefactoring guidelines in a talk at the Software Development Confer-ence, Jerry Weinberg made an interesting observation about some of the guidelines in this chapter. He stated that they revolve around the central principle of not throwing away information. For exam-ple, describing a price as a double, rather than as a Dollar, decreases the information about the price. Lumping a group of concepts into a single class, rather than splitting them into multiple classes, hides information. Now, if I only could have convinced my mother that my comic book col-lection was really information…

One of the dangers of making a perfect-looking GUI for a prototype is that the interface represents the program to the user. If the interface is complete, the user might expect that the system is almost complete. Some user interface experts suggest that interfaces be designed using whiteboards or Post-it notes. If you are programming in Java, you can use the Napkin Look and Feel (*http://napkinlaf.sourceforge.net/*). Tim and I created a rough-draft prototype of the screens for the uses cases we worked on with Sam (Figure 2-1). We went

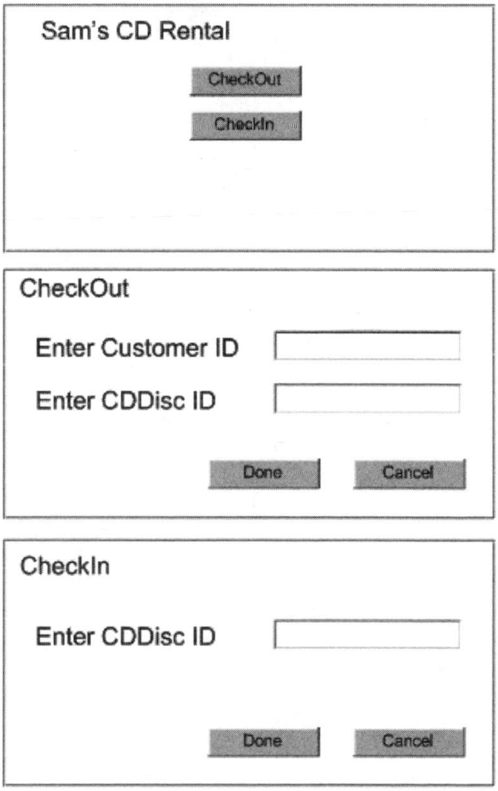

FIGURE 2-1. Rental screens

over it with Sam. The cases are simple, so he had no changes in its interface. He did note that the buttons should use a large font so that he could read them without his glasses.

PROTOTYPES ARE WORTH A THOUSAND WORDS

A picture of an interface, such as a screen, can be more powerful than just a description.

CHAPTER THREE

General Development Issues

BEFORE WE ANALYZE SAM'S SYSTEM IN DETAIL, we look at some general system development issues. These issues relate to all forms of software development, not just object-oriented design. We examine the big picture, interface contracts, communicating with code, simplicity, dealing with errors, and the spreadsheet conundrum.

Start with the Big Picture

The big picture refers to the broad perspective of a system in development. The big picture includes the system's overall architecture and business purpose.

Most successful systems have a single vision of the architecture. The vision can come from group consensus or from a single respected individual. Design decisions within a system should be consistent with that architecture.*

---

* For more information, see "The Third Principle: Maintain the Vision" by David Hooker at *http:// c2.com/cgi/wiki?SevenPrinciplesOfSoftwareDevelopment*.

As Tim and I develop Sam's system, we will keep in mind that its ultimate goal is to function as a multistore system. As the individual pieces of the initial system are developed, the choice between the various design approaches will be affected by that business purpose.

Sam's system is being created in an entirely new environment. Any components that we create (classes, display widgets, etc.) are going to be used in that context. If we attempt to develop components in a vacuum (e.g., without reference to their use), we might have a lot of vacuuming to do when we are finished.

For example, we are developing a new `Customer` class. Its purpose and interface are driven by its representation as someone to whom Sam rents a CD. An attempt to make the class more general (e.g., so that it can represent a purchaser of `CDDiscs`) not only would be unnecessary, but also would complicate its required purpose.

On the other hand, much software development occurs within an existing environment, which represents the even "bigger picture." The environment might consist of the entire enterprise, a single division, or a single department. Gaining knowledge of that environment before creating your own system helps save development time. The environment might have components that you can use in your system. It might have established frameworks that will make your system structure consistent with other systems in the environment.*

For example, the bigger picture might already contain a `Customer` class. If that class represents the concept that you want to use in the new system, to create another would be unnecessary duplication. This "bigger picture" also determines how you can develop components. If there were no existing `Customer` class, taking the effort to make your class more reusable might make sense.

THINK ABOUT THE BIG PICTURE

Decisions within a system should be congruent with the big picture.

Interface Contracts

A system is made up of interfaces that interact with each other. The interfaces can be implemented by object-oriented code or by procedural code. Yukihiro Matsumoto, the inventor of Ruby, suggests that the interface is everything to the user. I would add that the interface is everything to the developer.

---

* See *The Enterprise Unified Process: Extending the Rational Unified Process* by Scott W. Ambler, John Nalbone, and Michael J. Vizdos (Prentice Hall, 2005) for a discussion of enterprise frameworks and environments.

FINDING YOUR WAY IN THE DARK

We arrived at a camping area in the darkness of a new moon. We were looking for the campsite we had been assigned. We had a flashlight, but it yielded only a narrow beam of light. Relating what we saw in that narrow beam to the written directions was difficult.

The next morning, the sunlight revealed the big picture of the camping area. How the campsites were positioned in the area was apparent instantly. It would have been much easier had we had that big picture the night before.

Bertrand Meyer introduced the concept of Design by Contract in *Object-Oriented Software Construction* (Prentice Hall PTR, 2000). An interface has a contract with the user of that interface. The contract consists of preconditions and postconditions for every method in the interface. *Preconditions* are assertions that must be true when the method is called so that the method can perform its operations. *Postconditions* are assertions that should be true when the method finishes.*

For example, when you're writing to a file, a precondition is that the file must be opened, and a postcondition is that the file length has changed (if you're appending to the end of the file). A precondition can also apply to the value of an argument in a call; for instance, it must be between a given set of values. The called method should assure that the postconditions are met. Otherwise, it has not performed its job properly. The questions are who checks the preconditions and what should result if a precondition is not met.

Some designers feel that it is the calling routine's responsibility to make sure the preconditions are satisfied. For example, the calling routine should ensure that parameters are within the ranges the preconditions specify. If they are not, the called method has no responsibility to perform its contractual obligation.

I prefer that the called method specifically check for its preconditions in its code. The code is the record of the contract. Putting checking responsibility on the called method parallels the concept that a whole program is responsible for checking the input from the user.

The called method contains the most knowledge of the preconditions. Unless performance requirements dictate otherwise, the called method can check for all preconditions and report via an error notification mechanism if the conditions are not satisfied. Is a failure to satisfy a precondition a programming error or an inherent error in the domain? That depends on context. The called method likely has the most information as to "what" caused the precondition violation, but the caller has the most information as to the meaning of the precondition violation.

---

* Meyer also introduces the invariant condition, which must always be true for a valid object. An invariant condition typically involves the state of the attributes of an object. An example is that the value of an attribute must always be between two values.

Make the contract explicit. It should be visible in the code for the class and any derived documentation. To check the contract, you can use regular code style (e.g., if (parameter_value < 3), assertions (assert(parameter_value < 3)), aspects (see *http://aosd.net/* for details on aspects), or language-specific features.

CREATE INTERFACE CONTRACTS

Design with well-defined interfaces and enforce the contracts for those interfaces.

Validation

You should validate all input data before transferring it to internal processing. Violation of this rule has caused numerous web sites to be subject to attacks such as Structured Query Language (SQL) injection.*

You should convert input to its corresponding abstract data type as it comes into the system. For example, you should convert an input field that represents a dollar amount into a variable of type Dollar. Failures of conversion (such as an amount that has three decimal digits) can be reported back to the user immediately. There is no sense in processing an invalid Dollar.

All identifiers should contain self-validating values that can prevent most common entry errors. For example, if a PhysicalID was used to identify each CDDisc, it should contain a check-digit or other error-detection mechanism. Common typing errors can be caught at input, instead of being passed along as erroneous data.†

The most stringent rule is that the value of every parameter to every method should be subject to validation. The rule can be relaxed if the caller of the method (or its caller) has performed the validation. If an attribute is set from a method called from the outside world, the setting method should check for validity. If the value for the attribute is read from a configuration file, it should be checked. If the attribute is set by data read from a database and that data was placed there by the system, the checking needed is minimized. The data should have been stored only if it underwent validity checking. The paranoid developer might still want to check it.

---

* SQL injection involves using the entry fields on a web form to submit SQL commands to a database that is the backend for a web server. For more details, go to *http://www.nextgenss.com/papers/advanced_sql_injection.pdf* or search Google.

† It is ironic (or perhaps a rhyming term) that one of the most widely used identifiers, the Social Security number, has no check digit.

Paranoia is not necessarily a bad thing, unless it hinders code interpretation or performance. Some error-handling routines might never be invoked. That is not necessarily a bad thing. It is better for a doctor to double-check the blood types of a heart donor and its recipient before doing a heart transplant than it is for her not to double-check. If the double-check never fails because a mismatch never occurs, the error procedure ("Get another heart") is never executed.

For systems that involve two or more programs, such as a browser/web server, validation can occur in both programs. Validation in the server before further processing is mandatory. Validation in the browser provides error checking without round trips to the server.

On layered systems, validate at the boundary of each layer, according to the contract defined between the layers. For example, the model layer should validate the data feed from the display layer before processing it.

If the data is invalid, the method should report the error according to the "Decide on a Strategy to Deal with Deviations and Errors" guideline discussed later in this chapter. It should not pass along the invalid data, but terminate the processing of it.

VALIDATE, VALIDATE, VALIDATE

At each interface, validate that the input matches the contract.

Code Communicates

A primary purpose of code is communication. You are communicating with the computer, telling it what operations to perform. However, you are also communicating with the reader, showing him the steps you are taking to complete an operation. The most important issues to communicate are what are you doing and why you are doing it, not how you are doing it.

Code should communicate its purpose and your intention. On at least one level, code should read like a book, albeit one with stilted syntax. The client should be able to read the code to see if it follows the logic that he expressed in the requirements. The details of the implementation should be relegated to deeper levels.

When reading code, it is often difficult to determine intent. If the writer did not take particular care to make his intent clear, it might be buried in the details. The "micromanagement" of details can hide the flow of the logic.

For example:

```
if (a_customer.has_late_rental ())
    a_customer.suspend_rental_privilege();
```

This code does not show how the suspension of rental privileges is recorded. It states why the person is being suspended (because of a late rental). The client should be able to follow the logic involved, without getting buried in implementation details.

COMMUNICATE WITH YOUR CODE*

Your code should communicate its purpose and intent.

Code readability is measured by whether someone else can read it. The pair programming practice of Extreme Programming ensures that two people can read the code. If you are solo-programming, Nitin Narayan, a reviewer, suggests, "Readability of code is best verified when tested by two or three programmers who read the code and explain what it does to the actual coder. I call this the code readability test. The coder can then change his code to make it more readable based on the feedback he gets from the code readability testers."

Implicitness Versus Explicitness

Implicitness makes programs shorter, but can make them less readable by programmers who are less experienced in the language or who use many languages simultaneously. Implicitness requires that you make assumptions about the programmer's knowledge. Explicitness requires more writing, but uncertainty as to interpretation is minimized.

For example, in object-oriented languages that feature namespaces, you can refer to classes by using a fully qualified name (e.g., `java.util.Vector`), or by using an `import` statement (e.g., `import java.util.*`) and an unqualified name (`Vector`). Some coding standards suggest that you always use a fully qualified name. With the fully qualified name, it is clear to the reader to which package a class belongs, without having to have detailed knowledge of the packages.

You cannot be explicit about everything. You need to assume a common body of knowledge, such as the way the Java language is written. However, domain-related code requires more explicitness. You cannot assume that another programmer will know (or remember) every detailed piece of information you learned from the customer.

* See *Literate Programming* by Donald Knuth (Center for the Study of Language and Information— Lecture Notes 1992) and *The Elements of Programming Style* by Brian W. Kernighan and P. J. Plauger (Computing McGraw-Hill, 1978) for original discussion on communicating with code.

EXPLICITNESS BEATS IMPLICITNESS

Being explicit reduces misinterpretation.

A FEW MORE WORDS GIVE MEANING

Microsoft's MFC library has a method called `UpdateData( )`. The purpose of the method is twofold. It retrieves the values in display controls on the screen and places them into class members, and it sets the values in the controls from the member variables. Which operation it performs depends on whether the parameter is TRUE or FALSE. Now you tell me, if it is TRUE, should it retrieve the values from the text boxes, or set them? `UpdateData( )` is an example of a method that could use a better name. It would be more understandable if it were broken into two methods, such as `RetrieveValuesFromWindowControls( )` and `SetValuesOfWindowControls( )`. These names might be a little wordy, but they really express the meaning.

Jason Hunter provided an example from JDOM:

> The `Element.getText( )` method returns the text of the element. According to XML rules, it should return all whitespace. People often do not care about surrounding whitespace, so a method was needed that trimmed the whitespace. Some people proposed `getText(true)` where true indicates to trim the whitespace. However, the Boolean parameter did not have an obvious purpose.

What Hunter finally chose to implement was `getText( )` and `getTextTrim( )`:

> The XML purists were happy because `getText( )` followed the spec, and most people could add four characters and get what they really wanted. Furthermore, the method name explains what it does.

Later he added a `getTextNormalize( )` method that normalizes internal whitespace. That would have been hard using a Boolean switch.

Spell It Out

You might notice an emphasis on names in this book. Getting names to say what you mean and to be consistent makes code more understandable and readable. However, names appear in many places other than code: database column names, XML tags, and user documentation. Create meaningful names in the beginning and use these names in all these other contexts. Then the complete system will be more understandable and maintainable.

It might seem obvious, but you should avoid using names that differ only in a single character or that appear practically the same on the screen. Virus writers do that to fool unsuspecting users. A virus might be named *rundll.dll,* which is hard to distinguish from *rundll.dll* in the normal font on most systems. Following along the lines of error-detecting codes, there should be a noticeable distance between two names. At least two characters should be changed to convert one name into another. If you like to use single-character variables for loop indexes, pick letters that are distinctly different—e.g. *i* and *k*, rather than *i* and *j*.

READABILITY OR RDBLTY?

A few years ago, I developed some FORTRAN routines that manipulated orbital elements. Orbital elements describe the orientation and shape of a satellite's orbit. They are calculated from a satellite's position and velocity. The version of FORTRAN I was using allowed only six-character names. I created a routine that computed orbital elements and named it CMPORB. I created another routine that compared two sets of orbital elements and named it ORBCMP. Even though I created the routines, I could never keep straight in my head which one performed what operation. The parameter list gave a bit of a clue, but then the parameters themselves had only six-character names. Use readable names.

Modern languages have removed limits on variable names. The names themselves can communicate their meaning. Smart editors provide for autocompletion of names, so repeatedly typing a long name is not required.

You should use abbreviations and acronyms only if the client or the problem domain uses them. Names can be shorter if they are referred to only locally (inside a method). For example:

```
for (int m = 0; m < SIZE; m++)
    {
    // Use m inside of here
    }
```

However, any name that is exposed outside the method (such as parameter names) should be spelled out fully for readability.

Spellcheck Your Code

Many programs these days offer spellcheckers. Spellchecking ensures that your words are at least spelled correctly, even though they might not be used correctly. Compilers offer syntax checkers. They ensure that the words are used correctly, but they do not ensure that they mean anything.

You can run a spellchecker on your code to see whether the code terms have meanings in a particular language. You can parse *camelcase* words (SomethingLikeThis) or underlined words (something_like_this) into separate words prior to spellchecking. Before the spellcheck, you can add to the list of correctly spelled terms the acronyms and abbreviations that the developers and clients have agreed upon.*

---

* Go to *http://www.oreilly.com/catalog/prefactoring* for a simple spellchecker that runs on Unix/Linux.

Adapt Your Style to the Environment

Some relevant communication factors are people and time. If you are writing a program that only you are using, communication is much less of an issue. If you are writing a program that someone else will use or maintain, communication is a concern.

I use pseudocode to explain algorithms in this book. You can write pseudocode to look more like normal English, or you can stylize it to resemble actual code. I usually write pseudocode to determine how to approach a problem. If I am creating a quick little program to solve an immediate problem or to try out an idea, I might turn the pseudocode into comments and then code the implementation between the comments.

However, if I am writing a larger program, the pseudocode is transformed into the actual code. The names used in the pseudocode become the operations in the classes, with alterations for consistency or grammar. The operations spelled out in the pseudocode are implemented in methods and the implementation is placed within the methods. The pseudocode operations express the *what*. The methods describe the *how*.

Consistency Is Simplicity

Consistency is a form of simplicity. Consistency makes it easy to deal with the world. Can you imagine using your cell phone if every time you turned it on, another revision of the user interface was downloaded to it? However, too much consistency can inhibit creativity. You should apply consistency with a purpose. "A foolish consistency is the hobgoblin of little minds" (Ralph Waldo Emerson).

Consistency is not just following code style conventions.* It is doing similar things in a similar manner, unless there is a good reason to change. If you are going to use exceptions, come up with guidelines for what types of events are exceptions and what types are not. For example, should the failure to find a customer with a particular name be an exception or an expected condition? Is it the caller's or the callee's responsibility to check contracts? Will a dozen callers contain the same checking code that could be stored once only, in a single callee?

The development environment can provide consistency. For example, Borland JBuilder has a command that creates a listener for events. A separate listening class is created for each event, along with a separate method that is used to code the response to the event. This approach adds a level of indirection. However, once you're familiar with the approach, it is easy to determine which methods are event handlers.

---

* Gary K. Evans, a reviewer, tells programmers on his projects that the best they can do is to make their intent, or interface, intuitively obvious. The second-best thing they can do is to make it consistent, so once Evans learns it, at least it has consistency.

A consistent approach to style and solutions can make code easier to maintain.[*]

CONSISTENT FOR WHOM?

I worked with a group of programmers who programmed the menus in the ordering stations for a fast food chain. Being curious as to how the end user viewed the ordering process, I stopped at one of the franchises and queried the server. I asked how she liked the system. She said it worked fine until they introduced new menu items. Then she messed up orders for a few days. I asked why that happened. She said that she got used to the placement of the order items and would enter the order practically without looking. When a new menu item was introduced, the programmers rearranged the interface to put the item in its appropriate place. The programmers thought they were being consistent, but the consistency to the server was that the positions of the old items remain unchanged.

A Prefactoring Attitude

As you write your code, be conscious of the way you are writing it. Use a "prefactoring" editor attitude. It is OK to cut a block of code and paste it elsewhere. That usually means you're moving it to a better position: into a separate method, as detailed in Martin Fowler's Extract Method. If you find yourself *copying* and pasting a block of code, stop and analyze what you are copying. Should you place that code into a method? If so, why not place it there now, to prevent code duplication before it occurs?

Are you using the code you are copying as a template? Then why not create a template? A source code template is good for creating a common pattern in the layout of your classes. For example, if you decide that all classes should have to_string( ) and from_string( ) methods, set up a source code base that includes those methods. Whenever a developer creates a new class, she can copy that template into the new class source. This is "the exception to the rule" of copying and pasting more than a single line. In this case, there is a justifiable reason for the copy and paste: interface consistency. You can create a "wizard" to perform automatic text replacements. If your integrated development environment (IDE) supports an "implement interface" command, this template should be an interface. The act of implementing it creates the skeleton code for the methods of the implementing class.

---

[*] See Kernighan and Plauger's *The Elements of Programming Style* for an original discussion on this topic. One reviewer noted, "Uniform rules are invariably simpler."

When you find yourself writing a comment for a section of code, ask yourself why you are commenting it. Are you describing how you are implementing a particular algorithm within the method? If so, the section of code should probably be its own method. For example:

```
int [] array;
int odd_number;
// Find the first odd number in the array
for (int m=1; m < array.length; m++)
    {
    if (array[m] % 2  == 1)
        {
        odd_number = array[m];
        break;
        }
    }
```

This block could be turned into a method, such as the following:

```
int find_first_odd_number_in_array(int [] array);
```

Don't Repeat Yourself

The "Adapt a Prefactoring Attitude" guideline is a specialization of the "Don't Repeat Yourself (DRY) principle of Andrew Hunt and David Thomas (*The Pragmatic Programmer: From Journeyman to Master*, Addison-Wesley Professional, 1999). The concept is that information should have one authoritative source. If information is needed in multiple ways, a transformation process converts it from the single source into the other formats. By doing so, information needs to be changed only in one place. Dave Thomas says, "The idea is to try to plan ahead to prevent duplication, rather than to waste time removing stuff you've already done."

For example, an XML description of a data table can be transformed into SQL commands to create the table, as well as language-specific classes to access the table. Changes in the organization of the data table need to be made only in one place.

Documentation of Assumptions and Decisions

Keeping a journal is one way to learn from experience. In the journal, you can document the assumptions you made (e.g., the network is reliable) and the reasoning behind your design decisions. The journal can be separate from or part of the code source.

When you are faced with a design decision, you must have at least two alternatives. If you have only one option, you really have no decision to make. You might employ one of the guidelines in this book to aid you in your decision making. As you make decisions, document why you made them, especially for the more important ones. Later on, you can analyze those decisions and examine how your reasoning and assumptions worked out.*

The requirements outline what functionality your system needs to provide. The code itself says how you are technically providing that functionality. However, the code does not document why you chose that particular technical approach. The journal provides the "why." For example:

> "Sam stated that he never buys any CDRelease that has more than one physical CD. Therefore, there is only one physical CD that corresponds to a CDDisc and therefore only one ID associated with each CDDisc."

Suppose that later on, someone brings up the issue of CDReleases that contain more than one physical CD. You can examine the documented assumption and see whether it still holds true. If a multi-CD album was always rented as a whole package, the single-ID assumption can still be true. If the album were rented as individual CDs, now the assumption is false, and the design will need to undergo modification.

DOCUMENT YOUR ASSUMPTIONS AND YOUR DECISIONS
Keep a journal for retrospectives.

Dealing with Deviations and Errors

Dealing with error conditions is probably the hardest part of the development effort. Errors fall into at least two categories: conditions that arise in the normal operation of the program, and failures in the environment in which the program is operating.

I prefer the term *deviation* for an error that occurs during normal processing. A deviation is a departure from straightforward processing that can occur during normal program operation. Most use case logic deals with straightforward logic. The user does this, the system

---

* You can use the journal in the retrospectives discussed in Chapter 1. See also "Design decisions" at *http://www.agilemodeling.com/essays/agileDocumentation.htm*.

responds with that. In the normal course of processing, the system needs to deviate from this straightforwardness.

For example, it is possible that a CustomerID is entered that does not equal any of the IDs in the set of Customers. This could occur because the CustomerID was input incorrectly or the Customer was deleted because the customer had not rented for several years. If the collection of customers is kept on a server, causes include a network failure or server failure.

The first set of causes for a CustomerID not being found are deviations that can occur during normal processing. A correction mechanism can be suggested to the user (e.g., reenter the ID), though user action might not solve the problem.* The second set of causes (network or server failure) are errors, not deviations. They should not occur during normal operation. However, if the server or network were known to be unreliable, they could be handled as deviations.

Deviations should be dealt with at an appropriate level. The methods closest to where the deviation occurs often have the most information regarding what actions the user can take. If opening a nonexistent file signals an error, the caller of the open method usually knows the file's purpose and can add information regarding what might occur in the absence of that file. For example, suppose the file the method was opening was a configuration file. If the configuration file is nonexistent, the method might choose to use default settings. If the configuration file is absolutely required by the program, the method can signal an error.

Errors also should be dealt with at an appropriate level. There are two types of errors: fatal errors and nonfatal errors. *Fatal errors* are conditions for which further processing is probably futile. Examples of fatal errors include "out of memory" and "out of disk space." The user level is usually the place to deal with these errors. The internal code cannot correct them. *Nonfatal errors* are conditions for which the program can continue operation, albeit in a reduced capacity. An example is the inability to contact a service over a primary network. The methods in the level on which this error occurs should attempt contact over a backup network, instead of passing it up to a higher level. If sufficient nonfatal errors occur, they could turn into a fatal error. For example, if both the primary and backup networks go down, a fatal error should be signaled.

* For example, the failure could be due to an incorrect conversion from a String into a CustomerID. That failure is a program bug that should have been caught in testing. It is not a deviation.

DECIDE ON A STRATEGY TO DEAL WITH DEVIATIONS AND ERRORS

Determine for your system what deviations and errors are, and how to deal with both.

Whether deviations are signaled using return codes or exceptions is a matter of preference. If they are reported using exceptions, they should be classified into their own hierarchy to differentiate them from exceptions for unexpected conditions. If all possible deviations are coded as just regular exceptions, it becomes difficult to separate the expected from the unexpected.

Exceptions in many languages are divided into checked and unchecked exceptions. *Checked exceptions* are listed in the declaration of the method. The caller of the method must explicitly handle all checked exceptions by either catching them or passing them back to its caller. *Unchecked exceptions* are not listed and the caller might not even be aware that they are thrown. Unchecked exceptions are typically used for conditions that should cause termination, such as the inability to connect to a database.

Failure Distance

A large spread between the spot where an error occurs and when it is noticed makes the error harder to debug. For example, suppose an object reference is set to a null value. If this value is used to refer to an object, a program exception usually occurs. For example:

```
String reference = NULL;
// A few lines of code
reference.get_length( );
```

If the distance between the setting of the reference and its use is small, it is relatively easy to detect. If the distance is within a single method, often a compiler can identify the problem and issue a warning. However, if the reference is set in one method and is not used until many methods later, all the intervening methods have to be examined for bugs. The sooner the error is detected, the easier it is to correct it.

A concept of distance applies to the development process. The sooner an error is found, the easier it can be to fix. If abstract data types (ADTs) are used extensively, many errors can be detected at compile time in languages that support static type checking. For example, with a method such as:

```
get_abbreviation_for_state(String state);
```

any string can be passed to the method. With:

```
enumeration State {Arkansas, Alaska, ...}
get_abbreviation_for_state(State aState)
```

the compiler will signal an error if anything other than a State is passed.

WHAT'S AN ERROR TO YOU?

Deviations and errors are one way of classifying failures. Gary K. Evans, a reviewer, likes the term *deviation* but has grown accustomed to using *exceptions*, where an *error* is a kind of exception, but not conversely. He categorizes identified exceptions as 0 = no exception (no error); 1 = recoverable; 2 = unrecoverable; and 3 = fatal. He notes:

> Recoverable exceptions let you return to the main use case path and attain the goal of the use case. For nonrecoverable exceptions, you must abandon the goal. Fatal exceptions are moot. You are going down; you cannot attain the goal; and doing use cases for them is not very worthwhile. It has been interesting to me to group all exceptions according to these categories, and to address their implementation in ascending order. If I address only the *no exceptions* and *recoverable exceptions* categories in that order in my iterations, I still get approximately 80% coverage of the total exception space.

Another way of classifying conditions that occur is to consider whether they fall in the area of business rules or technology. Jim Batterson, a fellow consultant, divides errors into three categories:

- Things are not right but have been allowed for in the business rules. For example, what to do when someone enters a key that is not in the file, assuming your rules tell you what to do. They are not errors from a programming point of view, they are just something that takes us down a different path that we have allowed for in the program.

- Application problems are occurring that were not allowed for in the business rules, so your program does not know what to do with them, but still we are in the application domain here.

- We have problems that are in the technology domain. We cannot open a file or we run out of space on a drive somewhere. These were never mentioned in the requirements, but they are a problem. These problems can be classified as fatal or nonfatal errors.

User Messages

Messages reported to the user from deviations and errors should be meaningful to the user. They should include as much information as possible regarding how to work around or correct the error. Failures can be categorized into the meaning of the failure and how the user might react to the failure. The user message should designate the category of the failure.

For example, permanent failures imply that the user trying the same operation again will get the same error. Transient failures suggest that the user might attempt the operation again immediately and might complete it successfully. Temporary failures require some undetermined period of time before they are cleared up.

REPORT MEANINGFUL USER MESSAGES

Error messages should be reported in the context of what the user can do about the error, instead of in terms of what the underlying error is.

Implementation-related messages (such as a stack trace) should be captured, but not necessarily displayed to the user. You need to provide the means for developers to see the details. Otherwise, you cannot diagnose and fix problems, particularly intermittent problems.

Assertions

Assertions are statements about conditions that must be true while a program is executing. Some developers disable assertions when a program is used for production. If assertions in production code should be true during testing, they also ought to be true during production. Assertions should be removed only if there is a measured performance penalty.

The behavior of an assertion during testing usually causes the program to exit. For many applications, that behavior is appropriate. The user can be informed with a friendly terminating error message. For other applications, such as a server, that behavior might not be acceptable. In that case, assertions should be reported immediately and logged.

ORDERING PIZZA

You decide you want a pizza. Unless you have a specific pizza place in mind (a difference in implementation quality), you pick a pizza place out of the phone book, call them, and place an order.

"I'd like a large pepperoni with extra cheese," you say.

"Right. Address?"

"1 Elm Street," you reply.

"Thirty minutes," you hear, followed by a hang-up.

You ordered a pizza and got a response: it will be at your place in 30 minutes. If it does not arrive, it is a failure of the implementation.

This protocol symbolizes polymorphism. Almost any pizza place you call will require the same information. The speed at which they deliver might be different and the pizza might taste different, but the interface is the same.

What possible failures should you, the Hungry Customer, care about?

- **Closed: the pizza place does not answer.** You really do not know whether it is closed or whether their phone is not working. It really does not matter. You will not get a pizza from them today. This could be a temporary failure or possibly a permanent failure.

- **No longer make pizza:** the pizza shop has decided to concentrate on making calzones or subs. This is a permanent failure. There is no sense retrying.

- **Unable to make pizza at the current time:** you really do not care what the reason is. You have to try another pizza place. This is a temporary failure.

- **Unable to deliver pizza at the current time:** you can get a pizza, you just have to pick it up.

We have given user-meaningful names for these failures. You don't want implementation issues to slip back to the higher level. You don't care why they can't deliver the pizza, if there is nothing you can do to correct the situation. Their vehicle might have run out of gas or their driver might have gone on vacation.

The Hungry Customer should not have to deal with an OutofGas error. If the implementation uses bicycles rather than cars, a ChainBroken error might occur. The only thing that callers should deal with is an UnableToDeliver error. The more detailed errors should be handled at a lower level and rolled into the more abstract exception. The detail could be placed in an explanation and displayed to the user. The caller might find it amusing, but all they can do about it is to decide to pick up the pizza or find another implementation.

Speeding

Jerry Weinberg tells the story of two groups, both working on solving the same problem. Jerry's group created a solution that worked correctly but was slower than the other group's. The other group developed a solution that was fast but did not work for all input values.

The other group leader referred to the differences by belittling the correct solution for running so slowly. Jerry replied by asking when the other group would have a usable solution.

It is usually easier to transform a correctly designed "slow" system into a fast enough system than it is to alter an incorrect fast system. Even if the slow system cannot be transformed, it can be used as a reference platform for functionality tests.*

Do not waste time making assumptions about performance. Use a profiler to measure performance so that you can focus on a handful of key bottlenecks. Jim Batterson, a fellow consultant, tells the story:

> I know that when I was really concerned about efficiency, the best thing I had was a
> monitoring tool that would tell me where I was spending my time. It was always true
> that I was spending about 90% of my time on about 10 lines of code, or one little sub-
> routine or one read to a file that was done over and over again. You could optimize the
> hell out of the rest of the system and never get more than a 10% improvement, or you
> could optimize that one part and make that baby fly.

Once you have determined the location of the bottleneck, you can create a solution. Selecting a different algorithm often yields the greatest performance gains. For example, a quicksort algorithm works better than a bubble sort most of the time.

With object-oriented programs, high levels of abstraction can be the cause of bottlenecks. Fewer layers of abstraction decrease the number of method calls and thus the calling overhead. Sometimes more tightly coupled objects can eliminate overhead (e.g., sending messages in internal format between computer systems, instead of in a standard text format).

DON'T SPEED UNTIL YOU KNOW WHERE YOU ARE GOING

Make the system right, before you make it fast.†

OSF UNIX

The original OSF Unix was designed with several layers of abstraction. The virtual memory sub-system was written as an abstraction layer. This design made it easy to port the system between machines that used different virtual memory mechanisms. It turned out that this abstraction affected performance dramatically. To speed things up, direct use of the processor's virtual memory hardware replaced this abstraction.

---

* Andrew Koenig says, "When they tell you to avoid premature optimization, they don't mean it's OK to use a quadratic algorithm rather than a linear one, or even an n-log-n one."
† This is covered in *The Elements of Programming Style.*

The Spreadsheet Conundrum

The spreadsheet is an analogy for many design decisions you make during development. Consider the data on a spreadsheet, as shown in Figure 3-1. If you were to store the data in a linear manner in a file, you would need to decide whether to store the data by row or by column. Perhaps storing it by row seems most natural. What if programs that require the data in column order access it later? Row order makes that access inefficient.

CDDisc/Day	June 1	June 2
"Let It Be" copy 1	Rented	In-house
"Let It Be" copy 2	In-house	In-house
"Abbey Road" copy 1	In-house	Rented
"Abbey Road" copy 1	Rented	Rented

FIGURE 3-1. Spreadsheet of CDDiscs and days

If you knew that future programs were going to use column order, you should have considered that in your initial code. However, if you cannot reasonably foretell in what order data will be accessed, you cannot worry too much now how it should be stored. Just document your assumptions and later on, if you have to change your approach, you will at least know why you did it the other way.

Many facets of programs parallel the spreadsheet. For example, string resources and languages form a spreadsheet such as that shown in Figure 3-2.

Resource/Language	English	German
NAME	Name	Namen
CITY	City	Stadt

FIGURE 3-2. Spreadsheet of resources and languages

Typically the data in Figure 3-2 is stored with strings stored sequentially for each language. If you will be adding more languages, having the data stored in that manner makes sense. However, if you are always adding more resources, but never adding more languages, it could be more efficient to store the strings sequentially by resource.

THE SPREADSHEET CONUNDRUM

Recognize when you are making the row/column decision.

This spreadsheet conundrum is reflected in the organization of graphics packages. A package can be organized in two ways, which correspond to the rows and columns of Figure 3-3.

Device/Object	Rectangle	Circle
Screen	draw()	draw()
Printer	draw()	draw()

FIGURE 3-3. Graphics spreadsheet

A Graphics Example

For example, to draw a rectangle on a device, you could write the code as shown in Example 3-1.

EXAMPLE 3-1. Shape drawing self

```
class Rectangle
    draw(DeviceContext a_context);

class Circle
    draw (DeviceContext a_context);

Rectangle a_rectangle = new Rectangle( );
Circle a_circle = new Circle( );
a_rectangle.draw(a_device_context);
a_circle.draw(a_device_context);
```

Example 3-1 represents selecting the column headings as the shape performing the drawing. The alternative is to select the row headings to perform the drawing, as shown in Example 3-2.

EXAMPLE 3-2. Device drawing shape

```
class DeviceContext
    draw(Rectangle a_rectangle);
    draw(Circle a_circle);

DeviceContext a_device_context = new ScreenDevice( );
a_device_context.draw(a_rectangle);
a_device_context.draw(a_circle);
```

In Example 3-1, it is easy to add additional drawing shapes, such as a Triangle. You create a class for the new shape and implement a draw method. In Example 3-2, it is harder to create a new shape. You need to add a method to draw the shape to every implementation of the device context.

Who's in Charge

The same conundrum applies to the question of "Who's in Charge." For example, you could arrange the operation of dialing a phone number as shown in Example 3-3.

EXAMPLE 3-3. Phone does the dialing

```
class Phone
    dial(PhoneNumber a_number)

Phone a_phone = new Phone( );
a_phone.dial(a_phone_number)
```

Or you could arrange the operation as shown in Example 3-4.

EXAMPLE 3-4. PhoneNumber does the dialing

```
class PhoneNumber
    dial(Phone a_phone)

PhoneNumber a_phone_number = new PhoneNumber();
a_phone_number.dial(a_phone);
```

The distinction regarding who is in charge of dialing a phone number might not make any difference until you come across a situation in which you might want to send another set of digits to the phone (such as an account number):

```
class AccountNumber
    IntegerString number;
```

In Example 3-3, you would add another method to Phone. For example:

```
class Phone
    dial(PhoneNumber a_number)
    dial(AccountNumber a_number)
```

In Example 3-4, you would add a dial() method to the AccountNumber class to keep operations consistent with the PhoneNumber class.

```
class AccountNumber
    dial(Phone a_phone);
```

The tradeoff between these two approaches is not clear-cut. In one instance, you are asking a Phone to dial a set of digits. In the other, you are asking the object to dial itself on a Phone you provide. If you prefer one way, document your reason in your design journal. Later on, you might come across a situation in which the other approach seems more appropriate. You can review your previous decision and see whether the reasoning still makes sense in light of the new context.

The spreadsheet conundrum appears in many forms, which I will note throughout this book. Recognizing when you are making a tradeoff between two ways of organizing a class structure can help you to make better design decisions.

Tools Are Tools—Use Them Wisely

Many software development tools are available. They range from requirements documentation to modeling tools to IDEs (Integrated Development Environment). Tools are wonderful. They can automate many processes and ensure consistency and integrity.

Work with or Against the IDE

Particular features of IDEs or frameworks can influence how you develop your system. An IDE such as Microsoft Visual Studio makes it easy to develop handlers for graphical user interface (GUI) events. With a couple of mouse clicks, you can set up a function that is called when a button is clicked or when text is entered into an edit box. The IDE strongly suggests a stylistic pattern for handling and naming the functions. You are welcome to override that pattern if you have strong feelings concerning your own style. However, it is often easier to accept rather than to fight. It will add consistency to your programs. Other developers working on your system might not be as adamant about the style and might be much more willing to accept the default. So the default becomes the easiest form of consistent code. *

Multiple Tools

An old adage says, "Use the right tool for the job." When programming particular aspects of a system, usually certain tools are designed to perform specific jobs easily. For example, Perl performs string processing; XLST transforms XML from one form into another; Crystal Reports creates reports from databases. If you are familiar with the appropriate tool, it is quicker to code the operation with that tool. If you are not familiar with the tool and if the aspect of the program that requires the tool is relatively small, coding using the main development language might make more sense. For example, if you have a number of string manipulations, writing those manipulations in PERL makes sense. If you have only a few, code them in Java (if that's what you are using). Not only do you save tool-learning time, but also, the maintainers after you will not be required to know yet another language.

On the other hand, it is important to learn new tools. You learn new ways of solving problems. If you know more tools, you will be better able to pick the appropriate tools. If you know only a few, you will be forced to use those few tools, bending them into uncomfortable solutions.

* If you prefer your own style, select tools that do not impose their own style or allow you to customize their style. Eric M. Burke, a reviewer, gave the example of the Java Spring framework. Its persistence mechanism does not require you to code classes to be persisted in any particular style.

CHAPTER FOUR

Getting the Big Picture

WE CONTINUE TALKING WITH SAM TO GET A CLEARER UNDERSTANDING OF THE OVERALL REQUIREMENTS; in other words, we want to see the big picture. Then we start to create an architecture for a system to meet these requirements. We outline overall functional tests for the system to provide a reference for internal tests. We also consider the system's security aspects.

The Rest of the Story

To understand more fully the system we are creating, we sketch out the remaining use cases. Figure 4-1 shows a graphical view of the relationships between the different cases. The following use cases are written using the abstractions that Sam, Tim, and I agreed upon:

- Report_when_CDDiscs_are_overdue

    a. Clerk requests a report.

    b. System responds with a list of CDDiscs and a list of customers who owe overdue fees.

- Search_catalog

    a. Customer enters search criteria (artist, song title, etc.).

    b. System responds with CDReleases matching those criteria.

    c. Customer selects a CDRelease.

    d. System responds with songs on that CDRelease.

- Show_availability (extends Search_catalog)

    a. Customer requests availability of a CDDisc for a CDRelease (which store it is in).

    b. System responds with availability status.

- Provide_discounts (extends Checkout_a_CDDisc)

    a. When CDDisc is rented, give a discount to frequent renters.

- Charge_rental (extends Checkout_a_CDDisc)

    a. When CDDisc is rented, add charge to monthly bill for customers.

    b. At end of month, bill customer's charge card for total amount.

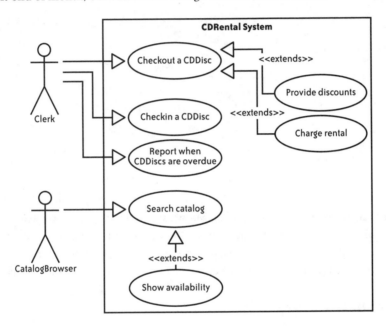

FIGURE 4-1. Use cases for Sam's system

For the first production release of the system, we want to ensure that we have the *minimum feature set* (MFS). The MFS contains the minimum set of requirements that will provide a usable program. For Sam's system, a program having a check-out feature without a check-in feature would be unusable.

Process

Analysis concerns describing the user requirements (the problem description), and *design* concentrates on creating a solution that meets the requirements (the solution definition). The exact boundary between the two is hard to determine, especially with iterative development. A feedback cycle occurs between the two phases.

Objects created in the design phase often reflect the real-world objects referred to in the requirements. If you state the object definitions in the requirements clearly, the software object definitions will be clear as well. Lack of clarity in what the software objects really should do feeds back into requirements clarification. For Sam's system, understanding the difference between a CDDisc and a CDRelease not only clarifies the requirements, but also yields two potential classes. As the CDDisc class is developed, questions regarding how its methods should work might help discover ambiguities in the requirements.*

Analysis Paralysis

Analysis paralysis occurs when you become stuck trying to complete your understanding of the requirements to be implemented. You become so stuck, always feeling that you *need* to learn yet one more thing, you cannot move on to design.

Gary K. Evans, a reviewer, points out, "Another cause is fear: fear that you might miss something. Some people have personalities that force them to try to anticipate and plan for every possible event before they are willing to move forward. Some organizations create cultures of impossible expectations where any failure is regarded severely, so people adapt by staying in the analysis mindset as long as possible. Some development processes force issues up-front that should not be considered until much later in the process, because the process tries to 'control away' the fear of failure."

You do not want to spend a lifetime specifying your system requirements. Nevertheless, you should spend some time understanding the basic abstractions, the basic use cases, and how everything interacts.

One cause of analysis paralysis is trying to specify every detail in a system. Some details are important, and others aren't. Determining what is important at each development step is key. Deciding what details are essential and unessential can be difficult. I found a few suggestions to be helpful. Any details dealing with appearance are unessential. You do not need to know the text for a label of a dialog box until you code it. Implementation details are usually unessential—for example, the particular database that will be used (Oracle or MySQL). The relationship count between two concepts is usually essential—for example, whether the relationship between CDDisc and CDRelease is one-to-one, one-to-many, or many-to-many.

Experience can help distinguish between the essential and unessential details. Examine your previous projects to determine which details discovered after the start of design and coding created major changes in the design.

---

* The design classes might not reflect the classes in the requirements precisely. They might differ by behavior, services, attributes, or relationships. However, the requirement classes do form a good initial starting point for the design classes.

Design Paralysis

Similar to analysis paralysis, you can also suffer from *design paralysis*. You are suffering from design paralysis if you do not want to start coding until the details of every class are determined. (Some people use the same term, analysis paralysis, to describe both of these situations.) One way to determine if you have a sufficient class design is to work through the use cases using the classes you created. If you can perform all the use cases, it's highly probable that you have captured the meaningful classes.

To work through each use case, you can create a Unified Modeling Language (UML) sequence diagram. An alternative fun way to perform the use cases is with a group of developers. Each developer takes on the role of one or more classes. One developer reads the use case, pausing at each step. The developers for the classes participating in the use case acknowledge the responsibilities of their classes in implementing each step.

Due to changes in requirements, a design might have to be changed. There is probably no fixed set of requirements for any given system.* However, the overall design that you create at the beginning should at least fulfill the initial use cases.

SAILING THE WAVES

When windsurfing over a series of waves, you need to think about the upcoming waves even while you are riding the current one. If you fail to do this, you might find your board's tip submarining into a subsequent wave, causing an unpleasant fall.

You know the waves will change, especially the ones farther away, but you are not sure how they will change. So the best you can do is to sail the current condition of the wave and be prepared to change your plans when the waves change.

The Initial Design

Everyone has their own way of coming up with an initial set of classes. You can start with the basic abstractions that were described during analysis. Some people examine the requirements or use cases for nouns, and turn those nouns into either classes or attributes of classes. Verbs that occur can be turned into responsibilities or methods of the classes. One ambiguity that exists in using grammatical syntax to discover objects is that an operation might be expressed as either a noun or a verb. The requirements might talk about a customer renting a CD or starting a CD rental.

Tim and I use a variation of CRC cards (see *Object Design: Roles, Responsibilities, and Collaborations* by Rebecca Wirfs-Brock and Alan McKean [Addison-Wesley Professional, 2002]) to formulate a starting set of classes.† CRC stands for *Class-Responsibility-Collaboration*. On an

---

* Changes in requirements are inevitable. Capers Jones (*http://www.softerra.com/files/conflict.pdf*) suggests that requirements change at a rate of 1% or more per month.

† See also *http://c2.com/doc/oopsla89/paper.html*.

index card, you list the class name, the responsibilities assigned to the class, and the other classes that it collaborates with to fulfill those responsibilities. Tim and I also jot a one-line description of each class on the card. Often we also capture potential attributes or other information that might have been referred to in the use cases or client discussions. Figure 4-2 depicts the CRC cards for Sam's CD rental system.

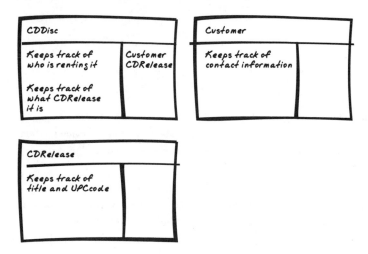

FIGURE 4-2. CRC cards for Sam's CD rental system

Tim and I often code class interfaces directly from the CRC cards. But since our handwriting can be unreadable to others, this book contains machine-written UML diagrams of our classes. UML diagrams are more formal than CRC cards and usually contain more precise declarations of the names of the methods and their parameters. Figure 4-3 shows the corresponding UML diagram for the class structure for Sam's system.

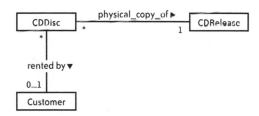

FIGURE 4-3. Class structure for Sam's CD rental system

Once Tim and I have agreed on the classes and their responsibilities, we create more detail regarding each class. The details show more specific information than the CRC cards. The following code shows the specifics for the classes illustrated in Figure 4-3. Note that the abstract data types (ADTs) specify meaningful types without addressing a specific design or implementation.

```
CDRelease /* A CD identified by its UPC*/
    CommonString title
    UPCCode upc_code
```

```
CDDisc /* Physical copy of a CDRelease */
    PhysicalID physical_id
    CDRelease cd_release
    static CDDisc find_cd_disc_by_id(PhysicalID physical_id)
    rent(Customer customer)
    return_a_rental( )

Customer
    CustomerID id
    Name name
    Address address
    PhoneNumber day_phone_number
    static Customer find_customer_by_id(CustomerID id)
```

> ### NOTE
>
> static is a keyword that denotes a classwide method. A classwide method
> does not operate on an object. It is typically used to return objects of a
> class.

Along with the class diagram, we write sequence diagrams or pseudocode listings to demonstrate that the proposed classes have sufficient behavior to implement the use cases. We
could create these documents for all the use cases. However, Sam is anxious to get a working system (the MFS). So we write down the complete details for only the first two use
cases:

Checkout_a_CDDisc

   Enter `customer_id` and `cd_disc_id` from keyboard or barcode scan:

```
CDDisc cddisc_rented = CDDisc.find_cd_disc_by_id(cd_disc_id);
Customer renting_customer = Customer.find_customer_by_id(customer_id)
cddisc_rented.rent(renting_customer); // Prints contract
```

Checkin_a_CDDisc

   Enter `cd_disc_id`:

```
CDDisc cddisc_rented = CDDisc.find_cd_disc_by_id(cd_disc_id);
cd_disc_rented.return_a_rental( ) // If overdue, print message
```

Before we move on, we need to get a little more information from Sam. I noticed that we
never discussed "overdue." Since that concept is mentioned at this high-level description,
it seems like an important detail.

I gave him a call.

"Sam, how do I know if a CDDisc is overdue?" I asked.

"Well, we allow the customer a base period. If the CD comes back after that period, we
charge him a late fee," he replied.

This is an example of the feedback that occurs between the design and analysis phases.
Often the complete understanding of a concept does not occur until someone tries to use
the concept.

Global Planning, Local Designing

You might be concerned that Tim and I are ignoring the other use cases. While we concentrate on a few of the cases in detail, we still review the others to help guide us in the design. One cannot deal with every facet simultaneously. We might have to alter our design when we get to the details of the other requirements. The requirements might change in the future and some use cases might go away before they are implemented. However, if our design cannot perform the other use cases, we need to redo it before proceeding.

After coming up with the initial set of classes, we examine each use case to see how it might affect the class selection. From our preliminary analysis, Search_catalog appears to be a fairly separate module. This case deals mainly with the CDRelease class. The Show_availability case will use CDDisc. In both cases, we feel the basic class layout should not need to be altered, although the classes themselves might require modification.

The Report_when_CDDiscs_are_overdue case creates a report. Since Checkin_a_CDDisc already checks for overdue rentals, the required information is probably already captured. From past experience, we know that reports are typically the easiest feature to write, since data states are not being changed. Therefore, we do not believe that this case will have a heavy impact on the classes.

REPORTS CAN DEFINE THE SYSTEM

Graham Oakes, a reviewer, suggests, "Reports often give the greatest insight into what information people really need from the system and to what exceptions might exist in the data. Some of the most successful projects I've worked on started from defining the reports that people needed to see and then defining the systems needed to collect that data. It might be worth thinking about: whether a system is information-centric as opposed to action-centric."

Charge_CDDisc and Provide_discounts revolve around how a rental is priced and paid for. They are an extension of Sam's current system. They are further down in the list of features to add. We know they will affect the current classes, since the classes do create a customer contract. If Sam wanted these features to be implemented as soon as the baseline system was created, Tim and I would explore them more fully before proceeding with the design. At this point, we need to replace his manual system first, and later we can get further into the rental policy details.

PLAN GLOBALLY, DEVELOP LOCALLY
Incremental implementations should fit into a global plan.

Testing Functionality

At each point in the system's development, you should create a rough draft of the tests.* The test outlines can cover the basic use cases, as well as any misuse cases that might come up in the discussion. A *misuse case* documents how a user might unintentionally (or intentionally, with malice aforethought) interact with the system.

Sam and I developed a first cut at the use cases. So now is a good time to examine some acceptance tests. Brainstorming the tests can bring up new issues that the client has not made part of his requirements. On the other hand, if you cannot imagine a test scenario that can determine that a requirement has been fulfilled, it is time to examine that requirement.

Sam, Tim, and I agreed on a preliminary list of acceptance tests that the system should pass before it is installed for production.

Use case: Checkout_a_CDDisc

- Scenario: RegularRental

  a. Enter a Customer ID and CDDisc ID.

---

* Eric M. Burke, a reviewer, noted, "Ideally you'd start writing tests, not just rough drafts. Also, start writing tools to automate the acceptance testing. If you develop the testing harness in parallel with the code, you will be more likely to write testable code. Failure to do this means you'll be able to write unit tests, but acceptance testing will be hard to automate."

b. System should print rental contract.

c. Check to see that CDDisc is recorded as *currently rented.*

- Scenario: AlreadyRented (Misuse)

    a. Enter CDDisc ID of CDDisc that is recorded as *currently rented.*

    b. System should respond with an error.

- Scenario: BadCustomer (Misuse)

    a. Enter Customer ID that does not exist in the system.

    b. System should respond with an error.

- Scenario: BadCDDisc (Misuse)

    a. Enter a physical ID that does not exist in the system.

    b. System should respond with an error.

Use case: Checkin_a_CDDisc

- Scenario: RegularReturn

    a. Enter CDDisc ID.

    b. System should respond that CDDisc has been returned.

- Scenario: OverdueReturn (Misuse)

    a. Enter CDDisc ID that is overdue

    b. System should respond that CDDisc has been returned with an overdue message

- Scenario: NotRentedReturn (Misuse)

    a. Enter CDDisc ID of CDDisc that is recorded as *not rented.*

    b. System should respond with an error.

IF IT CAN'T BE TESTED, DON'T REQUIRE IT

Every functionality requirement, whether formally or informally stated, should have a test created for it. If you cannot test a requirement, there is no way to determine whether you have met it.*

Often it is difficult to specify clear-cut tests for some requirements classified as the "ilities" described in Chapter 2. Requirements such as "easy to use," "quick to learn," or "maintainable" can be difficult to measure. So the guideline has been restricted to functionality tests.

* See *The Object Primer* by Scott W. Ambler and Barry McGibbon (Cambridge University Press, 2001).

Fractals Are Everywhere

A *fractal* is a geometric pattern that is repeated at ever-smaller scales. Likewise, the same software design pattern can appear in both a large scale and a small scale. For example, the overall framework for a system is input-process-output. In the early 1960s, IBM developed HIPO charts. HIPO stands for Hierarchical-Input-Process-Output. The chart depicted a functional breakdown of responsibilities. Each chart showed the input, process, and output for a given level of detail. From that level, you derived lower-level charts that gave more detail for the input/process/output sequence.

This same fractal principle is applicable to both use cases and tests. People normally think of use cases in terms of how the user interacts with the system. Although use cases generally are associated with a system as a whole, the technique can also be applied to interfaces and classes within the system. Use cases for a system define steps within a process. When the technique is applied to classes or interfaces, it yields a series of method calls. To distinguish between the two, I will use the term *work cases*, referring to the work that the implementation has to perform.

The work cases for the interfaces and classes are derived from the external interface's use cases. If you cannot come up with work cases for a class, perhaps the class has no purpose. If you do not know how you are going to use a class, it is hard to design it and test it.

For Sam's system, there is an external use case for checking in a CDDisc. From this external use case is derived a Check_in work case for CDDisc. Many of the misuse cases listed earlier also represent misuse cases for the CDDisc class. An example of a work case is the following. It appears similar to the use case from which it is derived since the use case involves mostly the CDDisc class:

Work case: Checkin_a_CDDisc for CDDisc

- Scenario: RegularReturn

    a. Find a CDDisc by ID.

    b. Return the CDDisc.

Since many functional tests are derived from use cases, the propagation of tests acts in a similar manner. Tests for the external interface show up as tests for the outer classes, which then appear as tests for classes deeper within the system.

The tests for each individual class should contain the appropriate subtests from the tests for the whole system. For example, the tests for the CDDisc class will include renting a CDDisc twice without being checked in. That test should produce an error response from the rental method. Tests for individual classes can also include ones based on the nonfunctional requirements for the whole system. An overall performance test such as a rate of transaction (being able to rent 100 CDDiscs in a minute) turns into a performance test for the CDDisc class itself.

You might have the time to make up unit tests for every single method of every single class. If you don't, you should at least make up tests that correspond to the work cases for that class. Often tests for individual methods are not meaningful. They can take place only in the context of a work case or multiple work cases. For example, with Sam's system, the test for checking in a Rental needs to be performed in the context of a checked-out CDDisc.

Another example of testing in context is a simple file class. You can write a test for just the open method. A successful result is meaningless if you are trying to determine if the file was opened properly. You cannot test for a successful open unless you do another operation on the file, such as a read or write. The open method cannot be tested fully by itself. It can be tested fully only in a context. Conversely, the read method cannot be tested fully by itself, except in the context of an open file.

PLAN FOR TESTING

Developing test strategies in advance can lead to a better design.

Testing Feedback

The concept of feedback applies not only to development, but also to testing. When users report bugs, you can write tests to check for those bugs in your current system. You can also analyze the bugs to see why they occurred and how they slipped through the tests.

You might want to alter your testing strategy in the next iteration. For example, if you find that the bugs are occurring when users have many other programs in operation, you can add tests for operating with limited resources to the appropriate class tests.

THE SKYDIVING GRANDMA

I consulted for a life insurance firm that was creating illustrations for life insurance. The illustrations depicted how the value of an insurance policy grew over the lifetime of the insured. The illustration program had hundreds of inputs, ranging from age, sex, and hazardous avocations (including skydiving) to the timing of loans that an insured intended on taking for expected events (e.g., college tuition). It was impossible to test all possible combinations of inputs (e.g., a skydiving 80-year-old female borrowing $10,000 for her grandchild's education in four years). The only way to perform full checkout was in the field.

The illustration program was distributed to thousands of life insurance salespeople. As the program ran, it recorded all inputs, some intermediate calculation values, and all outputs. The records were sent back to the development department and the actuaries for analysis. The illustrations that contained outputs that appeared anomalous (such as getting $1 million of life insurance for $1) were examined further. The inputs for those instances and the corrected outputs were used as test cases for the next version.

Testing Quality

Even if your use cases and misuse cases are numerous and complex, there is more to good testing than executing use cases. Use case testing focuses on the capability of the system; in other words, "can it work?" James Bach (*http://www.satisfice.com/*) says:

> Just as important is the reliability question: "will it work?" This is what makes testing difficult. We see that the system can work but we need to know if it will work under the requisite variety of circumstances, states, inputs, and outputs, now and in the future, for all the users we care about.

> So, we need to do a variety of tests, not just one. That is where creative and ingenious humans come in. Consider augmenting use case tests with a much more diversified approach to testing.

Bach describes an approach called exploratory testing, which invites the tester to use the information gained while testing to develop new tests (*http://www.satisfice.com/articles/et-article.pdf*). He notes that automated tests of any kind, while necessary, are rarely sufficient to validate the fitness of a product for release.

You might consider yourself a developer who leaves the testing to the testers. But you should be testing your developed modules to ensure they meet the desired functionality. For more information on testing, see *Testing Computer Software*, 2nd Edition by Cem Kaner, Jack Falk, and Hung Q. Nguyen (Wiley, 1999) and *Lessons Learned in Software Testing* by Cem Kaner, James Bach, and Bret Pettichord (Wiley, 2001).

Security

Sam asked me to stop by for a cup of coffee. He sat with a perplexed look on his face. I inquired about the idea that he was mulling over.

He said, "I watched a TV show last night about a guy who broke into a computer system and stole information worth millions of dollars. What happens if someone breaks into my system?"

"Well, how much is the information in your system worth?" I asked.

"OK, not millions, but maybe in the tens of thousands," he replied.

"We should perform a risk analysis, before we get too involved in the detailed design of the system," I responded.

Security encompasses a broad range of issues including access protection, attack prevention, data backup, and data security. You can find a detailed discussion of security issues in *Security Engineering: A Guide to Building Dependable Distributed Systems* by Ross J. Anderson and Ross Anderson (Wiley, 2001). You should consider security from the start of the design. You should perform a risk analysis to determine the risks, the probability of their occurrence, and the cost if the risks materialize. Once you've identified the risks, you can employ appropriate measures, including structuring the design to meet those risks.

Many books explain how to write secure code. Two are *Building Secure Software: How to Avoid Security Problems the Right Way* by John Viega and Gary McGraw (Addison-Wesley Professional, 2001) and *Secure Coding: Principles and Practices* by Mark G. Graff and Kenneth R. Van Wyk (O'Reilly, 2003). Determine how much effort you should spend on making code secure based on the vulnerabilities you find in the risk analysis.

Here is a portion of the risk analysis conversation I had with Sam. We were discussing the risks involved for the first two use cases.

"What's the worst thing you can think of that might happen?" I asked Sam.

"I could lose track of which customer rented which CD," he answered.

"That sounds pretty serious, but how serious is it?" I asked. "You would have to worry about dishonest customers who didn't return their CDs if they learned that this had happened. I don't think that would be a very high percentage.

"You're going to be doing daily backups, right?" I continued.

"Yes," Sam replied.

"So we should worry about the rentals and returns for a single day," I stated. "To spend a lot of money at this time worrying about dishonest people is probably not worth the cost. If you do have a disk crash, you can always enter the data again from the paper copies of the rental agreements."

"What we might worry about instead," I suggested, "is whether a customer could check in a CDDisc by himself and then just remove it from the store. We need to prevent this from occurring via physical security on the check-in computer, or software protection such as user passwords, or both."

If we decide to implement passwords, the login and logout processes ought to be added as either additional use cases or alterations of existing ones. The use case changes will affect the design by assigning additional responsibility to classes or by creating new ones.

IF YOU FORGET SECURITY, YOU'RE NOT SECURE

Security should not be an afterthought. Consider it during all phases of development.

CHAPTER FIVE

Got Class?

Now it's time to turn the initial draft of Sam's system into classes. We explore how concepts can be represented by single or multiple classes. We also examine different ways of dealing with data dependencies, and we consider how to use classes to perform collection-related responsibilities.

Categories and Classes

Sam came by and said, "Oh, by the way, the rental period is different based on the category of a CDRelease."

"What is a category?" I asked.

"Oh," he said nonchalantly, "it could be a Golden Oldie, New Release, or Regular. Didn't I mention that before?"

"You must have—I just didn't remember it," I noted dryly.

You can approach this issue in a couple of ways—using different classes and using different objects. Using different classes is often the solution for when a programmer learns about inheritance. Once you have a shiny new hammer, every problem is a nail needing to be pounded. But not every problem is, or should be, solved with inheritance. Often an extra attribute in a class will do the trick.

Different Classes

We have three different categories: NewRelease, GoldenOldie, and Regular. Because there are three names, a designer might make these three separate classes. Since they are CDReleases, a natural thing to do is to form an inheritance hierarchy with a base class from which to derive each class. Figure 5-1 shows what an inheritance-oriented class hierarchy might look like.

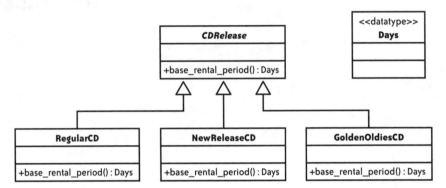

FIGURE 5-1. A CDRelease inheritance hierarchy

The CDRelease abstract base class defines the base_rental_period( )abstract method. This method is implemented differently for each type of CD. The base class and the three derived classes would look like those shown in Example 5-1.

EXAMPLE 5-1. CDRelease with inheritance

```
abstract class CDRelease
    {
    abstract Days base_rental_period( );
    };
class NewReleaseCD extends CDRelease
    {
    Days base_rental_period( )
        {
        return 2;
        }
    };
class GoldenOldieCD extends CDRelease
    {
    Days base_rental_period( )
        {
        return  4;
        }
    };
class RegularCD extends CDRelease
    {
    Days base_rental_period( )
```

EXAMPLE 5-1. CDRelease with inheritance (continued)

```
        {
        return  3;
        }
    };
```

Some solutions might use a concrete method for base_rental_period( ) and eliminate the RegularCD class.

The users of the classes illustrated in Figure 5-1 would use objects as outlined in Example 5-2.

EXAMPLE 5-2. Using derived classes

```
    CDRelease my_cd = new GoldenOldieCD( );
    Days rental_period = my_cd.base_rental_period( );
```

Different Objects

Having three classes whose behavior differs only in terms of the value of a property is an example of overclassification. The alternative is to have a single class with an attribute that denotes the type of CD. The class diagram in Figure 5-2 depicts this alternative.

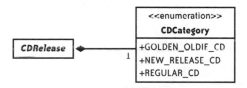

FIGURE 5-2. CDRelease using an enumerated category

The term *CDCategory* in Figure 5-2 might not specify exactly what we mean. The word *category* can be overloaded. However, if the client says that is what he wants, by all means, go with the client. It will make life a lot easier if you and your client are on the same page.

Using the CDCategory enumeration, the CDRelease class appears as shown in Example 5-3.

EXAMPLE 5-3. CDRelease using different objects

```
enumeration CDCategory {NEW_RELEASE_CD, REGULAR_CD, GOLDIE_OLDIE_CD};

class CDRelease
    {
    CDCategory category;
    CDRelease(CDCategory cd_category)
        {
        this.category = cd_category;
        }
    Days base_rental_period( )
        {
        /* Coming up soon */
        }
    };
```

Using different objects, the code corresponding to Example 5-2 is shown in Example 5-4.

EXAMPLE 5-4. Using different objects

```
CDRelease my_cd = new CDRelease(GOLDIE_OLDIE_CD);
Days rental_period = my_cd.base_rental_period();
```

The code for the base_rental_period( ) method in CDRelease that corresponds to the code for the derived classes in Example 5-1 looks like that shown in **Example 5-5.***

EXAMPLE 5-5. Base_rental_period method

```
static Days [] base_rental_period_per_category = {2, 3, 4};

Days base_rental_period( )
    {
    return base_rental_period_per_category [category];
    }
```

The real question is whether the three types really represent objects of the same class or of different classes. One rule of thumb you can use in making that decision is whether the objects differ in just values or in the logic of their methods.† If the former is true, one class might be sufficient. If the latter is true, different classes might be appropriate. We will examine inheritance again in a later section.

DON'T OVERCLASSIFY

Separate concepts into different classes based on behavior, not on data.

Declaration Versus Execution

Example 5-5 with arrays rather than separate methods illustrates the difference between using declarative-style and executable-style code to express an operation. The base_rental_period_per_category array is an example of declarative style. If you want to change the base period for a category, you do not change the internal operations of a method, just the values in a table. Because the values are in a table, this is often referred to as *table-driven code*. I use the term *declarative-style programming* to encompass any form of coding in which the design permits expected changes to be made in anything other than executable code. This includes table-driven code and configurable code.

---

* Example 5-5 was written to parallel the derived class example. We should apply the "Never Let a Constant Slip into Code" guideline so that the numbers are coded as BASE_RENTAL_PERIOD_FOR_NEW_RELEASE, etc.

† Scott Ambler suggests that this concept came from Responsibility-Driven Design. This topic was introduced in *Object-Oriented Design: A Responsibility-Driven Approach* by Rebecca Wirfs-Brock and Brian Wilkerson (Proceedings of OOPSLA, 1989).

With tables in source-code files, the code will have to be recompiled if the values change. Instead of hardcoding these values into the source, you could read in the values from a configuration file. The implementation of the configuration file could employ comma-delimited files, XML, or a database. The configuration data acts in a declarative-style mode. It contains information on what needs to be done, without specifying how it is done.

With a configuration file, the source program code does not change, even if a new CDCategory is added. We could add hundreds of new categories without an additional line of code. The configuration file would contain additional data on the new categories.*

DECLARATION OVER EXECUTION

Declarative-style programming can provide flexibility without code changes.

Appropriate Inheritance

When would we want to derive classes from CDRelease? When the classes behave differently. We want to deal with classes with a single interface (the base class), and not be concerned with the implementation in the derived classes.

A common indication that inheritance is desirable is the temptation to use switch statements in a class. For example, suppose Sam wanted to send an email to himself every time a CDRelease of type GoldieOldie or NewRelease was rented.

With only a single class, the code might employ a switch statement (or an equivalent set of if statements), as in the rental_notification( ) function shown in Example 5-6.

EXAMPLE 5-6. Rental_notification method with switch

```
void rental_notification( )
    {    switch(category_id)
        {
    case REGULAR_CD:
        break;
    case NEW_RELEASE_CD:
    case GOLDIE_OLDIE_CD:
        send_email( );
        break;
    default:
        throw new ProgramException( );
    }
```

---

* If Sam was going to be adding new categories or altering data for existing categories frequently, a separate CDReleaseConfiguration class should handle these functions.

With the array shown in Example 5-3, the creation of a new CDCategory involves just add-ing another entry to the array. With behavior dependent on the category such as in Example 5-6, each appearance of a switch statement needs to be changed. If we need one switch statement in the entire implementation of a class, we should consider inheritance. If the same switch occurs in multiple places, applying inheritance is in order. Suppose that Sam also wants an email when a GoldieOldie or NewRelease is returned. With different objects, the rental_return_notification( ) method would have a switch that parallels the switch in rental_notification( ). Using inheritance for CDRelease, as shown in Figure 5-3, eliminates these switch statements.

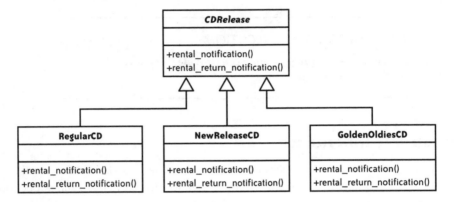

F I G U R E 5 - 3 . CDRelease with inheritance

Inheritance applied appropriately, such as in Figure 5-3, makes an excellent design. Using inheritance where it is not necessary, such as in Figure 5-1, can make designs harder to maintain.

AVOID PREMATURE INHERITANCE

Inheritance needs time to evolve.

As an alternative to inheritance, you can use delegation. The book *Design Patterns* strongly suggests that delegation is more powerful than inheritance. You can eliminate the inherit-ance of Figure 5-3 by delegating the behavior of CDRelease to classes implementing an interface (CDReleaseCategory) in a variation of the Strategy pattern (see *Design Patterns*). Figure 5-4 shows the class outline for this approach.

The constructor for CDRelease sets the cd_release_category attribute to an object of the cor-responding type. The methods in CDRelease delegate their actions to that object, as illus-trated in Example 5-7.

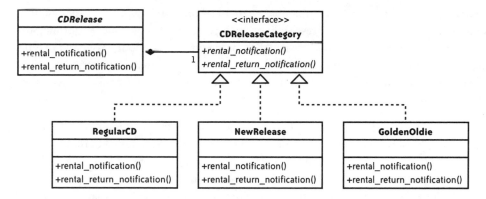

FIGURE 5-4. CDRelease with delegation

EXAMPLE 5-7. Example 5-7. CDRelease with delegation

```
CDReleaseCategory [] cd_release_categories = {
    new RegularCD(), new NewRelease( ), new GoldenOldie( )};
CDRelease (CDCategory cd_category)
    {
    cd_release_category = cd_release_categories[cd_category];
    }
rental_notification( )
    {
    cd_release_category.rental_notification( );
    }
rental_return_notification( )
    {
    cd_release_category.rental_return_notification( );
    }
```

Suppose aspects of CDRelease's behavior depended on a second attribute—say, the genre of music (classical, rock, or folk). With inheritance, you would have to create a second inheritance hierarchy based on that behavior. With delegation, you only need to create a second attribute that refers to another class of objects that contains the desired behavior.

Communicate with Text

Text is an excellent way to communicate between systems. You do not need to worry about the homogeneity of the systems. The physical representation of primitives, such as a double, in each of two systems can be different. The text form is the *lingua franca* into which each system translates its primitive values. The text can be unformatted or formatted, such as comma-delimited files or XML. In addition, the text form can be read by a human tester and can easily be created to fashion data-dependent tests.*

---

* See *The Art of UNIX Programming* by Eric S. Raymond (Addison-Wesley Professional, 2003) for a discussion on text.

Text inside a system is a different matter. When text strings are read into a program, they should be converted into the corresponding data types as soon as possible. Performing this conversion separates the external presentation of the information to the user and to other programs from the internal usage of that same information. If there is an error in the representation, the failure will appear in the translation process, not later on when you are trying to process the data.

We defined the CDCategories used in the previous section with an enumeration. If the values for a CDCategory were kept in a configuration file, it might be denoted in that file as the string "GoldenOldie." When reading in that data, this string value should be converted to the corresponding enumeration value. If the input string is misspelled or does not match one of the values for the enumerations, the error can be reported immediately, instead of trying to handle it in processing later.

Creating an enumerated data type is language dependent. If a language does not support enumerations, a class with class (static) attributes initialized to different values can give the same functionality. Conversion of those values to and from strings can be part of that class. Even if a language does have primitive enumerations, creating a class with those methods might be worthwhile for creating the to/from string conversion methods. For example:

```
class CDCategory
    {
    static String string_values [] = {
        "NewRelease", "GoldenOldie", "Regular"};
    static int corresponding_values [] = {
         NEW_RELEASE_CD, REGULAR_CD, GOLDIE_OLDIE_CD}
    static int NEW_RELEASE_CD = 0;
    static int GOLDIE_OLDIE_CD = 1;
    static int REGULAR_CD = 2;
    String to_string(int category)
        {
        return string_values[category];
        }
    int from_string(String a_string) throws BadValueException
        {
        for (int i = 0; i < string_values.length; i++)
            {
            if (a_string.equals(string_values[i]))
                return corresponding_values[i];
            }
        throw new BadValueException( );
        }
    }
```

TO TEXT OR NOT TO TEXT

Use text between programs, not within programs.

More Than One

You often work with more than one instance of an object. You can aggregate those instances using an array or a collection class. I like to distinguish between two types of aggregations. The first is termed a *group*, the second a *collection*. A group is a set of objects, typically coded using an array or a linked list. When I use the [] symbol in a class description, I am implying a group, not necessarily a particular implementation of a group.

A collection is a set of objects, typically implemented by a collection class or template (Vector, List, etc.). Operations on a collection can include performing an operation on the collection as a whole, such as calculating the average value of an attribute for all objects in the collection, or finding a particular object matching a key value.

If you find you are performing more operations on a group, other than just passing it to other methods or enumerating it, you might want to turn it into its own class. Creating a specific collection class, instead of using classwide (static) methods, separates the concerns of operations on all the objects in a collection, from those operations on a single object.*

For example, suppose that Sam wanted to keep track of the rental history of each CDDisc. You could keep the history of each rental in a RentalHistory object:

```
class RentalEvent
    Timestamp time_started
    Timestamp time_end
    Dollar rental_fee
class CDDisc
    RentalEvent [] rental_history.
```

If the only value Sam wanted to know was the number of times a CDDisc had been rented, there is no need for a collection. The number of times is simply the length of rental_history. However, if additional operations are to be performed with rental_history, it is time to make the attribute into its own class. For example, you might want to know the average time period for a rental, the shortest or longest rental, or the total revenue from the CDDisc. You can create a RentalHistory class to represent a collection of RentalEvents and add these methods to that class:

```
class RentalHistory
    Count number_of_rentals( )
    Dollar total_revenue( )
    Days short_rental( )
    Days longest_rental( )
```

The representation of a collection should be separate from the use of the collection. At coding time, RentalHistory can either be derived from a regular or a templated library class, or it can delegate its operations to an attribute that represents a library collection class.

---

* A reviewer noted that this is not true in languages such as Ruby and Groovy, which support closures. Closures let you apply arbitrary operations to generic collections without resorting to creating a specific collection class.

Likewise, CDDiscs exist within a CDDiscCollection. In Sam's Checkout_CDDisc and Return_CDDisc use cases, we need to find a CDDisc by its physical ID. Tim and I create a CDDiscCollection interface, which looks like this:

```
interface CDDiscCollection
    CDDisc find_by_physical_id(PhysicalID a_physical_id)
    CDDisc [] find_by_cd_release(CDRelease a_cd_release)
    // Standard collection operations:
    add(CDDisc a_cd_disc)
    remove (CDDisc a_cd_disc)
```

CDDiscCollection hides the implementation of how the collection is organized. In the actual implementation, we might use a library collection class, a database, or even a text file.

IF IT HAS COLLECTION OPERATIONS, MAKE IT A COLLECTION

Collections separate object usage from object storage and hide implementation of aggregate operations.

CHAPTER SIX

A Few Words on Classes

BEFORE CONTINUING WITH THE SPECIFICS OF SAM'S DESIGN, we look at object-oriented design in general. We review the class maxims of cohesion and coupling, along with the three laws of objects. Polymorphic behavior is demonstrated with both inheritance and interfaces. We examine reuse of implementation explicit naming.

Honor the Class Maxims

Highly cohesive, loosely coupled classes are a common goal for class design. A cohesive class encapsulates a single concept or idea. A loosely coupled class does not depend on the implementation of other classes.*

---

* Larry Constantine created the concepts of coupling and cohesion, and he and Edward Yourdon presented those concepts in *Structured Design* (Prentice-Hall, 1979). He presents the concepts in relation to object-oriented systems in an article he co-wrote with B. Hendersons-Sellers and I.M. Graham called "Coupling and Cohesion: Towards a Valid Metrics Suite for Object-Oriented Analysis and Design" (Object Oriented Systems, 3:143-158, 1996).

Cohesion

Each class should represent one abstraction. Each class should have a one-line description of the class's purpose and meaning. If you cannot describe a class briefly, it probably represents more than one abstraction. Responsibilities that are added to a class should fit within the description.

The CDDisc class just does not feel right. It appears that the class is mixing two concepts. Looking back through the requirements and use cases, we discover the term *Rental*. That term seems to be a missing abstraction. Note that a class can represent an event as well as a physical object. The one-line description of a Rental is:

Rental
    The loan of a CDDisc for a particular period

Tim and I alter CDDisc so that it has a current Rental if it is rented. Now the class looks like this:

```
class CDDisc
    CDRelease cd_release
    PhysicalID physical_id
    Rental current_rental
    rent(Customer a_customer)
    return_a_rental()

 class Rental
    Customer renter
    Timestamp start_time
    Timestamp end_time
```

FUZZY TIME

If a class has a fuzzy concept, the operations can appear mismatched. In my seminars, I introduce the Time class without giving it a definition. It has the hours, minutes, and seconds attributes. Some methods are applied to the class, such as to_string() and from_string().

Then the add_seconds(int number_of_seconds) method is added to the class. The carryover from seconds into minutes and minutes into hours goes without a hitch. Then the question arises: what should result if the hour count exceeds 23? At that point, the attendees recognize that the class mixes the concepts of both Time as clock time and Time as a period of time. If a one-line description of the class had been created in the beginning, the mix-up would not have occurred.

Coupling

Coupling measures how two classes interrelate. If two classes are coupled, a change in one class can force a change in the other class. There are three degrees of coupling: *tight*, *common*, and *loose*. Tight coupling means that a change in the implementation of one class forces a change in the implementation of the other. With common coupling, the second class uses the interface methods of the first class. If the implementation of the first class changes, the second class does not need to change. Loose coupling means that a class does not even rely on the interface of another class, only on its existence.

For most classes, you should aim for common or loose coupling. Common coupling follows a maxim stated in the book *Design Patterns:* "Design to an interface, not an implementation." Callers should rely only on the methods declared in the class interface and not on the implementation of those methods.

For example, the users of the CDDiscCollection class access it through the following interface:

```
interface CDDiscCollection
    CDDisc find_by_physical_id(PhysicalID a_physical_id)
    CDDisc [] find_by_cd_release(CDRelease a_cd_release)
    // Standard collection operations:
    add(CDDisc a_cd_disc)
    remove (CDDisc a_cd_disc)
```

The underlying implementation is transparent to the users. When a programmer calls the methods of this class, the programmer does not need to know about nor address anything about how they are implemented. No matter how radically the implementation might be changed in the future, as long as the methods continue to function properly, any code that calls them does not have to be changed.

HONOR THE CLASS MAXIMS

Make loosely coupled cohesive classes.

Three Laws of Objects

Isaac Asimov proposed three laws for robots in his book, *I, Robot.** Objects are a lot like robots. They are asked to perform certain operations with an expectation that those operations will be performed correctly. In addition to the maxims stated in the preceding section, you might consider the Three Laws of Objects. These laws can be applicable for a program as a whole, as well as for an individual object:

• An object shall do what its methods say it does

• An object shall do no harm

• An object shall notify its user if it is unable to perform a requested operation

---

* They are: 1. A robot may not injure a human being, or, through inaction, allow a human being to come to harm; 2. A robot must obey orders given it by human beings, except where such orders would conflict with the First Law; and 3. A robot must protect its own existence as long as such protection does not conflict with the First or Second Law.

Let us look at these laws in a little more detail:

An object shall do what its methods say it does

This law covers two concepts. The first is that a given method has a name that specifies what it does. This concept is covered in the guideline, "A Rose by Any Other Name Is Not a Rose." The second is that the method does what can be reasonably expected by that name. (This concept is also known as the "Principle of Least Surprises").

For example, what is the expectation for a method named "remove" versus one named "delete?" This dichotomy occurs in user interfaces as well as in collections. If a user "removes" an item from a collection (such as in CDDiscCollection), should he reasonably expect that the item still exists or should he expect that it has been erased completely? If the user "deletes" an item, does that operation delete the item as well as remove it from the collection, or does it just remove it? The terminology of many user interfaces corresponds with the first alternative for each of these answers. Consistency suggests that the methods you write work the same way.*

An object shall do no harm

A long time ago, I reviewed a package that created a set of graphical user interface (GUI) widgets on the screen. When the program created a widget, the widget object read its configuration from a file. The system seemed to work OK, until more than 20 widgets were on the screen. Then no more widgets were created. The reason was that the widgets closed the configuration file only when they were destroyed. The limit that was set on my operating system at the time was that only 20 files could be opened simultaneously. Perhaps the package had been tested on a system with a much larger limit.

These objects did harm. They hogged resources unnecessarily. Typical advice to object-oriented designers suggests that one acquire resources in the constructor and release them in the destructor. However, an object also needs to live within its means. It should not do harm by holding onto resources longer than necessary. If an object is not destroyed for an uncertain period of time (such as objects in Java), it needs to provide a method (e.g., dispose( )) that can be called to release resources.

Suppose that the underlying implementation of CDDiscCollection used a database. If the constructor opened a connection to a database, the destructor should close that connection.† Alternatively, CDDiscCollection might share a database connection with all the other collection classes.

---

* One reviewer suggested that keeping the meanings of words such as *remove* consistent across an application is difficult, especially in larger development groups. Local dialects make the consistent connotations of words difficult. A global dictionary can help but does not guarantee consistency.

† One reviewer commented, "Doing no harm includes not inconveniencing or potentially sabotaging neighboring objects, or objects that might be about to move into our application's object community."

An object shall notify its user if it is unable to perform a requested operation

An object should not fail silently. If the caller has passed inappropriate parameters, or the needed resources are not available, the object should report its inability to complete the operation. Whether the signal is throwing an exception or returning an error value depends on the language facilities and the programming guidelines of the development group.

For example, if the add( ) method of CDDiscCollection finds that it is adding an existing item, it should generate an error, instead of silently replacing the item. According to a reviewer, "The amount of debugging time this simple practice can eliminate is hard to overestimate. The amount of time saved in looking for points of failure alone can be staggering. Once you get used to programming in this style, you might begin to feel like you are surrounded by protective pillows."

NEVER BE SILENT

If a method encounters an error, it should report it, not remain silent.[*]

Need Determines Class

If a class contains all the data required by a method, that method belongs in that class. Another class should not extract data from a class, manipulate it, and then put it back into that class.

Conversely, if a method does not require any data from an object, the method is probably not needed as a member of the class. It is a candidate for a helper class or a general library class. With Sam's system, we might need to display the title of a CDRelease in multiple lines. We might leave the task of breaking up the lines to the display widget, or we might do it ourselves if we want more control over how the title appears. Suppose that CDRelease had a get_title_by_lines( ) method to return the title in separate lines:

```
class CDRelease
    {
    String title;
    static int CHARS_PER_LINE = 60;
    String [] get_title_by_lines()
        {
        return break_into_lines(title, CHARS_PER_LINE);
        }
    String [] break_into_lines(String text_to_break_up, int chars_per_line)
        {
```

---

[*] Herb Sutter and Andrei Alexandrescu cover this in *C++ Coding Standards* (Addison-Wesley Professional, 2004).

```
        // Break text into separate strings
        }
    }
```

The break_into_lines( ) method does not need to be part of the class. It does not manipulate any attributes directly. However, it looks like a useful tool for other classes. So the method seems appropriate for a separate utility class. For example:

```
class StringHelper
    {
    static String [] break_into_lines(String text_to_break_up, int chars_per_line)
        {
        // Break into separate strings
        }
    }
```

With this method placed in StringHelper, we would write the **get_title_by_lines( )** method as follows:

```
String [] get_title_by_lines( )
    {
    return StringHelper.break_into_lines(title, CHARS_PER_LINE);
    }
```

As an alternative to placing break_into_lines( ) into a utility class, you could create a class that inherits from String (if your language allows deriving from String). The line-breaking functionality would be an additional method. For example:

```
class MyString extends String
    {
    String [] break_into_lines(int chars_per_line);
    }
```

A call to the break_into_lines( ) method would look like this:

```
class CDRelease
    {
    MyString title;
    static int CHARS_PER_LINE = 60;
    String [] get_title_by_line( )
        {
        return title.break_into_lines(CHARS_PER_LINE);
        }
    }
```

It's up to you what method you choose. The disadvantage of inheritance is that MyString can become crowded with methods as more functionality is added (e.g., break_into_words( ), set_to_all_capitals( ), etc.). On the other hand, it might feel more natural asking title to break itself up, instead of asking another class to do the work.

Once you decide on the approach (a package of methods or inheritance) for adding functionality to strings, you can employ the same approach for adding functionality to other predefined classes.

Polymorphism

Polymorphism deals with manipulating objects of different classes using only the interface
that they have in common. There are two different uses for polymorphism. In the first case,
there are different implementations of an interface with the same behavior, such as with
printer drivers. In the second case, there are different behaviors with the same interface,
such as proxy classes with different operations.

You can code classes to be polymorphic in two ways.* One way is to use inheritance.
Derived classes share the interface of the base class. The second way is to implement interfaces in languages such as Java and C#.

Using Inheritance

A typical example of an inheritance hierarchy has a Shape base class. Shapes such as
Rectangle and Triangle are derived from Shape, as shown in Figure 6-1. A Square shape is
then derived from Rectangle, and an EquilateralTriangle is derived from Triangle.

An EquilateralTriangle and a Square have a facet in common that is not represented in this
inheritance hierarchy. They both represent regular polygons (all their sides are the same
length).

Using Interfaces

Instead of using inheritance, you could code the relationship with interfaces, as shown in
Figure 6-2.

When Squares and EquilateralTriangles are added, they can implement a RegularPolygon
interface as well as the Shape interface, as shown in Figure 6-3.

The disadvantage of using interfaces is that each class that implements an interface must
code each method in the interface. For example, EquilateralTriangle and Square both need
to have code for the set_length_of_side( ) method. If the code is the same, the common

---

* A reviewer noted that in Ruby, there is a third way called Duck Typing, whereby any class with a
  matching method name can handle a method. It does not have to implement an interface or
  extend a base class.

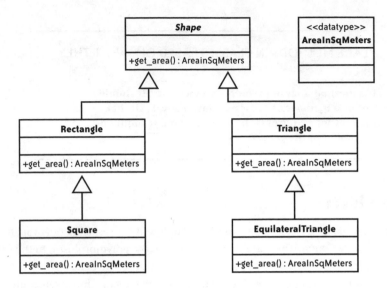

FIGURE 6-1. Shapes using inheritance

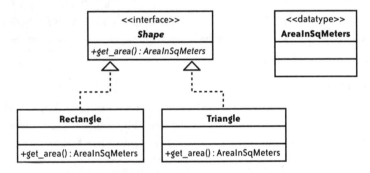

FIGURE 6-2. Shapes using an interface

code could be placed in a set_length_of_side( ) method in a RegularPolygonImplementation class. The set_length_of_side( ) methods in EquilateralTriangle and Square would call that method.

An advantage of using interfaces is that the relationship between the classes is fluid. After having experience in using the classes, you might find that RegularPolygons actually have a lot more in common than a Square and a Rectangle. Instead of prematurely creating an inheritance hierarchy that ties Square into Rectangle, thinking in interfaces allows these relationships to develop.

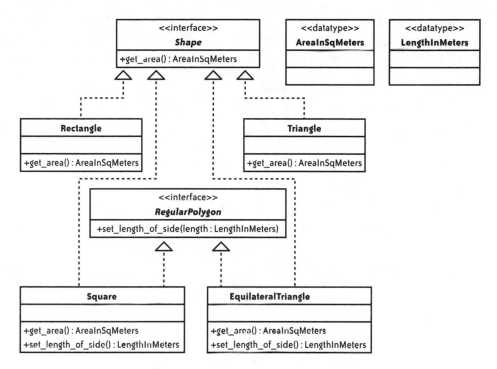

FIGURE 6-3. Shapes using an additional interface

THINK INTERFACES, NOT INHERITANCE

**Interfaces provide more fluidity in the relationships
between classes.**

Frameworks that use inheritance can often be designed with interfaces. For example, a Component class is often the base class of a GUI hierarchy, as shown in Example 6-1. With inheritance, it can be unclear which methods of the base class should be overridden by derived classes.

EXAMPLE 6-1. Component with inheritance

```
class Component
    {
    draw();
    hide();
    }
class MyComponent extends Component
    {
    // What should it override?
    }
```

Alternatively, the class could require that an interface be implemented, as shown in Example 6-2 and Figure 6-4. Custom components would implement the interface, which makes clear what methods need to be created.

EXAMPLE 6-2. Component with delegation to interface

```
interface Component
    {
    draw( );
    }
class BaseComponent
    {
    Component   a_component;
    draw( )
        {
        a_component.draw( );
        }
    }
class MyComponent implements Component
    {
    draw( )
        {
        // Particular draw
        }
    }
```

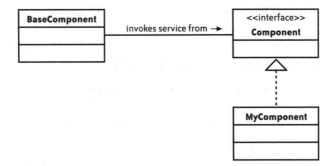

FIGURE 6-4. A framework using strategy

One Little Job

The framework of Unix pipes and filters is elegant. It is easier to create a program that does one simple job (a filter) than a program that does multiple jobs. For example, the word count program (*wc*) counts lines, words, and characters in the input file. The directory-listing program (*ls*) lists the files in a directory, one per line. To count how many files are in a directory, you pipe the output of the *ls* program into the input of the *wc* program and count the number of lines (e.g., ls | wc).*

---

* Unix commands represent another approach to the naming issue. The names are short. (Some people refer to them as cryptic.) Since these commands are typed over and over, the short names are reasonable in that contact.

Each class should capture one concept. Likewise, each method within a class should do one little job well. The Proxy pattern works in this way. Each proxy class can perform one operation (e.g., encryption or checking for security access violations). Once a proxy method has finished its task, it calls the corresponding method in another proxy object to perform further operations.

Multilevel delegation works in a similar manner. The lowest-level class performs simple operations. Higher-level classes perform more complicated operations, which are based on the lower-level operations. The lowest-level classes get used more often, and the higher-level classes are used less often, since they are designed for specific purposes.

For example, here is a File class that just reads a set of characters from a file:

```
class File
    boolean open (String filename)
    void close( )
    char read_a_char( )
    void write_a_char(char char_to_write)
```

The read_a_char( ) method internally might not read just a character from the operating system. The method might read an entire buffer and then return the characters one at a time. Performance is a quality-of-implementation issue, not an interface issue. However, if we found that we were calling read_a_char( ) in a loop in many places, we might add a more efficient interface method, such as read_array_of_char(char [] array). This is an interface performance issue, not an internal implementation concern.

On the next level up, we might want to read characters until a newline is read. Instead of modifying File, we create a new class to read lines, and delegate the actual file reading to File. For example, we might have the following:

```
class FileWithLines
    String read_line_up_to_new_line_and_toss_new_line( )
```

Alternatively, we could have added this method to the File class. If we took that approach for other operations, we would be burdening the File class with a number of unrelated methods. The File class should do its one job well. FileWithLines can incorporate other methods dealing with line-oriented input. For example, we could add get_count_of_lines_ read( ), set_line_terminator( ), and so forth.

In another project, we might read a file that contains keywords and associated values. The class might be as follows:

```
class KeywordPair
    String keyword
    String value
class FileWithKeywords
    KeywordPair read_next_keyword_pair( )
```

Once again, the file reading is delegated to the File class. If the keyword pairs were kept on separate lines, the reading might be delegated to the FileWithLines class.

Policy Versus Implementation

Following along with the concept of doing one job well, you should separate methods that
contain policy (what you are going to do) from methods that contain implementation
(how you are going to do it). A policy method contains the logic and reasoning for doing
something. An implementation method contains the details. For example, this code
checks for CDDiscs that are returned late and performs the appropriate action:

```
if (is_overdue())
    process_rental_which_ended_late()
```

The preceding code completely separates policy from implementation. Here's a version
that progressively mixes implementation and policy:

```
if (today > end_date)
    {
    process_rental_which_ended_late();
    }
```

Here's another:

```
if (today > end_date)
    {
    // Code for overdue actions
    }
```

The is_overdue() method in the first example might be reusable by other methods
employed by other use cases. If it is, the definition of overdue will be consistent among the
other use cases. Otherwise, some code might use today > end_date and others might use
today > start_date.add(base_rental_period). These types of inconsistencies can proliferate
quickly where teams of programmers are involved.

To separate out policy from implementation while creating code, write down what you
are going to do, not how you are going to do it. For example, first write:

```
if (a_customer.is_good_customer())
    a_customer.provide_discount();
```

Then write the is_good_customer() and provide_discount() methods.

Extreme Naming

In a previous section, you might have noticed an example of an extremely long method name:

```
class FileWithLines
    String read_line_up_to_new_line_and_toss_new_line( )
```

Suppose the method name was read_line. If I use read_line a lot, I might recall that it either does include or does not include the newline character. If the method is specifically named or has a parameter which denotes its operation (e.g., read_line(TOSS_NEW_LINE)), it is easier to remember the method's purpose.

Now you are probably saying: "this is extreme naming." You are right. If your group uses a method or variable often, a short name can be remembered more easily. However, if a method is rarely used, a long name is often better. The reader will not be scrambling for the documentation to recall what the method actually does.

COMPREHENDING DAVID COPPERFIELD

When I was in elementary school, I attempted to read Charles Dickens' *David Copperfield*. The book contained many words that were not in my vocabulary at the time. I read the book with a dictionary by my side. Every time I encountered an unfamiliar word, I looked it up in the dictionary. Needless to say, this cross-referencing destroyed the flow of the plot. If Dickens had written the book using familiar words, it might not have been a literary classic. However, it would have been more understandable.

Likewise, it is easier to read code that has methods with names that do not need to be cross-referenced.

Overloading Functions

In many languages, method names can be overloaded. Overloading allows two methods to use the same name, if they can be distinguished by their signature. A method's signature is defined by the number of its parameters and types. For example, you could have the following:

```
search(int an_int)
search(String a_string)
```

Why not use this overloading feature? If you use a text search to find one of the search methods in source code or other documents, you would wind up with matches that call all the methods with the same name.* You would have to examine each call closely to see if the call represents the method you are actually looking for. If you spell out the type of search in the name of each method, you can easily search for a particular method.†

In addition, making the search method name explicit permits searching for different attributes that have the same data type. For example, you could use the following:

```
search_for_first_name(CommonString a_string)
search_for_last_name(CommonString a_string)
```

Now notice the many ways the search term *search* appeared in this section. Could you keep track of all these meanings for *search*? By being more explicit in exactly what you are searching for, you make it easier for the reader to comprehend your code.

A related issue concerns overloaded operators, such as + and -, for languages that support overloaded operators. If overloaded operators are created, they should match their common meaning (e.g., + means adding two objects to create an object that represents a sum). Overloaded operators are only symbolic shortcuts. Unless they are used a lot, the meaning of the shortcut can be lost. A named method, rather than an overloaded operator, can keep the code more readable. Consider an overloaded + operator for a Time class:

```
Time t;
Time s = t + 5;
```

Does the 5 represent hours, minutes, or seconds to add to Time? Alternatively, a named method can be used:

```
Time t;
Time s = t.add_hours(5);
```

Now, there is no question that 5 hours are being added to the Time object.

OVERLOADING FUNCTIONS CAN BECOME OVERLOADING

By using unique names, functions can be more self-describing.

---

* Eric M. Burke, a reviewer, noted that a decent integrated development environment (IDE), including IntelliJ IDEA and Eclipse, provides a "find usages" function that searches for methods based on the structure of the code.

† One reviewer noted that you could have a single search method that takes a filter as its parameter. A filter denotes a function that is called by a search method to determine if an object is in the set of desired objects.

CHAPTER SEVEN

Getting There

WE ARE CLOSE TO CREATING THE FIRST ITERATION OF THE **CD** RENTAL SYSTEM. We address using separation of concerns to create reports. Planning for migration brings up some additional design issues.

Where We Are

Let us look at the classes we have developed so far. Figure 7-1 gives the overall picture, and the listing in Example 7-1 gives the details.

EXAMPLE 7-1. Class details for the system so far

```
class CDRelease
    CommonString title
    UPCCode upc_code
    CDCategory category
    Days base_rental_period( )
    Dollars get_rental_fee( )

class CDDisc
    CDRelease cd_release
    PhysicalID physical_id
    Rental current_rental
    start_rental(Customer the_renter)
```

EXAMPLE 7-1. Class details for the system so far (continued)

```
    end_rental( ) //

class PhysicalID

class CDCategory

class Rental
    Customer renter
    Timestamp start_time
    Timestamp end_time
    Days base_rental_period
    Boolean is_overdue( )

class CDDiscCollection
    CDDisc find_by_physical_id(PhysicalID a_physical_id)
    CDDisc [] find_by_cd_release(CDRelease a_cd_release)
    // Standard collection operations:
    add(CDDisc a_cd_disc)
    remove (CDDisc a_cd_disc)

class CustomerID

class Customer
    CustomerID customer_id
    CommonString name

class CustomerCollection
    Customer find_by_customer_id(CustomerID a_customer_id)
    // Standard collection operations
    add(Customer customer_to_add)
    remove(Customer a_customer_id) // Check to see no current rentals
```

We have two use cases that we are developing: Checkout_a_CDDisc and Checkin_a_CDDisc. Figure 7-2 gives an overall sequence diagram for the Checkout_a_CDDisc case.

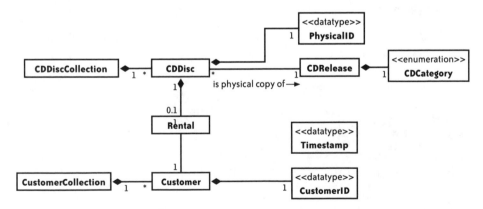

FIGURE 7-1. Class diagram for the system so far

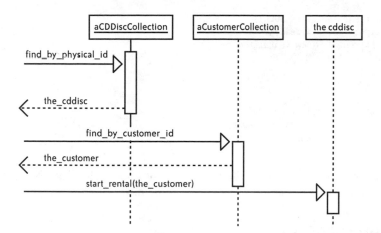

FIGURE 7-2. Checkout_a_CDDisc

Likewise, Figure 7-3 gives a sequence diagram for the Checkin_a_CDDisc use case.

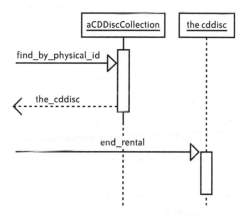

FIGURE 7-3. Checkin_a_CDDisc

For those who prefer pseudocode to document the flow of use cases, the pseudocode for the Checkout_a_CDDisc use case is:

```
CDDisc disc_being_rented = CDDiscCollection.find_by_physical_id(physical_id);
Customer renter = CustomerCollection.find_by_customer_id(customer_id);
disc_being_rented.start_rental(renter);
```

And for the Checkin_a_CDDisc use case we have:

```
CDDisc disc _rented = CDDisc.find_by_physical_id(physical_id);
disc_rented.end_rental();
```

The find_by... methods for the collections are straightforward, so details are not needed. For CDDisc, the pseudocode for the start_rental( ) and end_rental( ) methods looks like this:

```
start_rental(Customer the_renter)
   {
```

```
        if (current_rental != NULL)
            signal CDDiscAlreadyRented;
        current_rental = new Rental(the_renter);
        produce_contract();
        }
    end_rental()
        {
        if (current_rental.is_overdue())
            perform_late_rental_procedure();
        current_rental = NULL;
        }
```

We still have two operations that we have not examined in any detail: produce_contract() and perform_late_rental_procedure(). We look at those next.

Separating Concerns

The Model-View-Controller pattern that emerged from Smalltalk is similar to the batch-processing model of Input-Process-Output. Separating the concerns of how input is handled and validated from the way it is processed and then reported or displayed makes a program easier to maintain. This same separation of concerns is applicable to other facets of the system.

SEPARATE CONCERNS TO MAKE SMALLER CONCERNS

**Split responsibilities among multiple methods and
multiple classes to simplify each method and class.**

Sam's system needs to create a rental contract. Contract production can be separated into two steps: preparing the contract and printing the contract. The printed rental contract is a report. The steps for almost every report include the following:*

1. Calculate all values needed for the report, including counts and totals.

2. Create an output representation of the report using the appropriate formatting language (plain text, HTML, PostScript, etc.).

3. Display the output representation on the desired device (display screen, printer, browser window, etc.).

To clarify the distinction of the three steps, we create three separate methods.† Let us call the functions:

---

* Some report-writing tools, such as Crystal Reports, combine steps 1 and 2.

† Some operating systems tie the creation of the output representation and its display together. For example, when you prepare output for a particular printer, the operating system automatically passes that output to the spooler for printing on that printer. In that case, the create_rental_contract_report() method performs both functions for a printer and display_report() is needed only for nonprinter displays.

```
calculate_rental_contract( )
create_rental_contract_report( )
display_report( )
```

Separating the functionality into multiple methods lets us reuse many of the methods, even if the details in other methods are changed. In addition, by making the printing separate from the preparation, we can reprint the report in exactly the same form.

As we shall see in the following sections, these methods interact with each other as follows:

- `calculate_rental_contract( )` creates `RentalContractDTO`

- `create_rental_contract_report( )` creates `ReportPlainTextFormat` from `RentalContractDTO`

- `display_report( )` displays `ReportPlainTextFormat`

Calculating the Rental Contract

You could design the `create_rental_contract_report( )` method to pass all objects that contain data used in the report, or you design the method to require a Data Transfer Object (DTO) that includes only the data to display. If the `create_rental_contract_report( )` method does not call any calculation methods in the objects passed to it, the decision rests on how much you want the method to depend on the class interfaces. Suppose you pass individual classes to the `create_rental_contract_report( )` method. If those classes change, you will have to rewrite that method. If you use a DTO, you change only the code that creates the DTO.

We aim for extreme separation by having `calculate_rental_contract( )` create a DTO. The DTO can hold either the data required for the report in primitive types and abstract data types (ADTs, as defined in Chapter 2), or the data converted into `CommonStrings`. In the former case, `create_rental_contract_report( )` applies a string conversion method (such as `to_string( )`) to each data item. In the latter case, the values are converted into strings when placed into the corresponding DTO members.

An advantage of a DTO is that testing and creating the system's reports can proceed in parallel with development of the system's business logic. Test DTOs can be filled with values and the resulting reports given to the client for their approval of the format. DTOs can also be used in testing for correctly calculated values regardless of the format in which they appear in a report.

Here are the data values that Sam decided he wanted to have output on the printed contract:

```
Rental
    start_time
    due_time   // When the CDDisc is due
Customer
    name
CDDisc
    cd_release title
    physical_id
```

due_time is not currently part of the Rental class. Its calculation is clearly the responsibility of Rental, since that class contains all the information required. Therefore, we add an additional method to Rental:

```
Timestamp calculate_due_time( )
    {
    due_time= start_time + base_rental_period;
    return due_time;
    }
```

The DTO for the rental contract looks like this:

```
class RentalContractDTO
    {
    Timestamp rental_start_time;
    Timestamp rental_due_time;
    Name customer_name;
    PhoneNumber customer_day_phone_number;
    CommonString cd_release_title;
    PhysicalId cd_disc_physical_id;
    }
```

The calculate_rental_contract( ) method in Example 7-2 mostly moves data into RentalContractDTO. It calls any necessary routines to obtain the remaining values.

EXAMPLE 7-2. calculate_rental_contract

```
RentalContractDTO calculate_rental_contract(Rental rental,CDDisc cd_disc)
    {
    RentalContractDTO rental_contract_dto = new RentalContractDTO( );
    rental_due_time = rental.calculate_due_time( );
    rental_start_time = rental.start_time;
    customer_name = rental.customer.name;
    customer_day_phone_number = rental.customer.day_phone_number;
    cd_release_title = cd_disc.cd_release.title;
    cd_disc_physical_id = cd_disc.physical_id;
    return rental_contract;
    }
```

It can be hard to decide which class should contain a method that creates a DTO, since the data will probably come from several classes. The method could be in an entirely separate class, or it could be in one of the classes that provides the data. Since the report is a rental contract, it seems reasonable that Rental should contain calculate_rental_contract( ).

If we put the calculate_rental_contract( ) method into the Rental class, the first parameter is not needed, but Rental needs to know what the CDDisc is to create the contract. So we alter Rental to include an attribute for the CDDisc:

```
class Rental
    {
    CDDisc cd_disc;
    Rental(CDDisc cd_disc)
        {
        this.cd_disc = cd_disc;
        }
    };
```

If the method is part of the Rental class, all references to Rental disappear, as shown in Example 7-3. The cd_disc variable in Example 7-3 now refers to the attribute, rather than the parameter of Example 7-2.

EXAMPLE 7-3. calculate_rental_contract as a method of Rental

```
RentalContractDTO calculate_rental_contract( )
    {
    RentalContractDTO rental_contract_dto = new RentalContractDTO( );
    rental_due_time = calculate_due_time( );
    rental_start_time = start_time;
    customer_name = customer.name;
    customer_day_phone_number = customer.day_phone_number;
    cd_release_title = cd_disc.cd_release.title;
    cd_disc_physical_id = cd_disc.physical_id;
    return rental_contract_dto;
    }
```

Creating the Rental Contract

Next, we turn our attention to the method creating the report, create_rental_contract_report( ). The form of the report could be XML, HTML, RTF, plain ASCII text, or some other format. For our example, we create a plain-text report with the following method:

```
ReportPlainTextFormat create_rental_contract_report(
    RentalContractDTO rental_contract_dto)
```

This method can be implemented in numerous ways. It can create the report using formatted print statements. It can read a file that contained the report template with tags designating where to insert each value in the DTO. It can convert RentalContractDTO to XML, and then use an XSL transformation. (See *XML Bible*, 2nd Edition, by Elliotte Rusty Harold [Wiley, 2004]).

A more elaborate report might require a template format that mimics an Active Server Page (ASP) or Java Server Page (JSP). Those technologies have additional features such as the ability to loop over a group of items and to perform conditional formatting. Conditional formatting includes the ability to output one of an alternate set of strings, depending on the DTO values. For example, output could read "1 Widget" or "2 Widgets", instead of "1 Widget(s)".

ReportPlainTextFormat can have just a CommonString that contains all the characters to be displayed. Alternatively, it can be more structured, such as:

```
class ReportPlainTextFormat
    CommonString title
    CommonString [] lines
```

With this form of the class, more information is transferred, so the display method can be more flexible in its presentation. For example, if the report is being printed, the display method can place the title at the top of each page.

Displaying a Report

Now that we have a report, we need to do something with it. The final method takes the report and displays it on the appropriate device:

```
void display_report(
    ReportPlainTextFormat contract_report_plain_text_format)
```

Now the display_report( ) method's single job is to display the report on a particular device (e.g., a screen or a printer). That is an easy operation to test. You create an object of ReportPlainTextFormat and call the method. The report should display on the device. For example, if the device is the screen, a window could appear on the screen with the text in a read-only-style edit box.

To display a report on any one of several devices, we place this method in an interface. For example:

```
interface DisplayReport
    void display_report(ReportPlainTextFormat report_plain_text_format)
```

Each device that displays reports implements the DisplayReport interface in a manner appropriate to the device:

```
class Screen implements DisplayReport
class Printer implements DisplayReport
```

For example, if the device is a printer, and the operating system has a printer spooler, display_report( ) can transfer the text to the printer spooler and let the spooler handle any errors generated by the printer (offline, out-of-paper, network down, etc.).

Changes and Effects

Separating concerns, as shown in the previous subsections, makes it easier to deal with potential changes that might rear their heads down the line. Experience has shown that changes to reports are a frequent customer request. Some typical types of changes and their effects on the contract report are as follows:

The report layout changes
   The create_rental_contract_report( ) method needs to change

The items on the report require a different computation
   The calculate_rental_contract( ) method needs to change

New data is added to the report
   Both the create_rental_contract_report( ) and calculate_rental_contract( ) methods need to change

The system, including the report, is ported to a new platform or environment
   Only implementations of display_report( ) need to be altered

As you can see, the impact of a single type of change is generally limited to one method.

Migrating to the New System

Sam and I need to determine how to phase the new computer system into production. Often systems under development can be run in parallel with older systems. When a new system produces exactly the same results that the old system does, the old system is retired during a quiescent period, such as when the business is closed. We will take this approach with Sam's system.

Loading Current Data

For Sam's system, we need a way to get the current data into the system. That data includes the discs in the inventory, the customers, and the current rental data.

I met Sam for coffee. Sam is a coffee connoisseur. He can spout off the differences between beans from each country and each growing region. I can barely differentiate between regular and decaf. He ordered a *grande*. I wanted a large coffee (it might be a long discussion). When I ordered a supersize cup, the clerk looked at me quizzically.

"Sam, I've been thinking about how we're going to start up the system," I stated.

"I've been wondering about that also," Sam said.

"Since everything is currently on paper, you'll need to convert the information to digital form. I can specify a format that the information can be converted into so that it can be read into the system," I suggested.

"I'll take a look around for services that can scan in my current index cards to create these files," he offered.

"It will be hard to capture the current rentals. It will take time to scan the index cards. By the time they're done, the rentals will no longer be current," I said.

I told him we definitely need to create a machine-readable form of the data to initialize the values of Customers and CDDiscs. Since CDDiscs refer to CDReleases, we need to have data to initialize those objects as well. For these three classes, we add an additional method to their responsibilities:*

```
CustomerCollection
    add_customers_from_file(String filename)
CDDiscCollection
    add_cd_discs_from_file(String filename)
CDReleaseCollection
    add_cd_releases_from_file(String filename)
```

---

* Readers may note that putting these methods into the collections is a poor separation of concerns. Tim noted this issue and the methods were placed in separate classes, as you will see in the next chapter. Eric M. Burke, a reviewer, noted that the Apache Ant system was designed with knowledge of the XML project structure. Ant code cannot be easily reused with anything but an XML project.

Each method reads a file and creates objects initialized from the data in the file. At some later point, we will determine the best way to represent the data in these files. The format could be tab delimited, XML, or some other form.

Tim and I realize that these methods will also be helpful in testing the system. Test records can be kept in text files and read in to initialize the system. We get two uses for methods: migration and testing.

Since it is hard to capture the current rentals, Sam and I create a process for obtaining that information. As each CDDisc is rented, the information is recorded both on the current card and in the new system. After a few days, a printout of the current inventory of what is rented and not rented is checked against the actual physical inventory. This comparison helps us confirm that all the information was captured correctly in the conversion process.

The need for a current inventory printout in migration points out a feature that Sam had missed in his original specification for the system. The inventory printout is a needed feature for periodic inventory audits.

For CDDiscCollection, we add an additional responsibility: creating a DTO that contains the current inventory. The DTO includes every CDDisc that is in the collection with its PhysicalID, the CDRelease title, and the rental information, if currently rented. The DTO can be sorted by PhysicalID or by whether the CDDisc is rented or not, or both.

FIGURE OUT HOW TO MIGRATE BEFORE YOU MIGRATE

Considering the migration path might help you discover additional considerations in other areas of the design.[*]

Anticipating Potential Problems

A complete inventory is the only way that Sam can be assured that his rental data is captured correctly. Whenever receiving data that has been created elsewhere, you need to be concerned with the correctness of the data. Even if the data is coming from an existing computer system, you might still need to be concerned with data correctness. The data on the previous system might not have been validated. If the data required translation, the translation might not have been performed correctly. For example, suppose that we were migrating from a previous computer system. and that the previous system did not have a variable that represented the state of a rental. The initial value in the new system will have to be determined from some combination of other values in the previous system. That process of determination might not have been correct.

---

[*] A reviewer noted that this is discussed in *Rapid Development* by Steve McConnell (Microsoft Press, 1996).

When the conversion occurs for Sam's system, a number of possible errors can arise. We might not deal with them all at this time, but at least we should examine them to see the possible system ramifications. When we check the CDDisc inventory versus the real physical inventory, there are a number of possibilities:

- The ID on a physical CDDisc does not appear on the inventory
- The title on a physical CDDisc does not match the title on the inventory
- There is a CDDisc on the inventory report that does not appear in the physical inventory
- The status of a CDDisc on the inventory report does not match the physical inventory

These errors might be due to errors in the input data or errors in the program. We need to plan how to deal with the errors: either by reinitializing the data (and possibly saving the currently captured rentals) or by fixing our system. Since we will run a number of tests on it, it could not possibly be a programming error. Right!

Determining Uniqueness

Consideration of migration brings up the issue of uniqueness. We have already determined how we need to access items in the collections: by a unique PhysicalID for the case of CDDisc and Customer, and by UPCCode for CDRelease. When we are adding items to these collections during migration (or at any other time), we should check that each item being added does not already exist in the target collection. If the item being added does exist, we need to make up a consistent rule for handling that condition: either to overwrite the existing item or to signal an error. For example, if you add a CDDisc that has the same PhysicalID as an existing CDDisc, you probably want to signal an error to let the user know there is a duplicate.

On the other hand, Sam thinks some of his customers have multiple customer IDs. Since the system is paper based, it is hard to determine if that is the case. He figures that some customers who have been frequently late rental returners simply get another customer ID to start with a clean slate. When converting data from one system to the next, it is a good time to check for the uniqueness of that data, which brings up a new problem. We have to figure out a way to determine whether two customers are the same.

We might rely on the Social Security number, if the customers are willing to give us one. We can use credit card numbers, but customers could give us a different card number each time. Email addresses are even worse. Customers can give us so many different ones, we could wind up with hundreds of records for the same person. The driver's license number might work, as long as the customer does not move in or out of state. Since that identification is good enough for the state and the feds, it is probably the most useful for Sam as well.

In Sam's case, we might never know when a customer should be deleted from the collection. They could come back after a number of years to rent a CD. Customers who are refused rental privileges due to their excessive number of late returns or for other reasons should be kept in the collection forever so that Sam knows never to rent to them again.

It seems like there are at least three categories of Customers: Regular, Inactive, and NeverAgain. These definitely have different behavior. Whether these are represented as three separate classes, or as three states of a Customer, is something that we do not need to deal with at the moment. Sam has not even mentioned it in any of our talks. We will pass it by him after we finish the first iteration of the system.

KNOW WHO IT IS

Determine uniqueness criteria for objects that should be unique.

THE UNIQUE PASSENGER

When you take a commercial flight, the attendant checks to see that your identity matches the name on your ticket. When you make a reservation for a restricted ticket, you need to give your real name or else the ticket that is issued will not match your identity. However, for full-fare reservations placed through a travel agency, there was a little-known backdoor. You could change the name on the reservation up until the time the ticket was actually issued. Since the ticket did not need to be issued until immediately before the flight, the name could be changed up until that time.

If a passenger wanted to reserve a seat on a number of flights, his travel agent reserved the seats under different names. When the passenger finally picked the flight, the name on that reservation was changed.

Those who designed the reservation system wanted to determine if two passenger reservations with different names represented the same actual passenger. This turned out to be almost impossible to infer definitively. There was no easy way to determine the uniqueness of a passenger.

CHAPTER EIGHT

The First Release

TIM AND I CREATE THE FIRST RELEASE OF THE SYSTEM. A brief retrospective reviews how well our design approach worked. We explore issues that we addressed during development and the additional classes that we created during coding. We explain the areas where our practice did not match the guidelines presented in the previous chapters.

The Proof Is in the Pudding

At this point, Tim and I are ready to create the first release. We could continue our system analysis and design until we have covered every detail before commencing coding. However, it appears the undetermined details will not affect the overall class structure. We can fill in these holes in our information during coding.

A concrete implementation of the design demonstrates the guidelines that were described in the previous chapters. The design is general, so it can be implemented in any object-oriented language without much alteration. Since the design does not employ inheritance, it could even be implemented in other languages with a disciplined, object-based approach.

The complete set of classes is in Appendix B. Since Java has a standard graphical user interface (GUI) library, the implementation is in Java. The code looks much like C++ or C#, with the exception of the code for the GUI. The names of the methods have been changed to correspond with common Java coding conventions. Member variables of each class are prefixed with *the* and parameter names with *a*, if applicable.

Retrospective Time

Now that Tim and I have finished our first version of the system, it is time to perform a retrospective. A retrospective is a form of feedback. In a retrospective (*Project Retrospectives: A Handbook for Team Reviews* by Norman L. Kerth [Dorset House, 2001]), the team members analyze the team's personal interactions. They can also examine the design and architecture.

You can review your project journal and see where design decisions were made that had to be altered later. You might consider why a decision was made the initial way: speed, misunderstanding, or lack of information. You can try to modify the way decisions are made in the next iteration to decrease the amount of alteration required.

As occurs often in development projects, you might have to cut corners on your principles to create a working system quickly. At retrospective time, acknowledge those corners that you cut and determine whether they are severe enough to warrant refactoring. Cutting too many corners creates an illusion of greater velocity toward meeting the goal. It is like not eating so that you have more time to code. Eventually the lack of eating will catch up with you. I cannot overemphasize the power of retrospectives. Norm Kerth writes:

> The ritual of retrospectives gives vast insight into the actual technical decisions and discoveries made. I'm a strong advocate of patterns, and especially pattern languages. A retrospective is a great way to identify valuable patterns and systems of patterns. I have seen them lead to great advances in software architecture. I have also seen a retrospective as a natural tool to use in discovering the great refactoring opportunities available to a team.

> Through a retrospective, I've seen a community of minds understand the current structure of a system and collectively consider refactoring opportunities from a variety of viewpoints. The result is not just a better architecture, but also a group understanding of why the system is changing. Thus maintenance can be performed by a wider group of people; defects disappear; group ownership increases; and everyone involved becomes better programmers. Naturally the lessons learned from refactoring stay with the developers as they move on to other projects, thus the professionalism of software architecture and design continues to grow.

PERFORM A RETROSPECTIVE AFTER EACH RELEASE

**Examining your design and how you created it can
help in the next release.**

The more often you can perform a retrospective, the sooner you can use its feedback. You could hold a brief retrospective after every internal release and a longer retrospective after every major release.

The System as It Stands Now

The implementation of Sam's system contains many of the classes described in earlier chapters. Additional classes are explained in this chapter. The classes are divided into the following packages. Appendix B lists the details of the interfaces for each class. The entire source code is available at *http://www.oreilly.com/catalog/prefactoring*.

```
com.samscdrental.configuration
com.samscdrental.controller
com.samscdrental.dataaccess
com.samscdrental.display.adt
com.samscdrental.display
com.samscdrental.failures
com.samscdrental.helper
com.samscdrental.importexport
com.samscdrental.migration
com.samscdrental.model.adt
com.samscdrental.model.dto
com.samscdrental.model
com.samscdrental.reports
com.samscdrental.tests
```

Operations Interface

The com.samscdrental.controller package implements the CD rental system's operational interface via the following classes:

```
MaintenanceOperations.java
RentalOperations.java
ReportOperations.java
```

Tim and I added three operation classes to the model: RentalOperations, MaintenanceOperations, and ReportOperations. The methods in these classes represent the operations that can be requested by either the GUI or a test program. The class names use the term *Operations* rather than *Command* or *Controller*, since those terms have more existing connotations (e.g., the Command pattern and the Model-View-Controller pattern).

These operation classes are façades on the system's entire inner structure. They make a clean breaking point between the display and the model (see "Separating Concerns Makes Smaller Concerns"). Each operation on the user interface is represented in one of these façades. Each façade corresponds to different sets of user interactions that represent different types of users.

The RentalOperations class contains operations related to rentals: checkinCDDisc( ) and checkoutCDDisc( ). MaintenanceOperations contains the operations related to reading data from files into the collections. ReportOperations deals with report creation.

The methods in these façades declare their parameters as abstract data types (ADTs). This requires the GUI to convert an input string to the corresponding ADT before passing it to a method. Each ADT has a method that converts from a string and indicates whether the string is formatted properly. It is the GUI's job to call this method and report to the user if the format is incorrect.

Abstract Data Types

The abstract data types are contained in the `com.samscdrental.model.adt` package:

```
CustomerID.java
PhysicalID.java
Timestamp.java
UPCCode.java
Dollar.java
Name.java
```

The ADTs have no dependencies to the model. They are reusable in a number of different programs. They represent common data types: `CustomerID`, `PhysicalID`, `Timestamp`, `UPCCode`, `Dollar`, and `Name`.

Each ADT has methods for converting to and from strings. Two ADTs have corresponding display classes, since they appear in GUI dialogs. These two are `CustomerIDTextField` and `PhysicalIDTextField`. If the other ADTs appear in future dialogs, equivalent widgets will be created.

Configuration

Configuration classes are in the `com.samscdrental.configuration` package:

```
Configuration.java
DataAccessConfiguration.java
ReportConfiguration.java
```

The `Configuration` class represents data for configuring other objects in the system. For example, `DataAccessConfiguration` contains information for the `StoreDataAccess` object. The `StoreDataAccess` object receives a filled-in `DataAccessConfiguration` object from the `getDataAccessConfiguration()` method in `Configuration`. The source of the information is transparent to `StoreDataAccess`. `Configuration` retrieves it from preset values, but it could read it from a configuration file or database. The central configuration file is a variation of the Service Locator pattern (see *http://java.sun.com/blueprints/corej2eepatterns/Patterns/ServiceLocator.html* for details).

Testing

The automated acceptance tests are in the `com.samscdrental.tests` package:

```
CheckinCheckoutTests.java
TestOnlyOperations.java
```

The `CheckInCheckoutTests` class contains tests derived from the use cases and misuse cases. The tests run in the JUnit framework.* They are executed using collection instances (e.g., `CDDiscDataAccess`, `CDReleaseDataAccess`, etc.) containing a small amount of data. The data is initialized using the file import operation, which also serves in migrating data to the new system.

How many automated tests should you create? Let us differentiate between *testing* (determining if a system is functionally correct) and *debugging* (finding the source of failures). If the external interfaces to a system have a set of tests that check all functionality and the tests are successful, the system is functionally correct. If the tests are unsuccessful, the system does not work and the developer has to determine why.

It is possible to debug a system by tracing through the program driven by the external tests. For a complex system, the program tracing can involve numerous method calls and many classes. If there are no internal tests on a system's classes and modules, step-by-step debugging can be required to determine the cause of the failure.

The more tests performed on a system's internal classes and modules, the more confidence the developer can have that those items are not the source of failure. This permits skipping over the tested items during debugging. Having a full complement of tests on the internal items does not absolutely eliminate the need for step-by-step debugging. Failures can still occur due to the interaction between classes and modules.

Test Versus Production

The tests in `CheckinCheckoutTests` do not depend on the implementation of `RentalOperations`. However, to run the tests, it is necessary to perform operations that are not executed during normal operations. For example, the tests need to reinitialize the collections. Certainly, the ability for a regular user to remove all items from a collection is not something that should be permitted, even with multiple confirmations on the part of the user:

"You are about to destroy your data. Do you wish to continue? Yes/No."

"Are you sure? Yes/No."

"Last chance to stop this foolish act. Yes/No."

"OK, we warned you."

Such a drastic action should be part of an entirely separate interface to the system. If a language permits conditional compilation, this separate interface should not be compiled in production code. Tim and I created the `TestOnlyOperations` interface for those operations that should exist only during testing. The `collectionsClear( )` method is in that interface.

---

* Tests for the individual classes are not shown in the appendix. They duplicate much of the logic in the overall tests.

The `TestOnlyOperations` interface also contains the `setStartTimeForRentalBackSomeDays` method for setting the `start_time` of a `Rental` back a number of days. Without such a method, we could not easily test for late rentals. This method should not be part of the `RentalOperations` class, unless there is a justifiable use for it. We realized that for testing purposes, we needed to see if a `CDDisc` was rented or not. We added that method (`isCDDiscRented()`) to the `RentalOperation` class, since it seemed that it would be useful for other use cases in the big picture.

Individual classes might also have a separate test interface.* A test implementation of the class would support the test interface. A production implementation would not. For example, the collections classes have a `removeAll_TestingOnly()` method that is identified by name that suggests it should be used only during testing. An Extreme Splitter would place this in a test interface.

TEST OR PRODUCTION: THAT IS THE QUESTION

Place all test-only methods in a test interface.

Testing Flexibility

Flexibility can aid in testing.† The ability to choose different implementations of interfaces allows you to substitute test implementations for production implementations. For example, this system is tested using collections implemented with Java collection classes. The tests can run without the overhead of a database process. The production collections implementation can use any data persistence mechanism that supports the methods in the interface. Implementing this kind of flexibility requires, and so helps ensure, clean separation of the data persistence layer.

The `StoreDataAccess` class is where this flexibility has been concentrated. The methods in other classes do not refer to the individual collections directly. Instead, the methods refer to an appropriate member of `StoreDataAccess`. The constructor for `StoreDataAccess` can create a collection of the appropriate type (test or production) for each of its members.

---

* Eric M. Burke, a reviewer, notes, "If code is hard to test and you find yourself adding extra methods just to make it testable, this is often a 'smell' indicating something is wrong with the design. Well-designed code tends to be easier to test. Back when I first learned JUnit a few years ago, I would write a lot of package-scope methods just so that my tests could call them. Over time, I've found less and less need to do this."

† Flexibility is one manner of making something testable. See the testing reference mentioned in Chapter 4 for other testability ideas. Scott Ambler notes that testing flexibility is a core practice in Agile Modeling (*http://www.ambysoft.com/agileModeling.html*). Eric M. Burke notes, "Classes that are hard to test might be poorly designed."

Dealing with Deviations and Errors

As discussed in Chapter 3, any system has to deal with deviations and errors. Deviations are those conditions that can be expected to occur in normal processing. Errors are those conditions resulting from hardware or software malfunctions.

Signaling Errors and Deviations

Tim and I separated the conditions that occur during processing into errors and deviations. We needed to decide how to signal each type of condition. Errors from hardware and software malfunctions are generally not expected, so exceptions provide a clean way to handle those conditions. To signal deviations some groups prefer using exceptions and other groups prefer using return values from methods. Tim and I chose exceptions, since that is the common paradigm in Java.

Deviation Conventions

The `com.samscdrental.failures` package contains deviations and exceptions:

```
Deviation.java
CDCategoryFormatDeviation.java
CheckInDeviation.java
CheckOutDeviation.java
CustomerIDFormatDeviation.java
DollarFormatDeviation.java
ImportFileDeviation.java
ImportFormatDeviation.java
LateReturnDeviation.java
NameFormatDeviation.java
ParseLineDeviation.java
PhysicalIDFormatDeviation.java
PrinterFailureDeviation.java
StatusDeviation.java
UPCCodeFormatDeviation.java
SeriousErrorException.java
```

To separate deviations from exceptions, all expected errors are derived from `Deviation`, which in turn is derived from `Exception`, the base class for Java exceptions. The `Deviation` object contains an explanation that gives the user an indication of the error. For example, when converting from `String` to `CustomerID`, if the format is invalid, the `CustomerIDFormatDeviation` object that is thrown contains the reason.

Find methods for collections in Java return `null` if a matching object is not found. "Consistency is Simplicity" suggests that the collections in Sam's system also do so. If `CustomerID` is not found in `CustomerDataAccess`, the find method returns `null`. This situation might be a permanent error if the customer was removed from the collection. It might be a failure due to an error in inputting `CustomerID`. We might add a check digit or other error checking on the `CustomerID` to ensure that the string value is input correctly. That way, we would deal with the failure as close to the source as possible.

We created the `SeriousErrorException` class, which is an unchecked exception. An unchecked exception does not have to be indicated in the `throws` clause for a method. A method throws `SeriousErrorException` when an error occurs of such severity that the program should not continue. The exception represents bailout. There is no need to catch `SeriousErrorException` in intermediate methods. The user can do nothing to fix the problem indicated by the exception. The main program catches `SeriousErrorException` and displays its description to the user and then exits. If the user could do something to fix the problem, we would not exit the program, but allow for a retry.

Errors When Importing a File

Importing a file provides a whole series of errors that need to be handled. The interface contract (see Chapter 3) for the import needs to be spelled out in some detail. For example, when the file is read, what should occur if the file has bad or incorrectly formatted text in it? Should the program reject the entire file or just ignore the line with the incorrect format? When we are parsing the strings in the input file, we might get multiple errors on each line or we might have multiple lines with errors. Do we report each one or just the first one?

When a `CDDisc` object is to be added to `CDDiscDataAccess`, what should occur if there is already an object with the same `PhysicalID`? Should the current `CDDisc` object be overwritten or should the new `CDDisc` object be ignored? In the latter case, should the user be notified of the duplication?

No one solution is correct in all situations. The client and the users ultimately decide how to handle errors. However, for any solution, the user should not have to look inside the code to determine what went wrong. Any message displayed to the user should indicate what was wrong in the file, if anything, and how much of the file was processed if there was a problem.

A Little Prefactoring

We modified the design as the code was being written. The following prefactoring guidelines suggested these modifications.

Splitters Versus Lumpers

The `com.samscdrental.importexport` package contains classes related to importing the data from text files:

```
AddFromFileInterface.java
CDDiscDataAccessImportExport.java
CDDiscImportExport.java
CDReleaseDataAccessImportExport.java
CDReleaseImportExport.java
CustomerDataAccesstExport.java
CustomerImportExport.java
DataAccessImportExportHelper.java
```

Tim and I originally started to place the method to import data from a file in each collection class, such as `CustomerDataAccess`. If the external representation of the data changed, the method in each class would have to change. Taking the "Split Versus Lump" approach, the import methods were separated into their own classes (e.g., `CustomerDataAccessImportExport`). Each class with an external representation (e.g., `Customer`) has a corresponding class (`CustomerImportExport`) that contains the import method (`parseLine( )`).

The data file format is one object per line. Each line contains the attribute values separated by a vertical bar (|). The collection class, such as `CustomerDataAccessImportExport`, reads the lines and handles file-oriented errors. The corresponding `CustomerImportExport` class parses each line and deals with attribute value errors.

Adopt a Prefactoring Attitude

The collections are made persistent using Java object serialization. The stored values are read in the constructor of the collection and are written in the `dispose( )` method.

Tim wrote the deserialization code and serialization code for `CDDiscDataAccess`. He realized he would need the same code for the other collection classes. He was tempted to cut and paste the code and do a little alteration. However, he followed the guideline "never cut and paste more than a single line." So even before testing commenced, the code was separated into a class of its own: `DataAccessHelper`.

The First Released Iteration

Tim and I released the first iteration of our system to Sam. It features the first two use cases: rental check out and check in. This first iteration gives Sam and his staff an opportunity to work with the system and determine how well it meets their needs. The feedback they give us will be the first thing to work on in the next iteration.

Sometimes Practice Does Not Match Theory

If one has unlimited time and an unlimited budget, one might be able to make everything perfect. However, one is always limited in both dimensions. In respect to these restrictions, Tim and I left a few implementation issues outstanding.

Unintended Coupling

Tim and I did have to change the classes because of the way we stored them. This was not a major change, but one that had ramifications throughout the system. The collection classes were implemented using Java serialization. Thus, all of the data types had to implement Serializable. If the data had been kept in a database, this would not have been necessary. Sometimes implementation does affect the class definitions of upper-level classes.

We could have created a separate persistence class for each data class to restrict this change to only the persistence classes. The extra work in this instance would not necessarily result in any extra benefit.

Nothing Is Perfect

Prefactoring eliminates some refactoring, but it does not eliminate all of it. You will never see everything in advance. When writing the classes that perform the import of data from a file (e.g., CustomerDataAccessImportExport)), I found myself cutting and pasting an entire method (addCustomersFromFile( )) and modifying it for each collection. I knew it was wrong. I disregarded the "Adapt a Prefactoring Attitude" guideline.

Developing a template or a preprocessing script to create this common code would have been a far superior solution. The version of Java used to develop the program did not support templates. A preprocessing script should have been written to avoid the duplication. It was quick to copy the code that worked and perform the few modifications that were required. I justified this because readers who wanted to run the program would have to have the same scripting language installed on their computers.

However, the code works. If necessary, it can be refactored (or left as an exercise to the reader). Time and resource criteria often rank among the most critical factors in development choices and must be respected as valid engineering constraints.

NOTHING IS PERFECT

There is usually a better solution, but you can stop with good enough.[*]

There's Always an Exception

The following shows a combined operation:

```
collectionsInitialize(
        String customerFilename, String cdDiscFilename,
        String cdReleaseFilename)
```

This method really should be three separate methods that allow separate initialization of each file. The code is an example of getting lazy. Unless it is expected that the three must be initialized at once, the method should be "Split Rather Than Lumped."

A Little Misunderstanding

After Tim and I had the system coded, we recognized we used two terms interchangeably that really did not mean the same thing. They were *late* and *overdue*. The two words show up as synonyms in Microsoft Word®'s pop-up box. In relationship to this system, they really had two different meanings. A rental is "overdue" if it *has not been returned* by the due_date. The due_date is the start_date plus the rental_period. A rental is "late" if it *has been returned* and the end_date is greater than the due_date.

We make a note of this violation of "A Rose by Any Other Name Is Not a Rose." Before continuing development, we will examine every instance of *overdue* and *late* and ensure that they have been applied correctly. To separate out the two terms, we will describe them as OverdueRental and LateReturnOfRental. The extra words clearly differentiate the meaning.

ARE WE THERE YET?

We were driving with some friends to New York City. To provide some entertainment on the trip, the driver suggested that we bet on the exact time we would arrive in New York. Being the computer person, I said we had to agree on an exact definition of what arrival meant so that we could determine who won. I suggested that the moment the driver handed the toll to the toll taker at the Lincoln Tunnel would be the moment of arrival. We all agreed on this definition.

When we arrived at the Lincoln Tunnel, there was a backup at the tollbooth. The driver thought he was running a little late for the time that he bet as the winner. (We had covered the car's clock and removed all watches.) The lane next to us was empty, so he shifted over to that lane and pulled up to the booth. It was an automated pass booth, the kind where they read a bar code on your car. There was no attendant to hand the money to. He yelled out to the attendant in the next tollbooth, but she could not take his money. So he drove on through.

Now, by our definition, we never arrived in New York City. A clear definition helped avoid ambiguity and argument over who had won.

(One reviewer suggested that the person who had chosen the latest time could be perceived the winner. That person would be closest to the time that we next paid money to a toll taker at the Lincoln Tunnel. Of course, losers would want to take the Holland Tunnel instead.)

---

* James Bach has an article on "Good Enough Testing" at *http://www.satisfice.com/articles.shtml*. See also *http://www.agilemodeling.com/essays/barelyGoodEnough.html*.

The Rest of the Classes

To complete the picture, this section describes the remaining classes in the packages that have not been discussed in this chapter. In the `com.samscdrental.display.adt` package are the two display widgets that are tied to the corresponding ADTs:

```
CustomerIDTextField.java
PhysicalIDTextField.java
```

The `com.samscdrental.display` package contains the GUI classes:

```
CheckinDialog.java
CheckoutDialog.java
DisplayHelper.java
Main.java
MainFrame.java
```

The `StringHelper` class in `com.samscdrental.helper` contains string utility functions:

```
StringHelper.java
```

In the `com.samscdrental.migration` package is the main program for the migration of files into the system:

```
MigrateMain.java
```

The `com.samscdrental.model.dto`-package contains the Data Transfer Objects (DTOs) for the reports:

```
CDDiscInventoryDTO.java
CDDiscInventoryItem.java
OverdueRentalDTO.java
RentalContractDTO.java
```

The classes representing the model of Sam's system are in `com.samscdrental.model`. These classes, which represent the business model, were discussed in detail in the previous chapters.

```
CDCategory.java
CDCategoryValues.java
CDDisc.java
CDRelease.java
Customer.java
Rental.java
```

Lastly, the `com.samscdrental.reports` package contains the reports produced by the system:

```
CDDiscInventoryMain.java
CDDiscInventoryReportPlainTextFormat.java
ContractReportPlainTextFormat.java
OverdueRentalReportPlainTextFormat.java
ReportPlainTextFormat.java
Reports.java
```

CHAPTER NINE

Associations and States

SAM PRESENTS US WITH NEW REQUIREMENTS. We look at the existing design and see what alterations we need to make to meet these requirements. We explore using association classes in the system to implement the requirements. We examine how the state of objects in the system can be represented.

Sam's New Requirement

Sam met me for lunch at the local vegetarian bistro.

"You know, I was thinking," Sam began.

"Thinking up more things to do, I presume?" I replied.

"Well, yeah. I'd like to keep a report of what each customer is currently renting. Sometimes we get calls from customers who can't remember if they have any CDDiscs currently rented. They are a little absent minded," he stated.

"OK, it should just be an MM change," I said.

"An MM change?" he queried.

"Yes; a Major Minor change. It's a major change, since it involves keeping more information than we currently do. However, it's minor since we only need to rethink how our classes are arranged," I answered.

"That's good. So the other thing I was thinking about is probably an MM too," he said.

"What's that?" I asked.

"I'd like to keep track of all the CDDiscs that a customer has rented. I will be offering discounts to frequent renters in the future," he replied.

"Well, that's not quite as MMish," I said. "Tim and I will discuss it and get back to you."

Who's in Charge?

Are CDDiscs rented to customers or do customers rent CDDiscs? That might seem like a redundant question, but the decision of who is in charge underlies many design issues.

One Class in Charge

In the first version of the system, CDDisc had the start_rental and end_rental operations. When start_rental was invoked, it created a Rental. If we want to know what CDDiscs a particular customer is renting at the current time, we have to ask every CDDisc if it is rented to that Customer. CDDisc would need some additional methods:

```
class CDDisc
    {
    start_rental(Customer a_customer);
        // Begins a rental for particular customer
    end_rental();  // Ends the rental for that customer
    Customer retrieve_renting_customer();
    Customer [] retrieve_all_customers_who_rented();
    };
```

Should Customer keep track of what CDDiscs are rented to it? If so, at the time of the rental, we would call a method in the Customer class to record the rental and a corresponding method at the end of the rental:

```
class Customer
    {
    begin_rental(CDDisc a_cd_disc);
    end_rental(CDDisc a_cd_disc);
    Rentals [] retrieve_current_rentals();
    };
```

In Sam's current system, we have three classes: CDDisc, Rental, and Customer. A Rental object is currently a member of the CDDisc class. But Rental has a reference to the Customer class. So CDDisc is coupled to Rental and Rental is coupled to Customer. This organization worked OK when we had a one-to-one relationship between the classes. In essence, a

CDDisc was tied to a customer through a level of indirection. This tie was temporal. When the customer returned the CDDisc, the association was broken.*

Association Classes

We can approach the relationship between CDDisc and Customer in a different way. A rental represents the loan of a CDDisc to a Customer for a period of time. A rental that is completed could still exist. Its state would be different. Thus a rental can become a permanent association of a CDDisc to a Customer. For example:

```
class Rental
    Customer renter
    CDDisc cd_disc
    Timestamp start_time
    Timestamp end_time
    Dollar rental_fee
    Days base_rental_period
```

Association classes contain attributes that refer to two (or more) objects, as well as any data relative to the relationship. The objects that are linked typically represent different classes. Using an association class decouples the two linked classes. For example, in Sam's system, CDDisc no longer is coupled to Customer. Any methods in CDDisc referring to Customer are eliminated. (For more details on association classes, see *Object-Oriented Modeling and Design* by James R Rumbaugh et al. [Prentice Hall, 1990]).

Rentals are treated on an equal basis with CDDiscs and Customers. A RentalCollection holds the Rentals, and appropriate methods are created to retrieve the Rentals, based on Sam's new requests. For example:

```
class RentalCollection
    {
    RentalContractDTO start_rental(CDDisc a_cddisc, Customer a_customer);
    end_rental_of_cddisc(CDDisc a_cddisc);
    Rental [] retrieve_current_rentals_for_customer(Customer a_customer);
    Rental [] retreive_all_rentals_for_customer(Customer a_customer);
    Customer [] retrieve_customers_who_rented_a_cd_disc(CDDisc a_cd_disc);
    Rental retrieve_current_rental_for_cd_disc(CDDisc a_cd_disc);
    };
```

Figure 9-1 shows the class diagram for this approach.

The start_rental( ) method returns a RentalContractDTO. This is the same DTO that was produced in the previous system. Our reorganization of these classes does not affect the output reports. The reorganization affects only the CDDisc class and the RentalOperations class.

---

* Michael Green, a reviewer, suggested that one might discover a guideline in a retrospective: "Before discarding an association, check with the customer to see if it may be needed in the future. What kinds of questions might have been asked that would have helped foresee these changes and plan for them?"

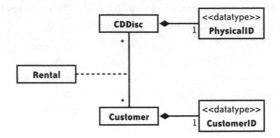

FIGURE 9-1. Rental association classes

DECOUPLE WITH ASSOCIATIONS

Association classes decouple the two classes being associated.

The State of an Object

Many objects have states. The behavior of such an object differs depending on its current condition: the state that it is in. Thinking in terms of states of objects, and what an object can do in each state, can simplify your code.

For example, the state of a file object can be **NotOpen**, **OpenForReading**, **OpenForWriting**, or **OpenForReadingAndWriting**. A file object in the **NotOpen** state cannot be read or written. Events, such as the calling of an object's method, can alter the state of the object. Calling the open method for a file object can transform the state into **OpenForReading**, **OpenForWriting**, or **OpenForReadingAndWriting**, or it might leave the state as **NotOpen**, if the file is unavailable.

State Diagrams

In Sam's system, a CDDisc has the state **Rented** or **NotRented**. A CDDisc that is **Rented** cannot be rented again. You can depict the transition between these states by using a state diagram, such as that shown in Figure 9-2.

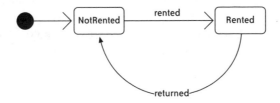

FIGURE 9-2. CDDisc state diagram

State diagrams are not just for developers. They also help users specify system behavior. They help explain how the system's state changes in response to operations, and they can clarify missing specifications. Suppose that Sam wanted to track lost CDDiscs. We prepare a state diagram (shown in Figure 9-3) to demonstrate the transitions between the Lost and InService states and the events that cause these transitions.

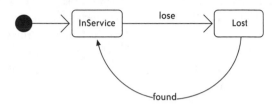

FIGURE 9-3. CDDisc service state diagram

This second state diagram for CDDiscs brings up a number of issues. Is the **Service** state independent of the **Rental** state? Can a **Rented** CDDisc become **Lost** only when it is **Rented**? Can you rent a **Lost** CDDisc? Thinking in terms of states can help clarify both the user and developer's understanding of the system.

Representing Binary States

You can represent an object's state in several ways. For a condition that has only two values, such as **Rented/NotRented**, the state can be kept as a binary value. If external methods require the value of the state, it is returned by a method to hide its actual implementation. For example, in the version of Sam's system prior to this chapter, the state was represented by whether the_rental attribute of CDDisc referred to null or to a Rental. The is_rented( ) method in CDDisc returns the result of this comparison.

With the Rental association introduced in this chapter, the state of a CDDisc is now represented by whether a current Rental for the CDDisc exists in the RentalCollection. The retrieve_current_rental_for_cd_disc( ) in RentalCollection indicates the state by returning either the Rental or null.

More Than Two States

For conditions that can take on a larger number of states, an explicit state mechanism is recommended. The mechanism can be separate classes, an attribute, or the State pattern (see *Design Patterns* by Erich Gamma et al.). For example, as noted in Chapter 7, the state of a Customer could be **Regular**, **Inactive**, and **NeverAgain**. The third value refers to customers who should never be allowed to rent due to their history of not returning rentals.

You could use three classes, such as RegularCustomer, InactiveCustomer, and NeverAgainCustomer, all derived from Customer. However, it is usually difficult to alter the class of an object when its state changes.

For classes for which the value of the state alters only a single behavior, an enumeration might be appropriate. For example, the state could be kept in an attribute of the type CustomerState:

```
enumeration CustomerState {Regular, Inactive, NeverAgain}
```

If there are more behavior differences between the states, the State pattern is desirable. With the State pattern, the behavior is delegated to objects that each represent a different state. The user sees objects of a single class (e.g., Customer), and not the state objects (e.g., RegularState, InactiveState, and NeverAgainState), as shown in Figure 9-4. It is easy to convert Customers from one state to another with the State pattern by changing the state object to which the behavior is delegated.

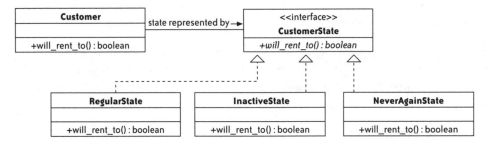

FIGURE 9-4. Customer with states

PRINTING THE UNPRINTABLE

I once worked with a company that programmed the reservation system for a large airline. When they first developed electronic ticketing, it was treated as a form of regular ticketing. The system had states for a reservation: reserved, ticketed, and so forth. It was pretty clear what ticketed meant: the ticket had been printed. A confirmation had come back from the ticketing agency that the printer had successfully printed the ticket. A number of decisions were based on ticketing, such as whether a person would be charged if he made a change to his ticket.

The question arose as to when an electronic ticket was considered ticketed. Since an electronic ticket was never printed, it was *never* considered ticketed. A passenger could make a change up until he boarded the plane and not be charged a change fee. (This condition has since been corrected.)

When using states, be sure that each state reflects the desired behavior. Don't force fit new states into existing ones.

SEE WHAT CONDITION YOUR CONDITION IS IN
Use state-based analysis to examine object behavior.*

Check All the Bases to See if Anyone Is On

Are there other states for a Rental? The late/overdue misunderstanding we discovered in the last chapter applies to the **Current/Completed** state. By the definitions of **Late** and **Overdue**, a Rental that is **Current** can be **Overdue** or **NotOverdue**. This condition is dynamic: it changes as time goes on. A Rental that is **Completed** can be **Late** or **NotLate**. This condition is static: once a Rental ends, it is forever going to be **Late** or **NotLate**. A **Completed** Rental cannot be **Overdue**, nor can a **Current** Rental be **Late**.

These states with their substates seem to cover all the bases for a Rental at this point. Depending on Sam's future desires for record keeping, we might create states for Rentals for other conditions, such as **EndedByLossOfCDDisc**.

THE BIG STATE SWITCH

I heard a story about one of the original designers of an AT&T telephone switch. He spent several months investigating all the possible states of a telephone call and what caused a transition from one state to another. The managers were getting concerned. All he did was walk around, talk to people, and scribble things on a pad of paper. They did not see any visible progress. One day, he announced that he was done. He turned the state diagram over to a coder. The coder completed the job in a few weeks. That program formed the basis for the AT&T switch for many years.

This is an example of how state-based design can result in a very maintainable system.

---

* A reviewer noted that Boris Beizer was an early proponent of state-based analysis and testing. See *Software System Testing and Quality Assurance* by Boris Beizer (Van Nostrand Reinhold/Wiley, 1984).

CHAPTER TEN

Interfaces and Adaptation

WE CREATE INTERFACES FOR SAM'S CATALOG SEARCH USE CASE that was introduced in Chapter 4. We explore how to test these interfaces. We adapt implementations to meet these interfaces, and we determine how additional interfaces can provide performance-oriented features.

The Catalog Search Use Case

My phone rang. I picked it up. Sam started talking immediately.

"Hello. I think I'd really like to get the in-store catalog in operation. Some of the customers have been asking for it. The printed listing of what CDDiscs we have in inventory works OK, but they'd like to be able to search for which CDDiscs have a particular song."

"Sounds fine. Let's get together and discuss the details," I suggested.

"I don't have much time, but I don't want to hold you up. I'm heading to the Caribbean in half an hour," Sam said in a hurried tone.

"All right. We need to work on the details," I replied.

"No time for details. I just want it searchable," he said.

"OK, I'll start to work on it. Can I get in contact with you if I have a question?" I asked.

"No. We'll be on a remote island without phones. But I trust you'll do the right thing," he replied.

"I'll tell you what; can I create a simple use case description and have you approve it before you go?" I queried.

"Yeah, go ahead, but make it quick. My taxi leaves in half an hour," he stated.

"Can I go with you?" I asked. "I hate to work on a project without the client available."

"Maybe some other time. I trust you'll make the right decisions," he replied.

I expanded the original Search_catalog use case to multiple use cases. This is an example of a hierarchical set of use cases. Search_catalog is at the top, and the following use cases fall underneath, each providing a detailed manifestation of the original use case:

Search_for_song

    a. User enters a string.

    b. System responds with all song titles that match that string.

    c. User selects one song title.

    d. System responds with all CDReleases that contain that song.

    e. User selects one CDRelease.

    f. User either exits or performs a Search_for_availability.

Search_for_availability extends Search_for_Song

    a. User has selected a CDRelease.

    b. If a corresponding CDDisc is available, system informs user of availability.

    c. Otherwise, system responds that all CDDiscs of the CDRelease are currently rented.

Now, one could imagine that later on, Sam might suggest using a sound-alike match or a wildcard format so that the user does not have to specify a name or title exactly. Such approaches are variations of the Search_for_song use case. In abstract terms, they are exactly the same use case, varying only by the definition of *match*, which could be any of the following: match exactly, match by sound-alike, or match with wildcards.

Do we need more detail for the Search_for_song use case? It contains some implicit requirements. There is an assumption that the system responds in a reasonable amount of time. If it takes 10 minutes to do a search, the system will be useless. It probably does not matter if it takes one one-hundredth of a second or one-tenth of a second. The user probably would not perceive that small a difference. However, there is a time period in the range of one-tenth of a second through 10 minutes for which the performance is not acceptable. The use case flow does not indicate this time period. That value should be captured in documentation accompanying the use case.

I emailed a copy of the preceding use cases to Sam. He sent back a third use case:

Search_by_performer

    a. User inputs a string.

    b. System responds with all performers that match that string.

    c. User selects one performer.

    d. System responds with all CDReleases by that performer.

    e. User either exits or performs a Search_for_availability.

I called up Sam to see if he wanted one more search, which seemed to complete the group: Search_for_CD_title.

He was rushing out the door. "Well, I hadn't thought of that, but it seems like a good idea," he said. "Go for it."

I wrote up the last use case:

Search_for_CD_title

    a. User enters a string.

    b. System responds with all CDReleases whose title matches that string.

    c. User selects one.

    d. User either exits or performs a Search_for_availability.

Designing the Interface

At this point, Tim and I were not sure how we were going to obtain the data for the catalog. Sam had mentioned a couple of Internet sites where it might be available. I figured a CD-ROM or two probably was available with the data. After all, a CD-ROM with equivalent information exists for books. At worst, we might put his staff to work when they had nothing else to do. They could input the information from the CD cases.

How we were going to implement the catalog was irrelevant at that point. What we needed was the search interface. Based on the use cases given in the previous section, we came up with a rough class outline that looked like this:

```
class Song
    CommonString the_title
class CD
    UPCCode the_upc_code
    CommonString the_title
    Performer [] the_performers
    Song [] the_songs
    // Other Info to display (e.g. producer).
class Performer
    Name the_name
```

Based on these classes, we developed the following interface. The return values are shown as groups (arrays). They could become collections if we started to add functionality to the groups (such as sort by producer).

```
interface CDCatalog
    Song [] search_for_song_by_title(CommonString string_to_match)
    CD []  retrieve_cds_for_song(Song a_song)  // From the song list
    Performer [] search_for_performers_by_name(CommonString string_to_match)
    CD [] retrieve_cds_for_a_performer(Performer a_performer)
        // From performer list
    CD [] search_for_cds_by_name(CommonString string_to_match)
```

What's a CD?

Now, what about the term *CD*? In the initial system design, we created CDDisc and CDRelease to distinguish clearly between those two concepts. Should this interface return arrays of CDReleases? Well, maybe.

The CD information retrieved from this catalog is not the same as the CDRelease in Sam's system. The CDRelease that Sam and I created contains just a UPCCode and a title, whereas the CD class additionally contains a performer list, a song list, and other information such as the producer. There is not a one-to-one correlation between CDs and CDReleases. CDRelease objects exist only for CDDiscs that Sam owns (or perhaps owned previously). However, CDs that are retrieved from the catalog can correspond to CDDiscs that Sam has never owned. Thus, the CD here is not a CDRelease. The two are separate concepts with separate purposes. It is easier to split them at this point and lump them later if we find we really are using these two classes in the same way.

Sam and I already agreed that *CD* is a nebulous term. So Tim and I needed to come up with another name for the CD class in the preceding example. If Sam thinks it is incorrect, a global search and replace can change it easily. We termed the concept CDCatalogItem. This is a little wordy, but certainly distinctive and easily searchable. The interface becomes:

```
class CDCatalogItem
    CommonString the_title
    UPCCode theupc_code
    Song [] the_songs
    Performer [] the_performers
interface CDCatalogItemCollection
    Song [] search_for_song_by_title(CommonString string_to_match)
    CDCatalogItem [] retrieve_cd_catalog_items_for_song(Song a_song)
        // From the song list
    Performer [] search_for_performers_by_name(CommonString string_to_match)
    CDCatalogItem [] retrieve_cd_catalog_items_for_a_performer(
        Performer a_performer) // From performer list
    CDCatalogItem [] search_for_cd_catalog_items_by_title(
        CommonString string_to_match)
```

A Little Premature Worry

A performance-concerned developer might worry about the performance of this interface. CDCatalogItem [] contains the matching CDCatalogItems. Each item in the list contains a good deal of information. The search system could take a big performance hit if CDCatalogItem [] returns a lot of matching items. In many cases, Tim and I believe, most of the information in each CDCatalogItem will never be viewed.

We could make CDCatalogItem do a lazy fill-in of its data (a *lazy lookup*). When an item on the list is created, the object will fill in only its identifier and the title. When the information on an item is actually requested, the object will go back to the catalog and read in the rest of the details.

Alternatively, the performance-concerned developer might change the interface. An additional class could be added that contains only the minimal information required for a display of matching CDCatalogItems (e.g., title). For example, we could create the CDCatalogItemInfo class:

```
class CDCatalogItemInfo
    Identifier the_identifier
    CommonString the_title
interface CDCatalogItemCollection
    Song [] search_for_song_by_title(CommonString string_to_match)
    CDCatalogItemInfo [] retrieve_cd_catalog_items_for_song (Song a_song)
        // From the song list
    Performer [] search_for_performers_by_name(CommonString string_to_match)
    CDCatalogItemInfo [] retrieve_cd_catalog_items_for_a_performer(
        Performer a_performer)
        // From performer list
    CDCatalogItemInfo [] search_for_cd_catalog_items_by_title (
        CommonString string_to_match)
    CDCatalogItem retrieve_item_for_cd_catalog_item_info (
        CDCatalogItemInfo cd_info)
```

An implementation of this interface will probably run faster than the previous one that does not use lazy lookup. Should we worry about performance at this time? For now, we could write down our concern, and the possible solutions, in our design journal ("Don't Speed Until You Know Where You Are Going"). Then we could code the first implementation, without the lazy lookup. When we test that implementation of the interface, we will see the actual performance. If it is too slow, we can implement lazy lookup for CDCatalogItem. If it is still too slow, we can try the CDCatalogItemInfo approach.

Interface Development

Sam and I did not have much time to discuss the new use cases introduced at the beginning of this chapter. The original Search_catalog use case in Chapter 4 seems to imply that the search should return only CDCatalogItems that Sam carries in inventory. Should that filtering be part of the CDCatalogItemCollection interface or should it be done on the list of CDCatalogItems that the interface returns?

Considering separation of concerns simplifies our decision. The job of the CDCatalogItemCollection interface is to find all CDCatalogItems that meet the search criteria for each method. The concern of another class, CDCatalogItemInStoreCollection, is to determine which CDCatalogItems correspond to CDReleases. The interface for CDCatalogItemInStoreCollection looks the same as that for CDCatalogItemCollection. CDCatalogItemInStoreCollection is responsible for checking that the UPCCode for each CDCatalogItem exists in the CDReleaseCollection and returns only CDCatalogItems for which that was true. Figure 10-1 shows the sequence diagram for a search using CDCatalogItemInStoreCollection.

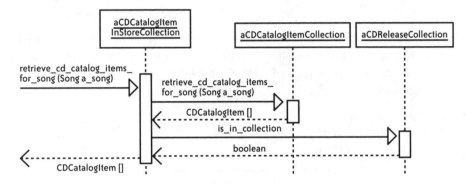

FIGURE 10-1. CDCatalogItemInStoreCollection sequence diagram

To check the usability of the search interface, Tim and I create a small class that implements the CDCatalogItemCollection interface and returns data for a very small number of CDCatalogItems and Songs. Text files are used to store the data so that it can be changed easily. Corresponding graphical user interface (GUI) displays are created to drive the interface. Then the prototype implementation is exercised to see how well the interface matches the user's expectations ("Prototypes Are Worth a Thousand Words").

Interface Testing

For CDCatalogItemCollection, we create tests based on the interface. The tests should include not only individual method tests, but also tests based on work cases that are derived from the overall system's use cases. These are the four use cases described earlier in this chapter: Search_for_song, Search_by_performer, Search_by_CD_title, and Search_for_availability.

For example, the Search_for_song use case exercises two of the methods in CDCatalogItemCollection. The tests based on this work case will call both search_for_song_by_title( ) to retrieve a number of songs and retrieve_cd_catalog_items_for_song( ) for one or more of the songs.

The tests are written against methods in the interface, not against a particular implementation of an interface. This permits substitution of any implementation during testing. For example, the prototype implementation should pass all the tests for CDCatalogItemCollection. Any real implementation should likewise pass these tests. A web-based implementation would take the search criteria, access a web site that performs CD searches, decode the returned HTML or XML, and place the data into the appropriate fields of CDCatalogItem.*

If a test invoked a method that was particular to a specific implementation, the implementation could not be substituted easily. Suppose the test called a method in the web-based implementation to set up an Internet connection. A non-web-based implementation such as the prototype implementation would not have that method, and would cause a compilation or link failure.

To validate the returned information, write a test that compares the results of two different implementations. Not using any implementation-specific methods makes it easy to substitute implementations for comparison.

TEST THE INTERFACE, NOT THE IMPLEMENTATION

Use the contract of the interface to develop the functional tests, not the implementation behind it.

This guideline does not imply that you are prohibited from looking at the implementation to come up with tests that might expose the implementation's weaknesses. That is a form of "white-box" testing. This guideline suggests that you should be able to run the tests you write to attempt to expose those weaknesses, on any implementation, not just on the current implementation.

Interface Splitting

The actions in the RentalOperations class introduced in Chapter 8 are definitely separate from the actions for searching a catalog. The search operations go into their own class, CatalogOperations. The only overlap is that methods in CatalogOperations need to find out if a particular CDDisc is rented, by invoking is_cd_disc_rented( ). That method is currently in RentalOperations.

Status operations do not affect a system's state. They are just reporting mechanisms for the state of an object. We split the current RentalOperations interface into two interfaces: RentalOperations and StatusOperations. The rental status operation (is_cd_disc_rented( )) is placed in StatusOperations.

Now, CatalogOperations needs StatusOperations, but it does not need RentalOperations, as shown in Figure 10-2. Splitting the interfaces allows us to better control the access to each function ("If You Forget Security, You're Not Secure"). The program used by a customer

---

* *http://Freedb.org/* and *http://www.gracenote.com/gn_products/cddb.html* both perform searches similar to the ones in our interface. The returned pages from those systems could be parsed for the results.

to perform catalog searches involves CatalogOperations, which has access to StatusOperations but not to RentalOperations.

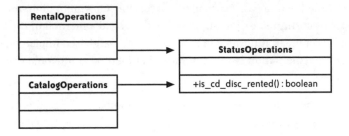

FIGURE 10-2. Split interfaces

SPLIT INTERFACES

Split a single interface into multiple interfaces if multiple clients use different portions of the interface.*

Something Working

The search interface we implemented is basic. It provides the needed functionality. We know that we might need to refine it. We could get bogged down in refinement details before creating the first implementation. Instead of doing that, when we have ideas for additional improvements while developing the first interface, we write them down in the design journal for later development.

The basic catalog lookup is working. The number of items returned by a given search criterion might be large. For example, if the user typed in the letter *A* or the word *The*, a large number of songs would be matched. The match processing could put restrictions on searches for common words. However, a large number of matches still would be possible. The display widget (e.g., a drop-down list or a web page) could have difficulty showing a large number of matches. We could refine the search mechanism to provide a limiting feature.

---

* A reviewer suggested that you could find more information on splitting interfaces in *Large-Scale C++ Software Design* by John Lakos (Addison-Wesley Professional, 1996).

GET SOMETHING WORKING

Create something basic before adding refinements. [*]

Placing Limits

One approach to the problem of dealing with a large number of matches is to place a hard limit on the number of matches. Placing limits on operations can be useful in getting something working. However, unnecessary limits on operations can be annoying to the user.

Instead of placing a hard limit on the number of matches, we can code our system to deal with large numbers of matches in small, easily handled batches. To that end, we wrap another interface around CDCatalogItemCollection. The methods in this new class parallel the methods in CDCatalogItemCollection. For example:

```
interface CDCatalogItemSearchByBatch
    CDCatalogItemSearchResults search_for_cd_catalog_items_by_title (
        CommonString string_to_match)
    CDCatalogItemSearchResults retrieve_cd_catalog_item s_for_a_performer(
        Performer a_performer)
    // and the other methods
```

The methods in CDCatalogItemSearchByBatch return objects of CDCatalogItemSearchResults. A CDCatalogItemSearchResults object works like an iterator, except it returns a batch of CDCatalogItems, not just a single CDCatalogItem. The class looks like this:

```
class CDCatalogItemSearchResults
    private CDCatalogItem [] results     // From the search.
    Boolean has_more_items()
    CDCatalogItem [] get_next_batch(int number_to_get)
```

The user calls has_more_items() to see if there are any remaining items. Then he calls get_next_batch() with the number of items desired. get_next_batch() returns null if there are no more items.

This is another example of "Separating Concerns Makes Smaller Concerns." The CDCatalogItemCollection class does not have to worry about keeping track of how many items were already returned as matches. CDCatalogItemSearchByBatch does not have to worry about how to find the matches.

---

[*] Danny Faught notes that although this is the key to being agile, "Before agile, I remember a suggested integration technique, taking a path from the top of the module hierarchy down to the bottom (with few side trips), so you can run an end-to-end test early on."

Common Code

The ability to iterate through a set of matching items seems appropriate for Songs and Performers. Therefore, we create additional classes (SongSearchResults and PerformerSearchResults) that are used to return batches of matches. The SongSearchResults and PerformerSearchResults classes have the same logic as CDCatalogItemSearchResults. The implementation of each class could delegate to a helper class the job of keeping track of which batch to return.

Since they differ only by the data type on which they operate, a mechanism for creating the duplicate logic seems appropriate. Templates and preprocessing code are two ways of creating this logic. A template is in the form of:

```
template <Item>
{
class SearchResults
    {
    private Item [] results;  // From the search.
    Boolean has_more_items();
        // next call to get_next_batch will return items
    Item [] get_next_batch(int number_to_get);
    }
}
```

We can use this template by specifying other text to replace the "Item" token. For example, we can declare:

```
SearchResults<CDCatalogItem> cd_catalog_item_search_results;
```

A call to a method for this object, such as cd_catalog_item_search_results.get_next_batch( ), returns an object of type CDCatalogItem [].

If the implementation language supports templates, we use that approach. If it does not, we can create a base source-code file and use a script to perform the substitution. The script can be part of the build process.

The template approach (either language based or script based) permits a set of code to be reused without cut and paste.

USE THE SAME LAYOUT TO GET THE SAME LAYOUT*

Use templates or scripts for classes and methods to create consistent logic.

---

* The page at *http://www.ambysoft.com/typesOfReuse.html* describes a wide range of reusable stuff.

CHAPTER ELEVEN

Zip Codes and Interfaces

SAM ASKS THAT THE SYSTEM KEEP TRACK OF CUSTOMER ADDRESSES. Addresses involve Zip Codes.*
We determine how to verify the Zip Codes. We also examine ways to keep track of the
information flowing through the Zip Code verification interfaces.

Adaptation

Sam stopped by for coffee. "You know, I forgot one thing."

"What's that?" I asked.

"I'd really like to keep customers' addresses in the database," he said.

"Well, we don't have a database. That's an implementation issue you shouldn't be concerned with," I replied.

"OK, you got me. I want to be able to keep track of a customer's address so that I can send
him mail," Sam stated.

---

* As an example of the difficulty of keeping consistent ("Consistency is Simplicity"), the United
  States Postal Service uses ZIP Code, while the O'Reilly stylesheet uses Zip Code.

"I think we can do that. You can have the staff enter each customer's address off your cards," I said.

"Yeah, but I also want to check whether my staff entered the addresses correctly. If they enter the wrong Zip Code, the post office might send the mail back. That's a waste," he stated emphatically.

"OK, we'll put Zip Code verification into the CD rental system," I said. "I'll look for a Zip Code verification system."

Then I asked, "What should the system do if the Zip Code is incorrect?"

He said, "Correct it," looking at me as if I were asking the dumbest question he had heard in the last year.

I followed it up with, "What should the system do if the Zip Code cannot be found?"

"Then I guess the user must have made a mistake, so we ought to ask him to correct it," he answered.

"What if the address is not in the Zip Code system yet?" I asked.

"Well, maybe you should keep track of that and try verifying it later," Sam replied.

Based on his responses, I came up with the following preliminary work case for the Zip Code verification system. A work case, as you might recall from Chapter 4, is a use case where the user is not a human, but another method:

Lookup_Zip_Code_for_address

    a. User supplies an address.

    b. If Zip Code is found for address, System replaces Zip Code in the address.

    c. Otherwise, System reports error

Of course, we need an `Address` to verify:

```
class Address
    {
    CommonString line_1;
    CommonString line_2;
    CommonString city;
    State state;
    ZipCode zip_code;
    }
```

A class interface derived directly from the use case might look like Example 11-1.

EXAMPLE 11-1. ZipCodeCorrectionService

```
class ZipCodeCorrectionService
    correct_zip_code_in_address(Address address_to_correct)
        throws ZipCodeNotFoundException
        // puts correct zip code into address_to_correct
```

It is not ZipCodeCorrectionService's responsibility to keep track of whether the system has verified the ZipCode. The best place to put that responsibility is in Address itself. The condition is a state of Address. So Address gets another attribute, appropriately set in the constructor.* We place the call to correct_zip_code_in_address( ) inside the verify_zip_code( ) method of Address:, as shown in Example 11-2.

EXAMPLE 11-2. Address class

```
class Address
    {
    boolean zip_code_verified = false;
    static ZipCodeCorrectionService zip_code_correction =
        new ZipCodeCorrectionService( );
    verify_zip_code( ) throws ZipCodeNotFoundException
        {
        zip_code_correction.correct_zip_code_in_address(this);
        zip_code_verified = true;
        }
    }
```

Why keep a state of verification in Address? You are going to ask the user again for the Zip Code, right? Who said the verify_zip_code( ) method is being called from a program that inputs the Zip Code from the user? Perhaps the method is being called to verify the Zip Code in a record in a database. Asking the database for a correction is tough. A service should not depend on the context in which it is called.

The correct_zip_code_in_address( ) method performs two operations that ought to be separated. The method looks up a ZipCode for an Address and then replaces the ZipCode in the Address. Separating these two operations creates another interface, ZipCodeVerificationService, as shown in Example 11-3.

EXAMPLE 11-3. ZipCodeVerificationService interface

```
interface ZipCodeVerificationService
    {
    ZipCode find_zip_code_for_address(Address address_to_check)
        throws ZipCodeNotFoundException
    }
```

The method in this interface simply finds and returns the ZipCode for an Address. The correct_zip_code_in_address( ) method calls an implementation of this interface and puts the returned ZipCode into the Address, as shown in Example 11-4.

EXAMPLE 11-4. ZipCodeCorrectionService

```
class ZipCodeCorrectionService
    {
    static ZipCodeVerificationService zip_code_verification =
        new ZipCodeVerificationServiceImplementation( );
```

* One reader questioned whether ZipCode should keep track of its own validity. You could take that approach. However, since you can determine the validity of a ZipCode only in the context of an Address, it seems more appropriate for the Address to keep the state.

EXAMPLE 11-4. ZipCodeCorrectionService (continued)

```
correct_zip_code_in_address(Address address_to_correct)
    throws ZipCodeNotFoundException
    {
    address_to_correct.zip_code = zip_code_verification.
        find_zip_code_for_address(address_to_correct)
    }
}
```

At this time, Tim and I are not sure which implementation will provide
ZipCodeVerificationService. We could purchase a Zip Code CD-ROM, subscribe to a Zip
Code web service, or create an HTTP command for the U.S. Postal Service web site and
decode the HTML response.

Whatever implementation we pick we will adapt to the ZipCodeVerificationService interface. Suppose that a third-party implementation already exists that performs a Zip Code
lookup. The method in that module might look like this:

```
String find_zip_code(String address1, String address2, String city, String state);
    // returns null if not found
```

We show in Example 11-5 an implementation of ZipCodeVerificationService
(Example 11-3) that calls this find_zip_code( ) method.

EXAMPLE 11-5. ZipCodeVerificationServiceImplementation

```
class ZipCodeVerificationServiceImplementation
    {
    ZipCode find_zip_code_for_address(Address address_to_check)
        throws ZipCodeNotFoundException
        {
        String zip = find_zip_code(address_to_check.line_1,
            address_to_check.line_2, address_to_check.city,
            address_to_check.state);
        if (zip == null)
            throw new ZipCodeNotFoundException( );
        ZipCode zipcode = new ZipCode( );
        zipcode.from_string(zip);
        return zipcode;
        }
    }
```

ADOPT AND ADAPT

**Create the interface you desire and adapt the
implementation to it.**

Pass the Buck

Tim and I implemented ZipCodeVerificationService for Sam using an third-party provider. After a little while, Sam came to me with a complaint.

"I'm spending way too much money utilizing that third party. I can't believe that it costs so much," he said.

I thought about comparing the amount he spent on the service to what he spent on his double latte each day. I quickly dismissed the idea.

"Can you log the requests to the service so that I can double-check that the number of lookups the service says it performed is equal to the number it actually performed?" he asked.

"Of course," I replied.

We do not want to alter the implementation that calls the service. It is time for the Proxy pattern, as described in Chapter 6. In the Proxy pattern, multiple classes implement the same interface. The methods in one proxy class perform some functionality, such as encryption or checking for security access violations. Then they call the corresponding method in another proxy class. Figure 11-1 shows the sequence of calls. The Proxy pattern allows you to preprocess, or postprocess, the functionality in the interface you are hiding behind the proxy. Since the proxy interface and the original interface are identical, the caller can be blind to which one is really being called.

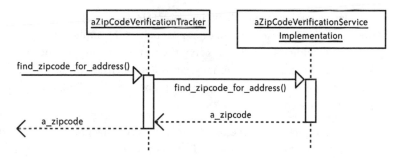

FIGURE 11-1. Proxy pattern for ZipCodeVerificationService

Example 11-5 shows the ZipCodeVerificationServiceImplementation. ZipCodeVerificationTracker also implements ZipCodeVerificationService, as shown in Example 11-6. It keeps track of the number of requested lookups.

EXAMPLE 11-6. ZipCodeVerificationTracker

```
ZipCodeVerificationTracker implements ZipCodeVerificationService
    {
    ZipCodeVerificationService next_implementation
        = new ZipCodeVerificationImplementation( );
    ZipCode find_zip_code_for_address(Address address_to_check)
        throws ZipCodeNotFoundException
```

EXAMPLE 11-6. ZipCodeVerificationTracker (continued)

```
      {
      track_this_call( );
      return next_implementation.find_zip_code_for_address(address_to_check);
      }
  }
```

We need to alter the `ZipCodeCorrectionServiceImplementation` (Example 11-4) to call the logging proxy.* We change the initialization of `zip_code_verification` to:

```
static ZipCodeVerificationService zip_code_verification =
       new ZipCodeVerificationTracker ( );
```

The only thing left is to decide what `track_this_call( )` should do. We need to determine what we want to track. We could record each call to `find_zip_code_for_address( )` in a log. Alternatively, we just could keep track of the number of calls and record that number at the end of the program.

DO A LITTLE AND PASS THE BUCK

Add proxies to interfaces to add functionality.

Unwritten Code

Suppose that we decided to log every call in `ZipCodeVerificationTracker`'s `track_this_call( )` method (Example 11-6). There are a number of possibilities for implementing a set of operations, such as a logging class. First, we can write just the features we need for the current situation (the YAGNI [You Ain't Gonna Need It] approach). Second, we can add features that we are sure we will need in the near term. Third, we can look for a prewritten and tested standard library component.

Tim and I have a logger library we have used on several previous projects. We found it as freeware many years ago. The user calls a method to output a comment and a value. The comment and the value converted to a string, along with the time, are placed on a line in a file. The library did the job and we have never had to investigate its internals.

---

* We would not need to change the method if we had implemented
`ZipCodeVerificationServiceFactory( )`, as discussed later in this chapter.

THE EASIEST CODE TO DEBUG IS THAT WHICH IS NOT WRITTEN

Never write functionality that already exists in usable form.

Aspect-Oriented Programming

Another way to avoid writing code is to use *Aspect-Oriented Programming* (AOP), if your language supports it. With AOP, you can easily add common functionality to classes. AOP modularizes *crosscutting concerns*, which is behavior that cuts across classes. These crosscutting aspects can include logging, security authorization, performance optimizations, and so forth. So instead of using proxies and a logging library as shown above, you can add logging as an aspect.

Here is a brief introduction to aspects. For more information on aspects, see *Aspect-Oriented Software Development* by Robert E. Filman, Tzilla Elrad, Siobhan Clarke, and Mehmet Aksit (Addison-Wesley Professional, 2004), or visit *http://aosd.net/*.

Aspects are coded using either a syntax that closely matches the program language, or XML. Either a preprocessor or a compiler creates extended classes that add the aspect functionality to the application classes.

At particular places in a program, called *join points*, the regular program and aspects meet. Types of join points include the invocation of a method, the construction of an object, or the execution of an exception handler.*

A *pointcut* identifies a set of join points. Advice specifies an action to take at a join point. An *aspect* contains the advice to apply to all the join points in a pointcut.

For example, you can denote a pointcut that identifies all methods. The advice could be to call a log routine. The aspect connects that advice to the pointcut. With a few lines of aspect definition, you add logging of all method calls. For Sam's system, we could identify the find_zip_code_for_address( ) method as the pointcut. The action of logging would not require any changes to the existing code.

More or Less

We decided we needed some more functionality in our logging system for Sam's application. In a few instances in the past, we had to write short programs to analyze the log for

---

* Depending on the implementation of aspects, you can also introduce a new method or attribute to all join points specified by a pointcut.

certain events. In particular, the ability to count events appearing in a log seemed to be a desirable feature.

We determined that the track_this_call( ) method in Example 11-6 could output a log message every time the method is called. We needed a report of how many times these messages appeared, as well as some other statistics.

We could create our own analyzer. Instead, we searched for a logging package that came with an analyzer that could easily perform the message counting. We found several packages that had many more features than we could imagine ever using. But sometimes, more is less. Often it is easier to take a tool that can do more than you need instead of developing an entirely new tool.*

We wrote an adapter to simplify the package interface only to those operations we required. The adapter also transformed the package's naming convention to the style of Sam's system.

MORE IS SOMETIMES LESS

Use a prewritten module with more features than you currently need and adapt it to your current needs.

Using a log to get a count might seem like overkill. But using features that already exist is not overdevelopment. We might find that using individual messages impinges on performance. Then we can make the implementation faster ("Don't Speed Until You Know Where You Are Going"). If the number of calls is high, track_a_call( ) might output a message every hundredth or millionth time it is called.

Indirection

An oft-quoted rule of computer science is "Most problems in computer science can be solved by another level of indirection." One might complain that too many levels of indirection can create maintenance problems. But like many other design facets, taking out indirection is often easier than adding it later. The Factory pattern (see *Design Patterns* by Erich Gamma et al.) is a common form of indirection. Instead of creating an object directly with a constructor, you obtain the object from a Factory class method. This method hides the actual implementation of the object's creation from the caller (see Example 11-7).

---

* One reviewer noted that sometimes tools have so many features, that it takes longer to learn the tool than it does just to write some code that does just what you want.

EXAMPLE 11-7. ZipCodeVerificationServiceFactory

```
enum ZipCodeVerificationServiceType {NORMAL, TRACKING};
class ZipCodeVerificationServiceFactory
    {
    static ZipCodeVerificationService get_instance
        (ZipCodeVerificationServiceType type_to_instantiate);
        {
        switch(type_to_instantiate)
            {
        case NORMAL:
            return new ZipCodeVerificationImplementation( );
            break;
        case TRACKING:
            return new ZipCodeVerificationTracker( );
            break;
        }
    }
```

We alter the initialization of zip_code_verification in Example 11-4 to call the factory get_ instance( ) method with the type requested (NORMAL or TRACKING):

```
static ZipCodeVerificationService zip_code_verification =
    ZipCodeVerificationServiceFactory.get_instance(TRACKING);
```

Note that the caller can choose his desired implementation type, but does not need to specify the name of the actual implementation. The caller specifies the *what*, but not the *how*.

If the decision to use logging should be made at execution time rather than compile time, the factory can read the type value from a configuration file. The factory code is changed, as shown in Example 11-8.

EXAMPLE 11-8. ZipCodeVerificationServiceFactory with configuration

```
enum ZipCodeVerificationServiceType {NORMAL, TRACKING};
class ZipCodeVerificationServiceConfigurationDTO
    {
    ZipCodeVerificationServiceType service_type;
    }
class ZipCodeVerificationServiceFactory
    {
    static ZipCodeVerificationService get_instance( );
    static ZipCodeVerificationServiceConfigurationDTO read_configuration( );
    }
ZipCodeVerificationService get_instance( )
    {
    ZipCodeVerificationServiceConfigurationDTO configuration =
        read_configuration( );
    switch(configuration.service_type)
        {
    case NORMAL:
        return new ZipCodeVerificationImplementation( );
        break;
    case TRACKING:
        return new ZipCodeVerificationTracker( );
```

```
        break;
        }
    }
```

In addition to using configuration information, the factory could check the environment in which the program is running and instantiate a logging class appropriate to that environment. In this example, the environment might permit an Internet connection. If so, the factory could instantiate a logging implementation that used a remote server.

Note that the configuration information in Example 11-8 has been removed by one level of indirection from the format of the configuration file. The read_configuration( ) method returns an object containing all the configuration information that ZipCodeVerificationServiceFactory requires.

WHEN IN DOUBT, INDIRECT

Indirection, using either methods or data, adds flexibility.

To avoid ZipCodeVerificationServiceFactory depending on a configuration file, we can alter the design to use Dependency Injection. Martin Fowler describes Dependency Injection (also called Inversion of Control) in detail at *http://martinfowler.com/articles/injection.html*. The user of a class injects data on which an object depends when the object is created. The dependencies are defined through constructor arguments, arguments to a factory method, or settable properties. The code using Dependency Injection appears in Example 11-9.

EXAMPLE 11-9. ZipCodeVerificationServiceFactory Dependency Injection

```
class ZipCodeVerificationServiceFactory
    {
    static ZipCodeVerificationService get_instance(
        ZipCodeVerificationServiceConfigurationDTO configuration);
    }
ZipCodeVerificationService get_instance(
        ZipCodeVerificationServiceConfigurationDTO configuration)
    {
    switch(configuration.service_type)
        {
    case NORMAL:
        return new ZipCodeVerificationImplementation( );
        break;
    case TRACKING:
        return new ZipCodeVerificationTracker( );
        break;
        }
    }
```

Logging

In pre-object days, I was adamant about having only a single return point for a routine. The return value could be logged before exiting the routine. With object-oriented code, my adamancy for a single return has dissipated. I can always add logging to a method with a proxy, as shown in this chapter. The calls to logging do not then intrude upon the logic for normal operations. The logging proxy can record the values of the input parameters and the return value.

Unit tests, or system use case tests, can check a system's functionality. However, these tests do not check a system in real life. Real users can generate sequences of operations or values of data not covered by automated tests. The interaction of modules in a multithreaded or multiprocess environment can be difficult to determine. Logging at major interfaces can provide the information needed to debug errors.

Paradigm Mismatch

Sometimes the paradigm of the underlying implementation does not match the paradigm of the interface you have created. Usually you can create an adapter that hides this difference. A dictionary holds pairs of keys with associated values. If you add a key that already exists, the value for the previous entry in the dictionary is overwritten silently. In other implementations, the duplication generates an error.

You might have created an interface that works one way. An implementation might work the other way. You can add logic to make that implementation work the other way. For example, if your interface assumed silent overwriting, the logic can check for the existence of the key and delete the current key before adding the new one.

You cannot adapt some paradigm mismatches in this manner. You might not be able to find an implementation that works in the paradigm of the interface you designed. In that case, you will have to rewrite the interface and redo the methods that depend upon it.*

---

* Eric M. Burke, a reviewer, noted that if you develop an interface without creating an implementation, you might create an interface that is impossible to implement in reality. Do not cast an interface in stone until you have developed and tested an implementation.

CHAPTER TWELVE

More Reports

SAM DECIDES HE NEEDS FANCIER REPORTS AND DIFFERENT REPORTS. We implement his requests using some of the guidelines already introduced. We also examine Sam's need to communicate data to the world outside the system.

Fancy Reports

Sam looked at the first version of the rental contract. "Well, it looks pretty plain to me," he stated.

"OK," I replied. "What else would you like on it?"

"How about a few graphics and making the due date stand out in bold with a larger font?" he queried. "Is that too much trouble?"

"No trouble at all," I answered. "What's the charge limit on your American Express?"

"I don't have a limit," Sam replied.

"Good, then there should be enough money to do it," I stated.

More Is Less

Handling graphics and different fonts, and laying out pages containing them, is a time-consuming process using procedural-driven code. We need to calculate the sizes of strings and compute where to position them. Fortunately, languages and modules are available that provide these necessary operations. These components contain a lot more than we need, but they make a lot less work for us ("More Is Sometimes Less").

One language that does the trick is the Hypertext Markup Language (HTML). The display modules are browsers and HTML-aware edit widgets. The create_report( ) method can create HTML-formatted text. We can display that text using an HTML-aware display module. We change our DisplayReport class to include a method for displaying an HTML report:

```
class DisplayReport
    void display_report_plain_text_format(
        ReportPlainTextFormat report_plain_text_format)
    void display_report_html_format(
        ReportHTMLFormat report_html_format)
```

ReportHTMLFormat contains HTMLString. HTMLString consists of properly formatted HTML:

```
class ReportHTMLFormat
    HTMLString contents
```

Spreadsheet Conundrum Revisited

The method for the existing rental contract is create_rental_contract_report( ). Now we are going to have two types of rental contracts—one in plain text and one in HTML—as well as additional reports, such as the late return report. The question is how these reports should be packaged. Do we keep all reports in a single class? If we separate them into separate classes, do we have each class handle all reports of a particular type (e.g., HTML, plain text, comma delimited), or should each class handle all the formats for a particular report?* This is another example of "The Spreadsheet Conundrum."

For example, we could have a class for each report, as shown in Example 12-1.

EXAMPLE 12-1. Class for each report

```
class RentalContractReports
    {
    ReportPlainTextFormat create_rental_contract_report_text_format(
        RentalContractDTO rental_contract_dto)
    ReportHTMLFormat create_rental_contract_report_html_format(
        RentalContractDTO rental_contract_dto)
    }
class LateReturnReport
    {
    ReportPlainTextFormat create_late_return_report_text_format(
```

---

* One reviewer noted another way to organize these reports. For example, since XML and HTML are really just text, you could have an interface representing TextReport. One of these is PlainTextReport.

EXAMPLE 12-1. Class for each report (continued)

```
        LateReturnDTO rental_contract_dto)
    ReportHTMLFormat create_late_return_report_html_format(
        LateReturnDTO rental_contract_dto)
    }
```

Or we could have a class for each output type, as shown in Example 12-2.

EXAMPLE 12-2. Class for each output type

```
class PlainTextFormatReports
    ContractReportPlainTextFormat create_rental_contract_report (
        RentalContractDTO rental_contract_dto)
    ReportPlainTextFormat create_late_return_report_text_format(
        LateReturnDTO rental_contract_dto)
    //... Other PlainTextFormatReports
class HTMLFormatReports
        ContractReportHTMLFormat create_rental_contract_report (
        RentalContractDTO rental_contract_dto)
    ReportHTMLFormat create_late_return_report_html_format(
        LateReturnDTO rental_contract_dto)
    //... Other HTMLFormat Reports
```

If we add a new type of report (e.g., XML), we have to redo all the report classes in Example 12-1. If we add a new report, we have to redo all the report type classes in Example 12-2. In our situation, it's easy to decide which organization to go with. We probably are going to add more individual reports than output types of reports. So the organization in Example 12-1 is the preferred option.

Oftentimes the tradeoff is subtler. If the creation of a report entails knowledge that is more specialized or is subject to frequent technology changes (e.g., from one version of HTML to another), the alternative organization (Example 12-2) might make more sense.

Change Happens

Sam dropped by. He began, "You know, one thing is bugging the staff and the customers a little bit."

"That's our job, to take out bugs," I replied. "What is it?"

"When the customer rents multiple CDDiscs, multiple rental contracts get printed. I'd like only one rental contract for all the discs rented at one shot," he said.

"Let's explore this more," I offered. "We separated out the printing of the contract from the rental itself. But now you want to change the concept of the rental contract. A rental contract, instead of being a printout of a single rental, is now a printout of multiple rentals. Is that right?"

"You've got it," Sam answered.

Sam and I developed an informal use case for this new procedure:

Rent_multiple_CDDiscs

    a. The user enters a `CustomerID` .

    b. The user enters one or more `PhysicalIDs`.

    c. The system prints a rental contract

I prepared a prototype for the new screens, as shown in Figure 12-1. Sam agreed that they captured his idea of how the new procedure would work.

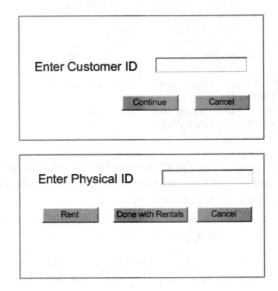

FIGURE 12-1. *Multiple-rental interface*

Now Tim and I are faced with reorganization. We have a new concept introduced into the requirements. If we were made aware of this in the beginning, we would have worked it into the design. The new concept is `RentalContract`. A `RentalContract` contains one or more Rentals:

```
class RentalContract
     Rentals [] the_rentals
```

This change provokes many questions. Should `RentalContract` contain `Customer` or should we just use the information in one `Rental`? We already have the `Rental` class working. Multiple `Rentals` in `RentalContract` have the same `Customer`. All the information is there, but it is duplicated.

Should `Rentals` be changed to refer to a `RentalContract`, rather than to a `Customer`? If we do that, what do we do about all the `Rentals` that we already recorded? What could the migration path be for those `Rentals`? Do we make up fake `RentalContracts` for them and point them to those fake `RentalContracts`?

We are unclear as to what is the true meaning of `RentalContract`. Is it a temporary item, just for the purposes of printout, or is it a persistent item? With all these questions, it's obvious we don't completely understand the problem. We check back with Sam.

"What's your definition of a rental contract?" we asked.

Sam replied, "A rental contract shows one or more rentals by a single customer at a single time."

"Is a contract just a piece of paper, or is it something we need to keep track of?" I asked. "Think carefully, because the answer will affect your pocketbook."

Sam pondered the question for a moment. "I'm not sure what you mean."

"About your pocketbook or the contract?" I asked.

"The contract," he stated.

"Once a rental has begun, does the system have to remember the contract on which it was printed?" I asked.

Sam replied, "I think I know what you are getting at. The contract is just a piece of paper. We file it away in date order, just in case a customer makes a stink. We probably look up a contract once a month. Since they're all filed by date and we can determine from the card when the customer rented a particular disc, it's pretty easy to find. So I don't want to spend a bundle, if that's what you're asking."

"Good," I replied. "I'd rather you save your money for more important things."

Our current concept of `Rental` remains the same. Now its creation appears in the context of `RentalContract`. However we already use the term, `RentalContract`, in the `RentalContractDTO` in Chapter 7. Should we alter `RentalContractDTO`'s details to apply it to a contract with multiple rentals, or should we create a new term? Once you have general agreement on the meaning of a term, altering its meaning can cause confusion.*

DON'T CHANGE WHAT IT IS

Create new terms rather than trying to apply new meanings to current terms.

A multiple rental contract has a different meaning than the current rental contract. So we create a new Data Transfer Object (DTO).

---

* An equivalent concept in methods is that is always easy to add new methods to a class, but it is difficult to alter the contracted behavior of existing methods. Other classes that depend on the current behavior will need to be altered.

```
class SingleRentalDTO
    Timestamp rental_start_time
    Timestamp rental_due_time
    CommonString cd_release_title
    PhysicalId cd_disc_physical_id
class MultipleRentalContractDTO
    SingleRentalDTO [] single_rentals
    Name customer_name;
    PhoneNumber customer_day_phone_number;
```

The new class that contains Rentals is MultipleRental. It has the responsibility of computing the total price for all Rentals, as well as creating the MultipleRentalDTO.

```
class MultipleRental
    private Rental []
    add_rental(Rental)
    Rental  get_rentals()
    Dollar compute_total_price()
    MultipleRentalDTO calculate_multiple_rental_contract()
```

We need to alter the user interface to appear as shown in Figure 12-1. The RentalOperation class needs operations involving multiple rentals. We also need to create and print the report using the MultipleRentalContractDTO.

```
RentalOperations
    MultipleRental start_new_multiple_rental(CustomerID customer_id)
    add_cd_disc_to_multiple_rental(MultipleRental multiple_rental,
        PhysicalID physical_id)
    MultipleRentalContractDTO end_multiple_rental(MultipleRental multiple_rental)
```

Exports

The Rentals in Sam's system are kept in RentalCollection. The information in Rental objects is used to produce the MultipleRentalDTO shown in the previous section, as well as the late return reports. If Sam wants to analyze the rentals for sales purposes, either analysis code has to be added to the system or the data has to be exported to an analysis program, such as SAS.

In keeping with the "Do a Little Job Well and You May Be Called Upon Often" guidelines, you should prepare systems to export data to and import data from other systems, such as analysis or accounting packages. Data can be exported periodically (snapshot) in standard formats for use in other systems. The export format can be XML, comma-delimited files, or some custom format. Data could also be made available in real time, as in an online ordering system that queries an inventory system for current availability of an item and notifies the inventory system when the order is placed.

We can use existing facilities of the underlying database to perform an export. Alternatively, we can create our own export methods. To demonstrate the alternative, for Sam's system we use export methods. There are two approaches to designing the export methods. We can use the existing methods in a class such as RentalCollection to retrieve a single

Rental or a group of Rentals. Then we can create an interface that exports these Rentals (see Example 12-3).

EXAMPLE 12-3. Export interface with groups of Rentals

```
interface RentalCollectionExport
    String export_rentals_as_comma_delimited_text (Rental [] rental_list)
    String export_rentals_as_xml(Rental [] rental_list)
```

With this interface, first the user calls a search method in RentalCollection and then passes the resulting group to the export method. Example 12-4 shows the RentalCollectionExport interface.

EXAMPLE 12-4. Using the RentalCollectionExport interface

```
Rental [] to_export =
    RentalCollection.retrieve_rentals_for_customer(a_customer);
String output = RentalCollectionExport.
    export_rentals_as_comma_delimited_text(to_export);
```

Alternatively, the export interface can implement methods that matched the retrieval methods in RentalCollection. This alternative interface appears in Example 12-5.

EXAMPLE 12-5. Export interface performing searches

```
interface RentalCollectionExport
    String export_rentals_for_customer_as_xml(a_customer)
    String export_rentals_for_customer_as_comma_delimited_text(
        a_customer)
```

These two alternatives represent a different form of the "Spreadsheet Conundrum." In Example 12-3, more ways to search Rentals can be added to RentalCollection without requiring any changes in RentalCollectionExport. In Example 12-5, existing mechanisms in the underlying database can be employed to export the data. If there were no database export mechanism, these methods would call the corresponding methods in RentalCollection. Adding new methods to search for Rentals to export would require additional methods to both classes.

In either case, the Rental data is made available to the other systems. These methods could be invoked by an ExportOperations interface, which in turn could be executed by an appropriately designed graphical user interface (GUI).

BE READY TO IMPORT AND EXPORT

Data should be available for use outside the system via a well-defined data interface.

CHAPTER THIRTEEN

Invoices, Credit Cards, and Discounts

SAM DECIDES IT IS TIME TO ADD THE ABILITY TO INVOICE CUSTOMERS and charge those invoices to credit cards. We explore interfaces to external credit card processors. We add computation of customer discounts in terms that Sam can understand. We also revisit security and privacy in the context of these changes.

The Next Step

"OK, what do you want next?" I asked Sam.

"A double cappuccino with latte," he replied eagerly.

"I meant for the system," I said.

"Oh, I'd like to get the charge system running, so I can bill customers monthly rather than for each rental. That will avoid leaving a lot of cash lying around the store. I also want to be able to offer discounts to frequent renters," Sam rambled on.

"OK," I said, "that sounds like two things. Which one do you want first?"

"Let's start with the charging part," he replied.

"We have at least two halves to that part: determining how much to bill the customer and then actually doing the billing. The determination part seems simpler: total up completed rentals and any late fees to compute a bill. The second part requires a bit more work. You need to sign up with an Internet-based credit card handler. That's another external interface, but a much more interesting one. You can't just test against that database willy-nilly. You don't want to charge customers for things they haven't bought," I stated.

"We need a new class. The one-line definition of this class is 'A charge to a customer for rentals during a period of time.' What do you want to call this class: Invoice or Bill?" I asked.

"I have a brother named Bill. So let's call it Invoice or else I'll get confused," he answered.

Here is the class that Sam and I created:

```
class Invoice
    Customer the_customer
    InvoiceDetail the_detail
    Dollar total
    submit_for_payment( )
    create_invoice_detail( )
```

InvoiceDetail represents the details of the charges on the invoice. I am not sure whether that will turn out to be a CommonString or a more structured class. So we denote it as a separate class ("When You're Abstract, Be Abstract All the Way").

The Customer class needs to know the customer's credit card number, so we add it to that class:

```
Customer
    Name name
    Address address
    CreditCard credit_card
    PhoneNumber home_phone_number
    Boolean on_charge_plan
```

On a monthly basis, Sam will create invoices for each customer and submit them for payment to the credit card company. Sam and I created a brief outline of the process for this activity:

Invoice_customers

   a. For each Customer on a charge plan in CustomerCollection, create an Invoice.

   b. Submit the Invoice to the credit card company.

   c. If the charge is approved, denote Invoice as paid.

Otherwise…

We stopped at the word *Otherwise*. Otherwise what? We need to handle this deviation. Does Sam keep charging unpaid invoices? Are they printed and sent to a collection agency? Sam can leave the decision up to a business rule. If we try to handle all the possibilities in this use case, it can get complicated. Sam and I fill in the ending:

Otherwise, denote it as an unpaid Invoice.

We deal with unpaid Invoices in another use case ("Separating Concerns Makes Smaller Concerns"). Sam is unsure what to do with them at this time, so we just note a simple process for this use case:

Handle_unpaid_invoices

    a. Produce list of unpaid Invoices.

Sam may later want to create an automated system to handle the unpaid invoices. At this point, we can use this list for testing purposes to ensure that the Invoice_customers use case works properly.

Dealing with Failure

Each invoice is submitted for payment to InvoiceProcessor. This interface represents the functionality for a credit card processor. The Invoice with the Customer and its CreditCard has all the information needed to make a credit card charge. The InvoiceProcessor interface looks like Example 13-1.

EXAMPLE 13-1. InvoiceProcessor

```
interface InvoiceProcessor
    process_for_payment(Invoice an_invoice)
```

If Sam requests the flexibility to use multiple vendors to process credit cards, we could separate out another interface ("Separate Concerns to Make Smaller Concerns "). The process_for_payment( ) method in InvoiceProcessor would use a CreditCardProcessor that represents the interface to a credit card processor. This interface could look like Example 13-2.

EXAMPLE 13-2. CreditCardProcessor

```
class CreditCardCharge
    CommonString first_name
    CommonString last_name
    Address billing_address
    PhoneNumber phone_number
    Dollar amount
    CommonString identifer
interface CreditCardProcessor
    submit_a_charge(CreditCardCharge a_charge)
```

The implementation of this interface needs to know Sam's merchant ID and other information specific to the vendor processing the charge.

We need to examine the possible situations that submit_a_charge( ) might encounter. These include the following.

`ChargeAccepted`
  The charge was processed successfully.

`UnableToContact`*
  There was a network or server failure.

`ChargeRejectedInsufficientFunds`
  This could be a temporary failure.

`ChargeRejectedAccountNotValid`
  This is a permanent failure.

We need to determine how to respond to these failure situations. In the event of `ChargeRejectedInsufficientFunds` or `ChargeRejectedAccountNotValid`, the `Invoice` is unpaid and is dealt with by the Handle_unpaid_invoices use case.

The `UnableToContact` event poses an interesting question. Is this failure a deviation, a non-fatal error, or a fatal error (see Chapter 3)? Since the service involves a connection to an outside server over a public network, failure can be expected to occur. Although a failure is expected, it should not occur during normal processing. If no backup network or backup server were available, the event certainly is a fatal error. Further processing is futile. The user should be informed of the situation. He might be able to do something to correct the situation (e.g., check the Internet connection).

CONSIDER FAILURE AN EXPECTATION, NOT AN EXCEPTION

Plan how operations should respond to failures.

Planning Tests

Tim and I know that the `CreditCardProcessor` implementation has to be tested carefully. `ZIPCodeLookupInterface` was relatively easy to test. We submitted a variety of addresses and compared the results to a definitive source of Zip Codes. Processing a credit card is a little more difficult. We need to test the implementation of `CreditCardProcessor` to ensure that it works according to the vendor-supplied protocol. Vendors have test servers to check that charges are submitted in properly formatted requests.

We need to check whether `CreditCardCharges` are being created accurately. We create our own test version of the `CreditCardProcessor` interface in Example 12-2. ("Build Flexibility for Testing"). Instead of submitting the charge to the vendor, the test version just creates a

---

* There is one other possibility: the charge was sent, but a reply was not received. This is a partial transaction. The charge needs to be resubmitted and the result returned. This can still be handled as an `UnableToContact` failure.

list of the charges. If the vendor's test system cannot simulate all the failure situations, this test version can be programmed to do so.

The vendor's test server and the production server provide the same interface to the real implementation of CreditCardProcessor. The only difference is that a charge submitted to the production server produces a real charge to a real credit card. CreditCardProcessor should work the same, regardless of the actual server. We need to have a way to check that this is the case. We will submit a set of small charges (e.g., $.01) to both servers. We check that the real server produces the correct results by examining the statement Sam receives from the vendor.

The Language of the Client

Sam came by to discuss the discount mechanism that he was thinking about. He started talking. I was listening with a pen in hand. He said something like this:

"I want to give a 5% discount if a customer rented more than six CDDiscs in the past month and another 5% if he averaged more than five rentals in the last six months," he said, without pausing for a breath.

"Say again," I asked.

He replied at the same speed, as though he thought that if he did not get it out fast enough, he would forget it.

I took out a clean sheet of paper and copied down what I was pretty sure I heard:

Start with discount_percentage = 0.0.

Compute number_of_rentals_in_last_month:

   If (number_of_rentals_in_last_month > 6) discount_percentage = 5.0

Compute average_number_of_rentals_during_last_six_months:

   If (average_number_of_rentals_during_last_six_months > 5) discount_percentage = discount_percentage + 5.0

I asked him if this was what he meant. He looked at it and asked what the > symbol meant.

I told him that it meant, "is greater than."

He said, "Great, that's exactly what I want."

"Is this what you'll want forever?" I asked.

"Well, probably not," he replied.

"I'll tell you what; I'm going to let you maintain this code," I said. "If those numbers change, you just change the numbers and I'll add it to the program."

"So I'm a programmer now?" Sam asked.

"Of course. We're part of a team," I replied.

Suppose Sam were fairly sure that the algorithm was not going to change, but the numbers were going to change. Then a configuration file would be appropriate. The values could be set in a dialog box and then written to that file. The algorithm would look like this:

Start with discount_percentage = 0.0.

Compute number_of_rentals_in_last_month:

> if (number_of_rentals_in_last_month > NUMBER_LAST_MONTH_RENTALS_FOR_
> DISCOUNT) discount_percentage = DISCOUNT_FOR_EXCEEDING_LAST_MONTH_
> RENTAL_LEVEL

Compute average_number_of_rentals_during_last_six_months:

> if (average_number_of_rentals_during_last_six_months > NUMBER_SIX_MONTH_
> RENTALS_FOR_DISCOUNT) discount_percentage = discount_percentage +
> DISCOUNT_FOR_EXCEEDING_SIX_MONTH_RENTAL_LEVEL:

Every variable in capital letters would have a corresponding entry in a configuration file. The configuration file in XML might look like this:

```
<number_last_month_rentals_for_discount>6
</number_last_month_rentals_for_discount>
```

If the algorithm were subject to additional changes, it is often easier to let the client be responsible for those changes. The developer's job is to provide the methods needed to perform the data gathering and computations needed by the client. For example, Tim and I might create more-general data-gathering methods, such as the following:

```
compute_average_number_of_rentals_during_previous_months(int number_of_months)
compute_total_number_of_rentals_during_previous_months(int number_of_months)
```

Sam could alter the number of months without contacting us. If Sam or his staff is maintaining the code and the indirection of using named constants was confusing, actual values might appear in the code. The code that he maintains might look like this:

```
Dollar compute_discount( )
    {
    Dollar discount_percentage = 0.0;
    number_of_rentals_in_last_month =
        compute_total_number_of_rentals_during_previous_months (1);
    if (number_of_rentals_in_last_month > 5)
        discount_percentage = 5.0;
    average_number_of_rentals_during_previous_months =
        compute_average_number_of_rentals_during_previous_months (6)
    if (average_number_of_rentals_during_previous_months > 5)
        discount_percentage = discount_percentage + 5.0;
    return discount_percentage;
    }
```

To the average programmer, this code seems a bit wordy. To Sam, it is understandable. These methods become a domain language for computing the customer discount. Even if Sam does not maintain the code himself, the code expresses his desires in his terms. He can look at the code to see whether it accurately reflects his business policies.

USE THE CLIENT'S LANGUAGE

Use the client's language in your code to make it easier to compare the logic in the code to the logic of the client. *

TYPE OR PRESS

Many years ago, I had a client who could never make up his mind whether a prompt should read, "Type any key to continue" or "Press any key to continue." For every release, he would switch his decision. Finally, I sent him a file that contained one of the phrases. I told him, "If you want to make a change, just enter it in that file, and send it back to me." The program incorporated that file as one of the source files for the executable. For further flexibility, the program could have read a file at star-tup time for the desired phrase. However, the client wanted to distribute only a single file.

The client was happy. He could make his own changes. So I was happy.

Business rules, such as for the customer discount, are rules created by businesspeople: those in finance, marketing, and other areas. Business rules can involve the price you charge for a product, the discount you give to customers, the action to take when an invoice is overdue, and so forth. The details of business rules can change frequently. Whether to create a separate class for business rules is another example of the "The Spreadsheet Conundrum". The compute_discount( ) method can go into the Customer class, since it relates to that class. However, the method could be put into a BusinessRules class to gather methods that a client is particularly interested in and that might change frequently.

If the business rules are complex, you can use a business rules language such as ILOG JRules, the open source Mandarax, or the Business Rules Markup Language (BRML).†

---

* A reviewer suggested that this is a concept in domain-driven programming. See *Domain-Driven Design: Tackling Complexity in the Heart of Software* by Eric Evans (Addison-Wesley Professional, 2003).

† Scott Ambler explains how business rules are another model at *http://www.agilemodeling.com/ principles.htm*.

Security and Privacy

Security and privacy are complicated issues. You need to deal with both administrative and development facets to make a secure system. Before implementing invoices and discounts, Tim and I consider the security and privacy issues.

Security

With the addition of CreditCard to Customer, CustomerCollection contains some sensitive data. We need to protect that data from prying eyes ("If You Forget Security, You're Not Secure"). Since we used CustomerCollection as the interface to the data, we can assign responsibility for protection of that data to that class and to classes with which it collaborates. We could apply a number of techniques to provide this protection. For example, we could encrypt all information in the collection in whatever persistence mechanism was used to store the collection. That way, the data would be relatively safe even if the file were copied. Only when a Customer is retrieved would the data be decrypted.

Security is not just a matter of encryption, but includes examination of all interfaces into a system. For example, CustomerCollection has a mechanism to search for customers by name. Sam needs to decide where to draw the line between ease of use and security. If the search allows the matching string to be a single character long, an errant user can find all names of customers with only 26 or fewer searches. If the search allows the empty string as a match criterion, a single search could produce a list of all Customers.

Privacy

Sam called me up. "A few customers have called me with concerns. They know about the federal law that doesn't allow rental stores to keep track of what videos a customer has rented. They want to know whether we keep track of the CDs they have rented."

"Sounds like a legitimate concern to me. Both Invoices and Rentals are related to Customers. We were thinking of tying Invoices back to Rentals. To alleviate that concern, we'll put the rental detail in InvoiceDetail and eliminate any other association between Invoices and Rentals. We will be sure to eliminate any paid Invoices. We'll keep unpaid ones, so we have all the information necessary to present to a collection agency, if it comes to that," I stated. "So we only have to worry about the Rentals. We can delete a Rental once it has been invoiced, but then we wouldn't have a record of the rentals for a particular CDDisc. Let's alter the Rental to relate to an anonymous Customer, once it's been invoiced."

"That sounds good to me," Sam replied hesitatingly.

I recognized I might have gone into too much detail. "In short, we'll be sure that any record of a customer renting a CDDisc is destroyed, once the rental is paid for," I explained.

"That's what I like to hear," Sam responded quickly.

Security and privacy concerns influence system design. For Sam's system, adding privacy is relatively simple. For larger systems, if security and privacy concerns are not addressed in the beginning, they can create a larger disruption when they finally must be addressed.

CONSIDER PRIVACY

Systems need to be designed with privacy in mind.

CHAPTER FOURTEEN

Sam Is Expanding

SAM IS EXPANDING HIS OPERATIONS. He is opening more stores, both locally and globally. His store is being featured on the Web. He returns to us for more development. We use many of the previously presented guidelines to develop our approach to this expansion.

The Second Store

Sam comes in and tells me he is opening his second store in the near future and he wants the system to be ready when that occurs.

I ask the leading question, "Are these two stores, or one store in two places?"

Sam stares at me with "the look."

He is already familiar with the reasons behind my strange questions. "What's the difference?" he asks.

"In the case of two stores, the system is almost ready to go now," I replied.

"And in the other case?" he queried.

"Then I've got some questions for you to answer."

"It sounds like the first case will cost less," he noted. "But go ahead with your questions."

"I wrote down the assumptions I made in the first system and the design decisions that were relevant to those assumptions. The assumptions are hard to decipher from the code itself, so I kept them as a separate document."

I continued, "A CDDisc was either in the store or not in the store. If it was not in the store and not part of a Rental, it was assumed lost. There was nowhere else for the Rental to go, except to be lost and never returned (like Charlie on the MTA). If CDDiscs were rented in only one store and were returned to that store, we could stop here."

"I like stopping; it is definitely cheaper. But what happens if I let them return a CDDisc to another store?" asked Sam.

"It makes things a little harder," I said. "Currently, when a customer returns a CDDisc to the store and the PhysicalID is entered into the system, the system might respond that the PhysicalID was not found. If that is the case, the staff has been instructed to enter the number manually. The assumption is that the scanner cannot read the bar code. If there is still no match, the CDDisc is set aside. At that point, the assumption is that the label is completely mucked up.

"With a set of stores, if there is no match, the system must determine to which other store the CDDisc belongs," I continued. "With only two stores, the staff can assume that an unmatched CDDisc belongs to the other store. With three stores we can determine which store by the easy way or the less easy way."

"The easy always costs less, right?" Sam asked.

"Yes, but it doesn't always give you flexibility for the future," I replied. "With multiple stores, there are two alternatives to how to store the data. One alternative is that the CDDiscCollection contains the CDDiscs in all stores and the RentalCollection contains the Rentals for all stores. The other is that there are separate CDDiscCollections and Rental-Collections for each store. With the former, we're dealing with a central server and networks. With the latter, we just need to add an interface that allows us to query another store to see if a PhysicalID is part of their CDDiscCollection. This is the easy way."

"Let's go with the latter," Sam stated emphatically.

"What about availability? Do you want the catalog search to show availability of a CDDisc in another store?" I asked.

"That sounds good to me," he replied.

"Think About the Big Picture" is an appropriate guideline to use when deciding how to proceed. Adding a central server provides a good deal of future expansion possibilities. For example, Sam could easily add all-store reports, instead of having each store prepare its own. If Sam's plans involved more features that suggested a central database solution, now would be a good time to implement the capability. A central server does have the disadvantage that a store with network difficulties cannot process rentals.

Sam has not indicated other needs that might favor a central solution. So Tim and I decide to create a peer-to-peer solution. Each store will query the other stores for information. The interface that each store's system provides to the other stores looks like this:

```
interface StoreServiceProvider
    Boolean is_physical_id_in_cddisc_collection(PhysicalID physical_id)
    Boolean show_availability_of_CD_release(UPCCode upc_code)
```

is_physical_id_in_cddisc_collection( ) is a wordy name for a method. It is almost as long as the logic in the method. It just calls the find_by_physical_id( ) method in CDDiscCollection and returns true or false. The show_availability_of_CD_release( ) method returns true if a CDDisc is available for the CDRelease.

When Tim and I sit down to discuss multiple stores, we realize we missed an abstraction in the first release: the Store. This abstraction contains the data relative to a location ("Clump Data So That There Is Less to Think About "):

```
class Store
    CommonString name
    Address address
    PhoneNumber phone_number
```

Since we have multiple stores, we have a StoreCollection that contains all the Stores:

```
class StoreCollection
    Store where_is_physical_id_in_cddisc_collection(PhysicalID physical_id)
    Store[] show_availability_of_CD_release(UPCCode upc_code)
    Store[] find_all_stores( )
```

StoreCollection knows how many Stores there are. The method show_availability_of_CD_release( ) queries each Store to find where a CDDisc belongs, by calling the is_physical_id_in_cddisc_collection( ) method in the StoreServiceProvider for each Store. Likewise, the show_availability_of_CD_release( ) method calls show_availability_of_CD_release( ) in the StoreServiceProvider for each Store.

A New Development

Sam called me up in an excited voice. "I've got great news."

"What? The coffee shop is having a special on double lattes?" I asked.

"Are they? I'll have to head down there," he replied. "My news is that I've hooked up with some web sites that catalog CDs. When someone gets to a CD that I have in stock, the web site posts a message telling the user that they can rent the CD at my store. I give them a cut of the rental in return."

"That sounds interesting. Are you going into the mail order rental business?" I asked.

"Not yet. But I'm getting ready," he answered. "I need you to work out the details with the web guys."

The Interface Contract

I called up the maintainers for one of the CD catalog sites. We discussed the interface operation and how we were going to communicate with each other. We created an interface with a single method: show_availability_of_CD_release(UPCCode upc_code). We also agreed on using Web Services as the communication protocol.

The show_availability_of_CD_release( ) method in StoreCollection is going to be exposed to the outside world. That calls for another interface, ExternalServiceProvider, to keep external services separate from internal services. The module in Sam's system that receives the request is:

```
interface ExternalServicesProvider
    StoreExternalDTO[] show_availability_of_CD_release(UPCCode upc_code)
```

StoreExternalDTO parallels the Store class. We make up a separate class so that we are free to alter the internal class, if necessary:

```
class StoreExternalDTO
    CommonString name
    Address address
    PhoneNumber phone_number
```

When the web service is invoked on Sam's system, the service calls the method in this interface to obtain the result to return to the other site.

Keep the Cold Air Out

Any interface that permits access by system outsiders needs to be designed carefully. All input should be validated and logged. Even if there is no value-level validation, such as a low and high range, almost any data should be subject to some form of checking.

For example, if the data is coming from a web page, or is on a web service request, the input should be converted to SymbolFreeStrings. The conversion would eliminate extraneous characters, such as ; and ?. Hackers commonly break into web sites by entering strings into form fields that contain characters that handling programs on the server might interpret as commands.*

Logging access from outsiders can help pinpoint problems that they are having in communicating with your system. Logs can also help determine what methods hackers might be using to attack your system. For example, the ExternalServicesProvider implementation will be monitored similar to the log of Zip Code lookups in Chapter 11 to ensure that it is accessed correctly by only authorized users ("If You Forget Security, You're Not Secure").

---

* Languages such as Ruby and PERL have the concept of "tainted" variables. Variables that are tainted have not yet been checked for validity. Once they have, they can be "untainted."

DON'T LET THE COLD AIR IN

**With interfaces exposed to the outside world, ensure
that input validation and logging occurs.**

Outside interfaces are particularly more vulnerable than internal interfaces. So this guideline emphasizes and extends the "Validate, Validate, Validate" guideline.

The Third Store

After Tim and I delivered to Sam the release containing the changes accommodating a second store, he gave me a call. "Well, I've got even better news," he said.

"The second store has been successful, so I'm thinking about expanding into either Canada or Mexico. How much of an effort will be required to make that change?"

"Are you talking Cozumel?" I asked.

"Well, I was thinking about that or Whistler. It'd be tough to have to go on a business trip to check out how the stores were doing," he replied.

"I think these systems will need a developer to install them," I stated.

"Only if it comes out of your pocketbook," he answered.

Currency Flexibility

If Sam picks Whistler (in British Columbia), Tim and I will not have to worry about translating the program into another language. We might even get away without any changes, since Canadians use dollars, albeit different ones from the U.S.

For an initial examination, we looked at all the places where the Dollar class is used. Since we have the separate class (and have not defined it as a double), it is easy to determine which attributes or variables represent dollars. We could add a couple of classes such as CandianDollar and MexicanPeso. However, that does not feel right. This sounds like a place to start adding some flexibility ("More Is Sometimes Less"). As long as we are going to add two variations, we might as well be prepared for more.

Tim and I change the Dollar class into a Money class. That adjustment should provide the limberness to adapt to either of the proposed expansion locations. We start by creating a single class that parallels the Dollar class:

```
enumeration CurrencyID
    {US_DOLLARS, CANADIAN_DOLLARS, MEXICAN_PESO}
class Money
    CurrencyID id
    Money(CurrencyID id)
    // Same operations and attributes as for Dollar.
```

Currencies differ only by data, not by behavior. So creating a single class makes sense ("Don't Overclassify"). The data differences include the symbol used for display, the side (left or right) on which the symbol is placed, and the format of the number itself (decimal point and thousands separator).

Sam's systems operate independently, so each system need only deal with the local currency. The actual currency can be read in from a configuration file, or we might obtain it from the locale. If we have to worry about exchanging currencies, we can create a CurrencyExchange class that transforms a Money amount in one currency to a Money amount in another currency.

Tim and I started by making up identifiers for the individual currencies. Since currencies are universal, we did a quick search on Google™ to see if a standard set of identifiers exists. We found the ISO 4217 set of currency identifiers. So the enumeration changes to this:

```
enumeration CurrencyID {USD, CAD ,MXN}
```

At the same time, we found a Currency class for Java. Since we began the implementation in Java, we will use that class ("Don't Reinvent the Wheel") to designate the currency in the Money class. We also found a Java CurrencyFormat class to which we can delegate the job of properly formatting Money. If we were coding in another language, we might still use those class interfaces and create an implementation for them in that language.

Now all we need to do is to substitute Money for Dollar everywhere we find Dollar in the current system. Then we try the system using tests for Money that parallel the Dollar tests.

If we had started our design by dealing with Money in the beginning, we might have been bogged down in the details of exchange rates and so forth. Since Sam's systems were being used in only one country, we coded for that currency only. Creating a more generalized monetary package would have been premature. Using the experience gained in developing the specific Dollar class helps us to design the Money class.

AVOID PREMATURE GENERALIZATION

Solve the specific problem before making the solution general.

You might find generalizations you want to develop before you need them. Write down your thoughts on the generalization in your design journal. You might heed Brad Appleton's suggestion (*http://c2.com/cgi/wiki?PrematureGeneralization*):

> Whenever I get such ideas to generalize this way, I don't necessarily do it. What I do is try to make sure I don't make any other design decisions which would preclude me from adding it later on. If I can't do that, then I at least try to do it in a way that doesn't require a *complete* overhaul if I need to go back and change it.

Language Flexibility

With multiple countries, we have to deal with more than just currency differences. Either Sam has to hire people who can read English, or the system has to present its displays and reports in the user's choice of French, English, or Spanish. When we coded our classes, we used the "Never Write a Constant in Code" guideline. We separated the contents of what was displayed from the reason for displaying it. For example:

```
String ERROR_CD_DISC_NOT_IN_COLLECTION =
    "CDDisc PhysicalID not in collection";.
```

There are at least two approaches to coding additional languages. This is another example of "The Spreadsheet Conundrum." We could provide translations of the strings in each class. A call to a configuration parameter could tell which strings to display. The pseudocode for retrieving strings would look like this:

```
CommonString error_string = get_string(CD_DISC_NOT_IN_COLLECTION);
```

The method would look like this:

```
enumeration StringID {
    CD_DISC_NOT_IN_COLLECTION,
    CUSTOMER_NOT_IN_COLLECTION};
CommonString get_error_string (StringID which_string)
    {
    static CommonStrings strings [][NUMBER_LANGUAGES] =
        {"English CD Not..", "French CD Not..", "Spanish CD Not..."},
        {"English Customer Not...", "French Customer Not ..",
            "Spanish Customer Not..."};
    index  = Configuration.get_index_for_current_language( );
    return strings[which_string][index]
    }
```

Another way to handle multiple languages is to create resource files. Each resource file contains all the strings for the entire program for one language. When the program is loaded, the resource file specified by the configuration is also loaded.

Most systems are developed using the resource file approach. From a translation standpoint, having a single file containing the content to be translated is much easier than having multiple files. However, every resource file will need to be altered every time a string is added or changed in a class. If the number of languages does not change, but the number of classes with strings changes frequently, keeping strings in the individual classes will localize the alterations required.

Unfortunately, many integrated development environments (IDEs) do not support multiple languages directly. In the Java implementation in Chapter 8, the IDE places strings directly into the code. To support multiple languages, we can alter the IDE-generated code to refer to a variable that represents the string.

Language is not the only thing that changes between countries. For example, the date format changes. With a single change in a configuration file, we would like to have everything change for us. The manner in which information is displayed is separate from the decision of what to display ("Separate Concerns to Make Smaller Concerns "). Many languages and operating systems support the concept of locale, so we incorporate that into our configuration mechanism, instead of creating a custom one.

Goodbye Sam

Sam and I met at the coffee shop.

Sam started, "I'll tell you what. Let me get you a fancy cup of coffee instead of the plain stuff you always gulp."

"OK," I answered.

"Make it a grande double breve sugar-free caramel mocha wet extra hot, please," Sam told the counter person.

I took a sip. "Not bad," I stated. "But at the rate I drink coffee, I'd be in the poorhouse if I took a fancy to this, especially since it appears we're done developing your system for a while."

"That's true. All the use cases we talked about in the beginning are complete, as well as the ones I came up with along the way," he said.

"I appreciate the opportunity you gave me to use your system to illustrate the guidelines in my book," I said. "However, some readers asked for examples using real-life systems. So it's time to say goodbye to you so that I can present a couple of other examples."

"Goodbye, and thank you for a great system," Sam replied.

Generality

Sam's system was created specifically for CDDiscs. You can use the underlying design for any system that needs to keep track of rentals of identifiable items. CDDisc can be generalized to RentableItem, which represents any rentable item that has a unique identity. CDRelease can be changed to CatalogItem, which represents a type of item identified by a UPC code. RentableItems are physical copies of CatalogItems. The RentalOperations interface, with RentableItems substituted for CDDiscs, provides the necessary operations. The specific methods in the CatalogOperations, just as searching by the recording artist, are not applicable to RentableItems. However, the separation of RentalOperations from CatalogOperations is generally applicable.

If we had tried in the beginning to make Sam's system general, we could have been bogged down in endless details. For example, the pricing mechanism for Sam's system was simple: three prices for three different categories of CDReleases and fixed rental periods. For a general system, the pricing would probably vary based on the rental period.

With Sam's system, we gained an understanding of the issues involved in rentals. Armed with the experience gained in developing that system, we could now tackle a more general problem such as a universal rental system or another industry-specific rental system.

CHAPTER FIFTEEN

A Printserver Example

THIS CHAPTER PRESENTS A CASE STUDY INVOLVING A REAL-WORLD SYSTEM that libraries use to charge for printouts of documents from personal computers. This chapter delineates where guidelines were employed in the design.

Introduction

EnvisionWare makes a print management system for libraries. The system enables patrons to pay to print documents in a variety of ways: prepaid, credit card, and so forth.

The current system is several years old and is being rewritten from scratch to allow for more flexibility and growth. I was called in as a consultant to help explore EnvisionWare's proposed object design, as a demonstrable system had to be created in less than 10 weeks for a trade show.

Rob Walsh, the cofounder of EnvisionWare, and I together examined the proposed design. We came up with a number of ways to increase the separation of concerns between portions of the system and to assign clear responsibility to each class involved. We did not incorporate every aspect of Extreme Abstraction and Extreme Separation to limit the number of changes that his programmers were experiencing at the time. Only the server side of the system was being recoded at that point. Re-creating the client side will occur down the road.

The System

In the EnvisionWare system, a library patron—say, Sandra—creates a document on a library's personal computer. She uses the Print command to submit the document for printing and then walks over to a release station to release the print job to the printer.

A printing client on the personal computer and a release station client both communicate with a central server. The central server uses a database to store user and print job information.

From Sandra's viewpoint, the system works as outlined in the following procedure. Incorporated into this activity flow are the message interactions that occur at designated points. The client sends the named message to the server and the server responds with the given message.

1. Sandra decides to print from the application she is running. Using the application's print functions and dialog, Sandra selects a printer and indicates her desire to print the document.

2. The system validates Sandra.

   a. The print client asks Sandra for her UserID.

   b. The print client sends the UserID to the central server to validate the user and to obtain the charging rate for the user:

      `AuthenticateUserRequestMessage` sent; `AuthenticateUserReplyMessage` returned.

3. The print client calculates the price from the page count for the print job and the user's charging rate. It displays this information to Sandra.

4a. Sandra can choose to accept the charges and print:

   a. The print client submits the print job to the central server. The central server notifies the print client at which release station the job will be printed:

      `NewJobMessage` sent; `ConfirmJobMessage` returned.

   b. The print client displays the Job Confirmation dialog and tells the user how to collect the job at the release station.

   c. Sandra goes to the release station and enters her UserID.

   d. The release station requests the jobs for that user from the central server. The central server responds with a list of print jobs:

      `GetJobsMessage` sent; Series of `PrintJobMessages` returned.

   e. The release station displays the available jobs in a dialog box.

   f. Sandra selects the jobs she wants to release.

   g. The release station requests the central server to release the jobs. The central server submits each released print job to the printer. For each job:

      `ReleaseJobMessage` sent; `JobPickUpMessage` returned.

4b. If Sandra chooses to cancel the print job without submitting it:

    a. The print client tells the central server to cancel the print job. The central server cancels the job:

        `CancelJobMessage` sent; `SuccessMessage` returned.

    b. The print client displays a dialog confirming that the job was cancelled.

If an operation fails, `FailMessage` is returned as the response. The client can retry the operation or inform the user of the failure.

Both the printing computer and the release station have a graphical user interface (GUI) associated with them. The GUI is a thin layer on top of the messaging system.

The Message

In this library system, the underlying mechanism for communication is the `Message`. A `Message` contains a header with a message identifier, and parameter values or response values corresponding to the message type. Each operation performed by a print client or a release station client is transformed into one or more `Message`s that are sent to the central server. The server responds to each `Message` with a `Message` back to the client. The client takes action appropriate to the operation and the response. It might display information on the GUI, report an error, or continue to send other `Message`s. `Message`s are transmitted between the two systems in text ("To Text or Not to Text"). The `Message` class has a well defined interface ("Create Interface Contracts") and looks like this:

```
class Message
    ComputerID computer_id
    UserID user_id
    Timestamp timestamp
    abstract Integer get_message_type_id( )
    abstract convert_from_text(String text)
    abstract String convert_to_text( )
    abstract Message handle( )
```

`computer_id` identifies the source of the message. `user_id` identifies the user at the client. `timestamp` is used for logging and tracking purposes. The `convert_from_text( )` and `convert_to_text( )` methods convert the attributes in derived `Message`s to and from text. The `handle( )` method processes the message. `get_message_type_id( )` returns the type identifier assigned to each message type.

Particular Messages

Every message is derived from `Message` and includes the attributes for a particular type of message. Each derived `Message` overrides the four methods in the base class. The organization of each message looks like *ParticularMessage*:

```
class ParticularMessage extends Message
    // Attributes for the message
    // Overrides of abstract methods
```

MessageEncoderDecoder converts the entire Message from and to text:

```
class MessageEncoderDecoder
    Message decode_from_text(String text)
    String encode_to_text(Message a_message)
```

The decode_from_text( ) method decodes the header text, determines the message type, and creates the corresponding message. Then it calls convert_from_text( ) to convert the remainder of the text to attribute values for a *ParticularMessage*. encode_to_text ( ) works in reverse to create the header text and calls convert_to_text( ) for the corresponding message.

The actual format of the textual representation is hidden behind this interface. It could be in comma-delimited form, XML or a custom format The text is used just to communicate between the systems. The only consideration in the underlying textual representation is that all clients and servers need to agree on it. It is possible for a server to understand two different formats of messages. It just results in a little more code on the interpretation side. Since the clients were not being rewritten, we used the format that was on the current system. Vertical bars separate the text representing each attribute.

We could convert the messages to and from text using a common method that takes a table instead of creating executable code in each convert_to_text( ) and convert_from_text( ) method ("Declaration over Execution"). The implementation of the table is language dependent. However, if all message attributes were declared as an abstract data type (with corresponding to_string( ) and from_string( ) methods), the implementation could be relatively simple.

Handling a Message

The handle( ) method for a *ParticularMessage* does all the work using the attributes of the *ParticularMessage*. The method is invoked by a series of communications from the GUI through the network and to the server, as shown in Figure 15-1 ("Separating Concerns Makes Smaller Concerns"). Here are the interfaces and classes that work together to perform an operation requested by the client and return a response:

```
interface MessageReceiver
    Message process_message(Message message_to_process)
interface TextSender
    String send_text(String text_to_send)
interface TextReceiver
    String receive_text(String text_to_receive)
interface Operation
    Message do_particular_operation( )
class ClientMessageDispatcher implements MessageReceiver
    Message process_message(Message message_to_process)
classClientSocket implements TextSender
    String send_text(String text_to_send)
class ServerSocket
    Implements a receiving socket
class ServerMessageReceiver implements TextReceiver
    String receive_text(String text_to_receive)
class ServerMessageDispatcher implements MessageReceiver
    Message process_message(message_to_process)
```

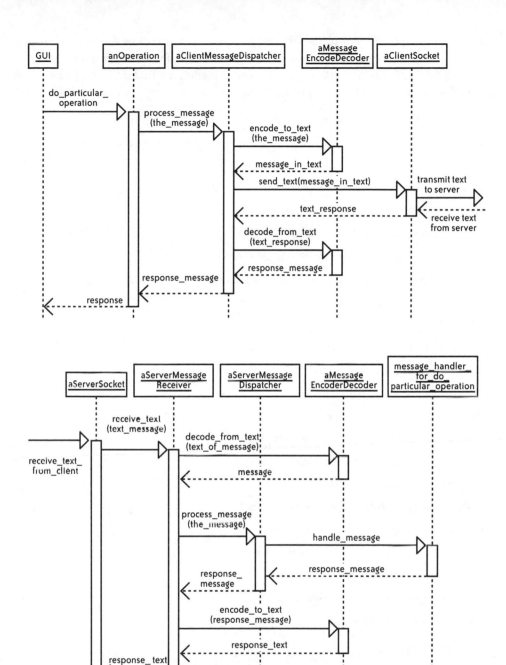

FIGURE 15-1. Sequence diagram for handling a message

The sequence diagram in Figure 15-1 shows the overall flow. The flow details are shown in the following list. When the user commands the GUI to perform a particular operation, the flow is initiated. The GUI calls the appropriate operation method in the Operations interface, shown as *do_particular_operation( )* in the example.

- Operations *do_particular*_operation( )

  Creates a Message of the appropriate type with the appropriate values

  Calls ClientMessageDispatcher.process_message( )

  Returns values in response Message back to the caller

- ClientMessageDispatcher.process_message( )

  Calls MessageEncoderDecoder.encode_to_text( )

  Calls ClientSocket.send_text( ) with encoded text

  Converts received text to Message using MessageEncoderDecoder.decode_from_text( )

  Returns Message

- ClientSocket.send_text( )

  Sends the text over the network to the server

  Returns received text

- ServerSocket

  Receives text over the network

  Calls ServerMessageReceiver.receive_text( )

  Sends returned text back over the network to the client

- ServerMessageReceiver.receive_text( )

  Calls MessageEncoderDecoder.decode_from_text( )

  Calls ServerMessageDispatcher.process_message( )

  Calls encode_to_text( ) for the returned Message

  Returns the text

- ServerMessageDispatcher.process_message( )

  Calls handle( ) for the Message

  Returns Message

Each class has one simple job to perform. The only classes that need to be aware of particular messages are the methods in the Operation interface and the handle( ) method for each particular message.

Environment

To use this message system on a particular computer, the client and I set up two environment classes: ClientEnvironment and ServerEnvironment. The details in these two classes can be summarized as follows:

```
class ClientEnvironment
    ComputerInformation (computer name, server IP address)
    UserInformation (logged on user id)
class ServerEnvironment
    ComputerInformation (computer name)
    Database (test or production)
```

The client-side classes have a reference to ClientEnvironment and the server-side classes have a reference to ServerEnvironment. By changing the member references in each environment, we have a flexible testing situation ("Build Flexibility for Testing").

Example Messages

Here is a concrete example to help understand the overall flow. When Sandra prints a document on her personal computer, a PrintJob is created and sent to the central server. Sandra then goes to a release station. She enters her UserID. The release station displays her PrintJobs in a dialog box. She selects a job to print. The release station submits a ReleaseJobMessage to request the job to be released. The central server releases the job to the printer and returns a JobPickupMessage that indicates where the printer is located. The messages are as follows:

```
class ReleaseJobMessage
    Integer jobNumber  // job to release
class JobPickupMessage
    String printer_location
class FailMessage
    String explanation
```

On the release station, the method that sends the ReleaseJobMessage to the server looks like this:

```
String release_job_operation(Integer jobNumber)
    {
    ReleaseJobMessage releaseJobMessage(jobNumber);
    MessageReceiver messageReceiver =
        ClientEnvironment.getMessageReceiver();
    Message returnMessage =
        messageReceiver.process_message(releaseJobMessage);
    if (returnMessage is_type_of JobPickupMessage)
        return (JobPickupMessage) Message.printer_location;
    else if (returnMessage is_type_of FailMessage)
        return (FailMessage) Message.explanation;
    else
        return ERROR_SERVER_COMMUNICATION;
    }
```

On the server side, you find the following code, which I've simplified a bit, to handle the ReleaseJobMessage message.

```
class ReleaseJobMessage
    {
    Message handle( )
        {
        PrintJob printJob=
            ServerEnvironment.getJobDB( )->getJobByNumber(jobNumber);
        if (printJob == NULL)
            return FailMessage("Print Job Not Found");
        else
            {
            printJob.releaseToPrinter( );
            Printer printer = printJob.printer;
            return JobPickUpMsg(printer.location);
            }
        }
    }
```

Testing

The entire testing procedure is beyond the scope of this book. Following is a short summary of how the tests proceed. The client and I developed our testing strategy as the design was being developed ("Plan for Testing"). Because we applied the guidelines of Extreme Separation, there are only a few methods to test in each class.

1. For each *ParticularMessage*:

   a. Ensure that convert_to_text( ) and convert_from_text( ) both work.

   b. Create a message with test values, call handle( ), and check that the returned Message is of the correct type and has the appropriate values.

2. For each set of Messages involved in an operation method, such as *do_particular_ operation( )*:

   a. Call *do_particular_operation( )*.

   b. Check the return values from *do_particular_operation( )* to see if they match the testing oracle (the definitive source of what should be the results of a test).

3. For a sequence of operation methods:

   a. Call the set of methods.

   b. Check the values along the way to see if they match the testing oracle.

You can run the second and third tests in a variety of environments by varying the implementations of TextMessageDispatcher, ClientEnvironment, and ServerEnvironment.

The classes that implement interfaces allow for mixing and matching of implementations during testing ("Build Flexibility for Testing"). Both ClientMessageDispatcher and ServerMessageDispatcher implement the MessageReceiver. To test that the handle( ) method for each Message works correctly, *do_particular_operation( )* can call the implementation provided by ServerMessageDispatcher directly. Testing can proceed without involving the network or decoding/encoding text.

Both ClientSocket and ServerMessageReceiver implement TextReceiver. ClientMessageDispatcher can talk directly to the ServerMessageReceiver implementation. Now the flow can be tested with the addition of conversion to and from text.

Test versions of TextSender and MessageReceiver can be created that return failures to see if *do_particular_operation( )* responds correctly.

Testing is about being able to alter one little thing and see the differences in the results. Regardless of how things are hooked up (in any one of three ways), the results should be the same, if there is no network failure.

With the flexibility in the design, you can test *do_particular_operation ( )* multiple ways:

- It can be on the same machine as the server and connect via the localhost socket (127.0.0.1).
- The client *do_particular_operation( )* method can run a different machine than the server.
- Multiple instances of the client *do_particular_operation( )* method can run on the same or different machines by using different ClientEnvironment.ComputerInformation. This checks for how well the process of dealing with multiple simultaneous users works.
- Tests can be run with either a test or a production database.

Logging

On the EnvisionWare system, message logging occurs at the interfaces ("Plan Your Logging Strategy"). Since the implementations are simple, we made logging part of the implementation, instead of using a proxy. In particular, the classes containing logging calls are:

```
class ClientMessageDispatcher implements MessageReceiver
    Message process_message(Message message_to_process)
class ServerMessageDispatcher implements MessageReceiver
    Message process_message(message_to_process)
```

ClientMessageDispatcher logs all outgoing requests and returned responses. ServerMessageDispatcher logs all incoming requests and returned responses. The logs are created in a searchable format by adding a convert_to_keywords( ) method to each Message class and a encode_into_keywords( ) method to MessageEncoderDecoder—the convert_to_keywords( ) method creates attribute/value pairs (e.g., NumberPrintJobs=2) for each attribute. encode_into_keywords( ) adds attribute/value pairs for the base Message class attributes. The attribute/value pairs make it easier to search and filter logs for particular messages with particular values.

One potential addition is to create decode_from_keywords( ). You would use this method to decode each entry in a log. You could use the decoded entries to create a stream of messages that would duplicate a real or simulated stream. You could use this stream of messages for debugging and regression testing.

The `ClientEnvironment` and `ServerEnvironment` methods might also perform logging—for example, for the client whenever the UserID was changed, or for the server whenever the database was accessed.

Still More Separation

The design described in this chapter can have even a little more separation. You can split the `Messages` into two classes ("Splitters Can Be Lumped Easier Than Lumpers Can Be Split"). You can call the classes `Command` and `Response` (or `ClientMessage` and `ServerMessage`). The two classes would behave in a similar manner, except they would reference different environments (`ClientEnvironment` and `ServerEnvironment`). They could both be of a common abstract type, such as `Message`, or they could remain completely separate types. The separation would clarify which messages were client generated and which were server generated.

Another possible design change deals with separation. Particular client messages in the current EnvisionWare system, generate multiple messages in response. The client requests are for a list of items, such as print jobs. The current system uses a protocol that works like an enumeration. The messages involved are as follows:

Request is `InitialRequestMessage`

   Response is `ListShortMessage`

Request is `SendNextMessage`

   Response is `NextItemInListMessage`

Request is `SendNextMessage`

   Response is `ListCompleteMessage`

The server has a message queue mechanism for creating the appropriate responses to `SendNextMessage`. On the client side, the operation method keeps requesting items until it receives a `ListCompleteMessage`. As an example, `GetJobsMessage` results in multiple jobs. The sequence is as follows:

Request is `GetJobsMessage`

   Response is `ListStartMessage`

Request is `SendNextMessage`

   Response is `PrintJobMessage`

   This repeats until all `PrintJobs` are returned

Request is `SendNextMessage`

   Response is ListCompleteMessage

An abstraction has not yet been captured. There are both LogicalMessages and a PhysicalMessages. For messages that will return multiple items, these two are different. A LogicalMessage contains a collection of items that are generated from PhysicalMessages. For messages not containing collections, the LogicalMessage and the PhysicalMessage are the same.

In this example, the ListStartMessage, PrintJobMessage, and ListCompleteMessage are PhysicalMessages. Using LogicalMessages, two new messages—GetJobsLogicalMessage and PrintJobsLogicalMessage—would be created. The operation on the client side would send a GetJobsLogicalMessage. The handle() method on the server would create a single PrintJobsLogicalMessage, rather than individual PrintJobMessages. The translation into corresponding PhysicalMessages and back from the PhysicalMessages would be handled by the framework.

If there were both LogicalMessages and PhysicalMessages, operation methods on the client and handler methods on the server would create and examine only LogicalMessages. LogicalMessages would create the corresponding PhysicalMessages. If multiple items were expected as the return Message, the LogicalMessage would send the appropriate SendNextMessages to receive all the PhysicalMessages.

By using LogicalMessages, you can change the underlying mechanism for handling multiple-item messages without affecting the operation methods. On a message-by-message basis, you can change the format from enumeration-style multiple physical messages to a single physical message that contained the multiple items.

Now comes the question as to whether this is a big enough issue to make the appropriate switch ("Separating Concerns Makes Smaller Concerns"). Clearly, there is a separation between LogicalMessages and PhysicalMessages. But if almost every LogicalMessage corresponded to a single PhysicalMessage, this separation, although noteworthy, provides little additional benefit. We would be handling parallel message spaces and simply transforming one message object into another.

If only one or two Messages contained multiple items, having specific code to deal with the enumeration is not a problem. If the percentage of multiple-item Messages becomes large (where large is relative to your level of tolerance), creating a separation between the two becomes beneficial.

Epilogue

The Envisionware system was successfully demonstrated at the trade show. Applying the guidelines as shown in this chapter allowed the system to be quickly developed and tested. Since the show, it has grown and matured with little change in design.

CHAPTER SIXTEEN

Antispam Example

THIS CHAPTER EXAMINES HOW EMAIL IS TRANSMITTED AND RECEIVED. It presents a proposed design for an email receiver and spam detector and demonstrates where the guidelines have been used in the design.

The Context

Spam mail needs no introduction. Everyone has probably received some that has leaked through spam filters. This chapter's case study looks at a program designed to check for and trap incoming spam. Many programs receive mail and many programs analyze mail for spam. So why create another one? This design shows some alternative ways of assigning responsibilities in a system. It demonstrates the guidelines in a different context.

The Environment

Several processes are involved in email delivery. The *user agent* (e.g., Outlook, Eudora, etc.) interacts with the user to create messages and to display received messages. The user agent sends outgoing messages to a mail server. The mail server (SendingMailServer) transmits the messages to the receiving mail server (ReceivingMailServer). The receiving server queues the received mail for a particular user. The user agent for the recipient picks up the received mail and displays it to the user. Figure 16-1 shows the email delivery process.

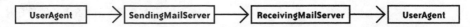

| UserAgent | → | SendingMailServer | → | ReceivingMailServer | → | UserAgent |

FIGURE 16-1. Process of delivering email

Mail also can be transmitted by programs that send messages to a list of people (e.g., Mailman). These programs, often called *list servers*, typically send the messages to a SendingMailServer for delivery.

A spamming program acts as a SendingMailServer. It contacts ReceivingMailServers to deliver the spam to the end user. It is not easy to control the senders, so the bulk of the responsibility for spam prevention falls on the receiver. In this chapter, we describe a ReceivingMailServer that identifies spam and reacts to it. The ReceivingMailServer must try to distinguish between a legitimate message and an illegitimate message. The server can examine a message to see if it resembles spam. The server can also identify SendingMailServers that transmit mostly spam and establish by policy that all messages from those servers are illegitimate.

It is also incumbent on legitimate SendingMailServers not to send spam. At the end of this chapter, we examine a design for a SendingMailServer that reuses the spam detection classes of a ReceivingMailServer.

SMTP

A SendingMailServer and a ReceivingMailServer communicate using the Simple Mail Transfer Protocol (SMTP). SMTP is described in RFC 2821 (*http://www.ietf.org/rfc/rfc2821.txt*). The basic protocol consists of a sequence of commands and responses between the sender and the receiver. The SMTP is a text-based protocol ("To Text or Not to Text"). To keep this description within reasonable bounds, I show only the basic SMTP sequence of commands to transfer a message in the following steps. All ReceivingMailServers must support the commands in this sequence and all SendingMailServers must be prepared to send to receivers who understand only these commands.*

Here is the basic SMTP sequence of commands and responses:

1. ReceivingMailServer:

   Awaits connection from sender.

   On connection, sends greeting.

2. SendingMailServer:

   Sends **HELO *SendingHost***.

3. ReceivingMailServer:

   Sends response.

---

* You also can use SMTP as the protocol between a user agent and the SendingMailServer. To avoid being classified as a spammer, a SendingMailServer should authenticate user agents that use it to transmit email messages and should perform other operations to ensure that spam is not transmitted through it.

4. SendingMailServer:

   Sends **MAIL FROM: <*SendingUser*>**.

5. ReceivingMailServer:

   Sends response.

6. SendingMailServer:

   Sends **RCPT TO: <*Recipient*>**.

   Multiple recipients are established by executing this command repeatedly.

7. ReceivingMailServer:

   Sends response.

8. SendingMailServer:

   Sends **DATA**.

9. ReceivingMailServer:

   Sends response.

   This intermediate response indicates a readiness to accept data.

10. SendingMailServer:

    Sends data (the email message).

    Data ends with EndofData (a period [.] all alone on a single line).

11. ReceivingMailServer:

    Sends response.

12. SendingMailServer:

    Sends **QUIT**.

13. ReceivingMailServer:

    Sends response.

The response is indicated with a numeric value, as well as optional text. Response values fall into three main categories: **Success**, **PermanentFailure**, and **TemporaryFailure**. If the response is **PermanentFailure**, the SendingMailServer usually sends a message back to the *SendingUser*. If the response is **TemporaryFailure**, the SendingMailServer attempts the transfer again later. It might also send a message back to the *SendingUser*. If the response to the end of the data for the **DATA** command is **Success**, the ReceivingMailServer has accepted responsibility for delivering the message to the recipients.

The *SendingUser* and the *Recipient* are email addresses. The combination of the *SendingUser* and the list of *Recipient*s is termed the Envelope. The email addresses in the Envelope do not have to agree with the "From:" or "To:" addresses listed in the message header.

To complete the basic protocol, SendingMailServer can send four additional commands.

EHLO

> This requests that the ReceivingMailServer respond with additional (extended) commands that it supports. For the purposes of the design in this chapter, this works the same as **HELO**.

VRFY

> This requests that the ReceivingMailServer verify an email address. Many ReceivingMailServers do not support this command.

RSET

> This clears the Envelope. **MAIL FROM:** also does this.

NOOP

> This is sent just to get a response from the ReceivingMailServer.

State Diagram

A state diagram can clarify the sequence of states for a ReceivingMailServer ("See What Condition Your Condition Is In"). The states shown in Figure 16-2 are **AWAITING_HELO**, **AWAITING_MAIL_FROM**, **AWAITING_RCPT_TO_OR_DATA**, **INPUT_DATA**, and **TERMINATE**.

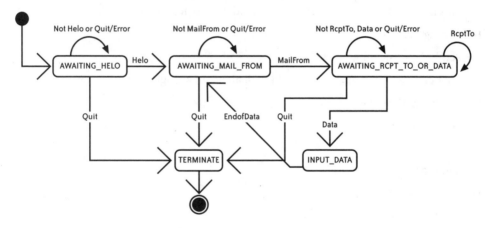

FIGURE 16-2. State transition for SMTP for the ReceivingMailServer

The transition events are **Helo** (a **HELO** command), **MailFrom** (a **MAIL FROM** command), **RcptTo:** (a **RCPT TO:** command), **Data** (a **DATA** command), **Rset** (a **RSET** command), and **Unrecognized** (an unrecognized command).

I was originally tempted to name these events **Hello**, **ReceiptTo**, etc., to make them real words. However, the "Use the Client's Language" and "Consistency Is Simplicity" guidelines suggested that they should be named corresponding to the commands.

The **INPUT_DATA** state ends when the EndofData is received. No transition events are recognized within this state. Upon completion of **INPUT_DATA**, the state is set to **AWAITING_MAIL_FROM**. When the **TERMINATE** state is reached, the ReceivingMailServer terminates the connection to the SendingMailServer. If the amount of data received while in **INPUT_DATA** exceeds a maximum limit, the ReceivingMailServer might go to **TERMINATE**.

If an unknown command is received, the state does not change. A count of unknown commands (across all states) is kept and when more than `MAXIMUM_UNKNOWN_COMMANDS_ALLOWED` is reached, the state goes to `TERMINATE`.

Spam Checking

The `ReceivingMailServer` class performs two actions. It receives the mail and it examines the mail to see if it is spam. The spam checking is delegated to whatever programs or objects the mail server administrator or a user desires ("Separate Concerns To Make Smaller Concerns"). These actions can be separated into two processes: one that receives the mail and one that checks the mail for spam. However, the reason for checking for spam during mail receipt is that any responses that indicate rejection of a message (i.e., **PermanentFailure**) are sent to the `SendingMailServer` immediately for delivery to the user that sent the email. A legitimate `SendingMailServer` will deliver the rejection notice to the user. A spamming program will probably ignore the rejection.

A legitimate sender should be informed with a bounce message by the `SendingMailServer` that his email message was rejected because it appeared to be spam. That way, the sender can either alter the message or use an alternative means of communication to the recipient. Remaining silent by dropping a message and not informing the user can cause communication difficulties ("Never Be Silent"). You can imagine the exchange that begins with "I sent you an email. Are you telling me you didn't get it?" With an assured means of informing the message sender that he was identified as spam, spam filtering by the `ReceivingMailServer` can be more aggressive. It can have more false positives (messages erroneously identified as spam), since false positives will be reported back to the sender.

If spam checking is performed after the connection between the `SendingMailServer` and `ReceivingMailServer` is terminated, it becomes problematic to send a message back to the sender of a message identified as spam. All of the information in an email can be faked. Sending a rejection notice to a faked sender (especially with the message body attached) simply propagates the spam. The only reliable information is the `IPAddress` of the `SendingMailServer`. However, a message sent to the postmaster at that `IPAddress` might not be relayed back to the sender. There might not even be a `ReceivingMailServer` at that `IPAddress`, so even the connection could fail.

The considerations outlined in this section make `ReceivingMailServer` more complicated than if it simply received mail and placed it in a queue for delivery. Sometimes designs cannot follow the "Separate Concerns To Make Smaller Concerns" guideline.

The ReceivingMailServer

The `ReceivingMailServer` creates a `ConnectionHandler` for every `SendingMailServer` that connects to it. The `ConnectionHandler` directs the overall flow of the command/response operation. Commands are both used as the event that determines the next state and processed. We separate these actions by having both a state processor and a command processor. The state processor ensures that the commands are presented in a valid order, according to the state table (Figure 16-2). The command processor interprets the command, which for the most part involves updating the MailDTO, to be discussed shortly. The overall view of ConnectionHandler appears in Figure 16-3.

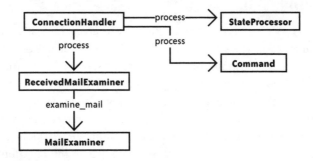

FIGURE 16-3. ConnectionHandler communication diagram

The ConnectionHandler class looks like this:

```
class ConnectionHandler
    Connection connection
    ReceivedMailExaminer received_mail_examiner
    StateProcessor state_processor
    MailDTO mail_dto
    MailReport mail_report
    handle( )
    send_greeting( )
    Command receive_command( )
    write_mail( )
    process_command(Command command)
```

The Connection class represents the connection to the SendingMailServer. It looks like this:

```
class Connection
    CommonString read_line( ) throws ConnectionException
    write_line(CommonString line) throws ConnectionException
    drop( )
```

Both read_line( ) and write_line( ) throw ConnectionException if an error occurred when sending or receiving characters. This is an unrecoverable error, for which the only appropriate action is to terminate the connection ("Decide on a Strategy to Deal With Deviations and Errors").

The receive_command( ) method of ConnectionHandler receives a line from the connection and converts it into a Command. The Command class looks like this:

```
class Command
    CommonString remainder_of_command_line
    abstract Response process(MailDTO received_mail_dto,
        MailReport received_mail_report,
        Connection connection)
```

A class derived from Command represents each command. We will examine the process()
method for each command shortly.

The StateProcessor ensures that the sequence of commands is in accordance with the state
table shown in Figure 16-2 ("See What Condition Your Condition Is In"). The class looks
like this:

```
class StateProcessor
    Count number_of_unknown_commands
    ReceivedState current_state
    StateProcessor()    // initializes current_state to AWAITING_HELO
    Response process(Command current_command)
```

The spam policy (i.e., whether to reject an email message because it is probably spam) is
dictated by the ReceivedMailExaminer, to be described shortly ("Separate Policy from Implementation").

Example 16-1 shows the overall flow for the handle() method of ConnectionHandler.

EXAMPLE 16-1. ConnectionHandler overall flow

```
handle()
    {
    try
        {
        state_processor = new StateProcessor();
        received_mail_examiner = MailExaminer.get_instance();
        mail_dto = new MailDTO();
        mail_report = new MailReport();
        send_greeting();
        while (true)
            {
            Command current_command = receive_command()
            Response response = process_command(current_command);
            if (response.mail_complete && response.result == REQUEST_OK)
                {
                write_mail();
                }
            if (response.reset_dto)
                {
                mail_dto = new MailDTO();
                mail_report = new MailReport();
                }
            connection.write_line(response.to_string());
            if (response.terminate_connection)
                {
                connection.drop();
                break;
                }
            }
        }
    catch(ConnectionException exception)
        {
        // Log the broken connection
        }
    }
```

The handle( ) method begins by calling send_greeting( ) to send the desired greeting. It creates a new StateProcessor whose initial state is **AWAITING_HELO**. Then it receives commands and processes them in a loop. In a reverse of the normal policy/implementation split ("Separate Policy from Implementation"), the called methods determine what to do and the handle( ) method executes those decisions. If the state processor, the command processor, or the mail examiner determines that the connection should be terminated, it is dropped and the loop exits.

If mail input is complete (mail_complete is set by the **DATA** command), handle( ) calls write_ mail( ) to write the message and the examination report to the ReceivingMailQueue (described later in this chapter). A "Received:"header line is added to the message that specifies the ReceivingMailServer domain name and the time of receipt. If response.reset_ dto is set, handle( ) initializes the mail_dto and mail_report to unfilled objects.

The Response

The Response class represents what a MailExaminer, the Command processor, or the StateProcessor suggests should be reported back to the SendingMailServer. This class has the following structure:

```
enumeration Result {REQUEST_OK, MAILBOX_UNAVAILABLE, ... }
class Response
    Result result
    CommonString explanation_text
    boolean terminate_connection
    boolean reset_dto
    boolean mail_complete
    Response(SymbolicReturn symbolic_return, CommonString text_to_return)
    Response combine(Response other)
        // Creates a Response with the most severe result.
    CommonString to_string( )
```

The response sent to the SendingMailServer for a command has the following syntax:

numeric_value_string explanation_text_string

An example of a response is:

502 Command not implemented

The meanings of *numeric_value_string* are defined in RFC 2821. The *explanation_text_ string* is free-form. The Response attribute result is turned into the *numeric_value_string*. The Result enumeration separates the representation of the return value from the meaning of the return value ("Never Let a Constant Slip into Code"). The Response attribute explanation_text is the text to send back as the *explanation_text_string*.

In the standard SMTP, the ReceivingMailServer should never terminate a connection until the SendingMailServer issues a **QUIT** command. However, in the case of spammers, we might want to terminate a connection to prevent wasting our processing power. Any method determining that the SendMailServer is a spammer can set the terminate_connection attribute.

The Process Method

The pseudocode for the process_command method of ConnectionHandler looks like the code shown in Example 16-2.

EXAMPLE 16-2. ConnectionHandler process_command method

```
Response process_command(Command current_command)
    {
    Response response;
    response = state_processor.process(current_command);
    if (response.result == REQUEST_OK)
        {
        response = current_command.process(mail_dto,
            connection);
        if (response.result == REQUEST_OK)
            received_mail_examiner.process(mail_dto,
            mail_report);
        }
    return response;
    }
```

First, a command is checked to see if it is valid according to the state processor. Then the appropriate command process method is invoked to check the data supplied with the command and to update the MailDTO, which is described in the next section. If the command is valid, the received_mail_examiner checks the mail for spam.

MailDTO

The MailDTO class represents the logical information contained in an email message.* The format of a mail message for SMTP is described in RFC 2822 (*http://www.ietf.org/rfc/rfc2822.txt*). MailDTO separates the external physical representation of an email message from its logical representation ("To Text or Not to Text"). Each command alters the MailDTO. Example 16-3 shows what the class looks like.

EXAMPLE 16-3. MailDTO

```
class MailDTO
    Greeting the_greeting
    Envelope the_envelope
    MessageData the_message_data
    Message the_message
    Status the_status
```

The individual parts of MailDTO use the following abstract data types (ADTs) ("When You're Abstract Be Abstract All the Way"). Each ADT represents a logical type. The classes with String in their name have appropriate validation methods to ensure that the corresponding objects have the correct format.

```
    class DomainNameString
    class EmailAddressString
```

---

* DTO, you might recall, stands for Data Transfer Object.

```
class MimeTypeString
class HeaderString
class IPAddress
class EmailAddress
    EmailString identity
    EmailString domain
class MimeType
    MimeTypeString content_type
    MimeTypeString content_subtype
enumeration HeaderCategory {FROM, TO, SUBJECT,... X_FIELD}
```

These ADTs are used in the following classes that declare the attributes of the MailDTO of Example 16-3:

```
class Greeting
    IPAddress sending_ip_address
    DomainNameString hello_host_name
class Envelope
    EmailAddress sender
    EmailAddress [] recipients
class HeaderField
    HeaderCategory category
    HeaderString name
    CommonString value
class BodyPart
    HeaderField [] header_fields
    Byte [] data
class Message
    HeaderField [] header_fields
    BodyPart [] body_parts
class MessageData
    CommonString [] raw_data
```

An email message consists of a header, which contains HeaderFields with name/value pairs and a body. The lines that constitute the HeaderFields are separated from the body by a blank line. There are standard HeaderField names and nonstandard field names. Standard field names will have the category set to the appropriate value of HeaderCategory. Non-standard names will have the category set to X_FIELD, which represents that those fields should begin with the letter *X*, as stated in RFC 2822.

HeaderField could represent a base class with each standard field having a corresponding derived class. However, there are no significant behavioral differences between the headers, so inheritance is not employed ("Avoid Premature Inheritance"). The category attribute was created to help with simple validity checking of the fields (e.g., no more than one "From:" field.). If validity checking of the individual HeaderFields were implemented, this would be an appropriate place to employ inheritance.

The body can consist of a single part (e.g., just a text message) or multiple parts (e.g., a message with attachments). Each BodyPart can have its own header fields. One field describes the MimeType of the part. A MimeType consists of a content_type and a content_ subtype, such as "text/html". Each BodyPart can be examined to see if it contains a virus or other nefarious data.*

The MessageParser class parses text one line at a time and fills in the Message part of the MailDTO. This class could be reused by other message processing programs:

```
class MessageParser
    parse_line(MailDTO mail_dto, CommonString line)
```

The raw_data attribute of MessageData contains the message as delivered by the sender. The attribute is included in the MailDTO for MailExaminers (to be defined shortly) that perform their own message parsing.

The Status class is an enumeration that indicates how much of the MailDTO contains data. The MailExaminers use it to determine how much of the MailDTO to examine for indications of spam.:

```
enumeration Status {EMPTY, GREETING, ENVELOPE_SENDER, ENVELOPE_RECIPIENT, ...}
```

Command Processing

The process( ) methods for the individual commands alter the appropriate parts of the MailDTO:

HeloCommand

Sets the_greeting.sending_ip_address.

Sets the_greeting.hello_host_name.

MailFromCommand

Sets the_envelope.sender.

RcptToCommand

Adds the address to the_envelope.recipients.

DataCommand

This command works differently from the other commands. It has an intermediate response and it reads multiple lines. After sending an intermediate response back to the SendingMailServer, it performs the following until it receives EndofData:

a. Reads a line from the connection.

b. Adds the line to the_message_data.raw_data.

c. Converts the received line into the appropriate part of a Message by calling MessageParser.parse_line( ).

At the end, the command sets response.mail_complete if the data was successfully received and sets response.reset_dto.

---

* In a complex message, BodyParts can contain BodyParts (in a hierarchical pattern). The representation has been simplified for this example.

If the data exceeds `MAXIMUM_SIZE_DATA`, or the `SendingMailServer` takes too long to send the data, the command can terminate with an error.

QuitCommand
> Sets response.terminate_connection.

RsetCommand
> Sets response.reset_dto.

Alternatives

Should the `handle()` method of `ConnectionHandler` (Example 16-1) process received commands or should it process received lines? Almost all commands are single lines, so distinguishing between a command and a line is a matter of abstraction. The `receive_command()` method reads a line and creates a `Command` from it. The `process_command()` acts on that `Command`. The methods could have been written as `receive_line()` and `process_line()`, with one exception.

The **DATA** command is the exception. It needs additional lines to fulfill its operation. If `handle()` processed lines, the method would have to keep track of which commands required additional lines. It is easier to give responsibility to each `Command` object to process all input for a command. Thus, the `Connection` is passed to each `Command`, so additional lines can be read. Only the **DATA** command requires the connection.

ReceivedMailExaminer

The responsibility of the `ReceivedMailExaminer` is to examine the mail and determine if it is acceptable. The `ReceivedMailExaminer` delegates the actual examination to objects implementing the `MailExaminer` interface ("Separating Concerns Makes Smaller Concerns"), shown in Example 16-4.

EXAMPLE 16-4. MailExaminer interface

```
interface MailExaminer
    UnacceptableRating examine_mail(MailDTO a_mail_dto,
        MailReport a_report)
```

The `UnacceptableRating` returned by the `examine_mail()` method of `MailExaminer` is compared by the `ReceivedMailExaminer` to a configuration setting to see if the mail should be considered spam. If so, the appropriate response is returned to the `ConnectionHandler`.

On construction, the `ReceivedMailExaminer` calls the `MailExaminerFactory`. The `MailExaminerFactory` method checks configuration information to see what examiners are requested, creates the appropriate examiners, and returns a reference to an examiner. This reference might be to the only one, to a composite one, or to a `DefaultMailExaminer`.

The composite pattern (see *Design Patterns* by Erich Gamma et al.) is used if multiple `MailExaminers` are desired. If the configuration calls for multiple examiners, `MailExaminerFactory` creates a `MultipleMailExaminer`:

```
MultipleMailExaminer implements MailExaminer
    add_examiner(MailExaminer an_examiner)
    // plus methods in MailExaminer
```

The MailExaminerFactory adds each specified MailExaminer to the MultipleMailExaminer object.

When an examine method is called, the MultipleMailExaminer object calls each MailExaminer that has been added and returns the highest UnacceptableRating that is reported by any of them.[*]

Alternative Interface

An alternative interface for MailExaminer is to have multiple methods, as shown in Example 16-5. Each method is called based on the_status of the MailDTO.

EXAMPLE 16-5. Alternative MailExaminer interface

```
interface MailExaminer
    UnacceptableRating examine_greeting(Greeting a_greeting,
        MailReport a_report)
    UnacceptableRating examine_envelope_sender(Greeting a_greeting,
        EmailAddress sender, MailReport a_report)
    UnacceptableRating examine_envelope_recipient(Greeting a_greeting,
        EmailAddress sender, EmailAddress recipient, MailReport a_report)
```

The two approaches to the MailExaminer interface (Examples 16-4 and 16-5) are another example of the "Spreadsheet Conundrum." In Example 16-4, the single method is passed an object that has information on how much data it contains. In Example 16-5, each individual method designates how much data is being used.

Alternative Responsibility Assignment

An alternative assignment of responsibilities is to make the MailDTO class more active. For example, the method that adds a recipient to an Envelope could also call the examine_mail( ) method in ReceivedMailExaminer. This would tie MailDTO to ReceivedMailExaminer. This coupling makes MailDTO less usable in other contexts that do not require spam checking ("Obey the Class Maxims"). In addition, MailDTO, along with the associated ADTs, has enough work to do to ensure the validity of the message format ("Do a Little Job Well and You May Be Called Upon Often").

This separation also makes testing easier ("Plan for Testing"). The ReceivingMailServer can be tested without any MailExaminers. The individual MailExaminers can be called with MailDTOs that are assembled from a collection of messages. The performance of each MailExaminer in identifying spam can be analyzed easily in a context other than in the act of receiving mail.

---

[*] There are at least two types of mail examiners: those that examine a message for spam and those that accept a message unconditionally. An example of the latter is checking the sender against a whitelist of senders that a user is willing to accept mail from, regardless of its contents. A MailExaminer of that type can return a value corresponding to UnconditionallyAccept. If one did so, further MailExaminers need not be called.

MailReport

A `MailReport` represents the examination methods' findings. Each `MailExaminer` adds an instance of `ExaminerResults` to the `MailReport`. These classes look like this:

```
class ExaminerResult
    CommonString examiner_name
    UnacceptableRating unacceptable_rating
    CommonString [] explanation
    HeaderField [] headers_to_insert
class MailReport
    ExaminerResult [] results
```

The `MailReport` is stored along with the message in the `ReceivedMailQueue` (to be described shortly). When the message is delivered to the recipient's user agent, the `MailReport` can be appended to it, based on user configuration settings. A recipient can use this information for further message filtering.

MailExaminers

Each method in the `MailExaminer` interface determines whether an email message is spam, based on the information currently available. The following examples list some ways that a `MailExaminer` can examine a `MailDTO` to determine if a message is spam. The list is based on current spam filters (such as sendmail milters) plus comments made in an antispam mailing list (spamtools).

The Greeting *can be examined to:*

- Check that the `sending_ip_address` is not listed in a black-hole list. Black-hole lists are maintained by several organizations. They contain the `IPAddresses` of hosts that have been reported as sending spam.

- Check that the `hello_host_name` is formatted properly.

See if the reverse name lookup for an `IPAddress` matches the `hello_host_name`.

The Envelope *can be examined to:*

- Check that the sender is not on a blacklist that is global to the `ReceivingMailServer`.

- Keep track of how many recipients were invalid. If the number exceeds `MAXIMUM_NUMBER_INVALID_RECIPIENTS`, return response with an appropriate result.

For each recipient:

- See if the `sending_ip_address` or the sender is on a blacklist for the recipient. If either is the case, the recipient can be removed from the_envelope.recipients.

- See if the recipient is a *honey pot*. A honey pot is an email address that is placed on web pages or in news groups specifically to attract spammers who use automated tools to generate mailing lists. Appropriate action can be taken.

The Message *can be examined to:*

- Check for spam by executing a program that uses rules or Bayesian analysis to determine a spam score and take appropriate action ("The Easiest Code to Debug Is That Which Is Not Written"). SpamAssassin is an example of a rule-based spam judge.

- Check the headers to see if the "Received" headers form a proper sequence from user agent through final delivery.

- Check for viruses by executing a virus checker to see if the message contains a virus ("Don't Reinvent the Wheel").

- Check the_envelope.recipients and the Greeting to make user-based spam determination.

> **NOTE**
>
> One aspect of SMTP in regards to spam is that the DATA command can be accepted or rejected only as a whole. If users were allowed to create their own configuration commands (e.g., accept anything), some users might reject a message while others accept it. If this were the case, the mail administrator has a quandary: whether to return **Success** or **Permanent-Failure**. A common policy for messages that are accepted (**Success** returned) is to tag the message with a header line and deliver it to the users who wanted to reject it. Another alternative could be to send back a **PermanentFailure** response with the textual explanation that the message was not delivered to all recipients, but to deliver the message to any recipients that did not reject it ("Never Remain Silent").

To check on individual users, the RecipientCollection is accessed:

```
interface RecipientCollection
    Recipient find_recipient(EmailAddress recipient)
interface SpamConfiguration
    should_this_message_be_accepted(Greeting a_greeting, Envelope an_envelope)
class Recipient
    EmailAddress email_address
    SpamConfiguration spam_configuration
```

These interfaces are implemented by accessing the appropriate user information on a particular operating system ("Adapt or Adopt"). For example, on Linux/Unix, a datafile (e.g., /etc/passwd on an unsecured system) is searched for the recipient by the find_recipient( ) method. The SpamConfiguration information can be read from a file in the user's home directory.

Efficiency Considerations

It is possible that the MailExaminers are slow to examine a message. SendingMailServers do not wait forever for a response. The time it takes to determine a response to most commands is short. However, if the amount of data in the Message is large, it could take longer to check for spam than the SendingMailServer is willing to wait. In that case, the sender might terminate the connection and attempt to resend the email later.

If an examination of the logs shows that a faster response to the **DATA** command is needed, several solutions might present themselves ("Don't Speed Until You Know Where You Are Going"). The MailExaminers could be given a fixed amount of time to create an UnacceptableRating. If that time was exceeded, the rating could default to an acceptable one. As another alternative, a listener interface could be implemented. At particular points within the receipt of the email message, the DataCommand process() method could call DataCommandListeners. The interface is as follows:

```
DataCommandListener
    UnacceptableRating on_received_line(CommonString line, Byte [] bytes)
    UnacceptableRating on_end_of_header(MailDTO mail_dto)
    UnacceptableRating on_end_of_content_part(MailDTO mail_dto)
DataCommand
    DataCommandListener data_command_listener
```

The DataCommand.process() method creates a listener by calling the following:

```
DataCommandListener data_command_listener =
    DataCommandListenerFactory.get_instance()
```

The DataCommandListenerFactory method checks the configuration file, and creates a listener, a composite listener, or a DefaultDataCommandListener (if there are no listeners in the configuration file). "Consistency Is Simplicity" suggests that this pattern should follow the MailExaminer pattern.

At each appropriate point in receiving data, the DataCommand.process() method executes the appropriate method in DataCommandListener. If the UnacceptableRating exceeds a configuration setting, the process() method is terminated and an appropriate Response is returned.*

Separation of Concerns

The main method of ReceivingMailServer creates a listening socket on TCP port 25, the SMTP port. When a connection is received, it creates a thread that handles the connection. The logic for the ConnectionHandler as shown in Example 16-1 handles a single connection. Each connection from a SendingMailServer could be handled serially. However, that would tie up the ReceivingMailServer for long periods.

So ConnectionHandler.handler() runs in the context of a thread. Each connection from a SendingMailServer operates in a different thread. The logic of ConnectionHandler.handler() does not change regardless of whether it runs serially or in a thread.

The portion of the program that creates the separate threads can keep track of the number of connections from a particular SendingMailServer. If that number exceeds MAXIMUM_NUMBER_OF_CONNECTIONS_FROM_SENDING_MAIL_SERVER, subsequent connection attempts could be dropped immediately and handle_connection() would not be called.

---

* A composite DataCommandListener that calls multiple DataCommandListeners might need to organize those calls so that implementations that are quick to execute are called first.

This separates the processing of a single thread from the processing of a group of threads ("Do a Little Job Well and You May Be Called Upon Often").

The Full Flow

The design example presented in this chapter separated responsibilities into a SendingMailServer and ReceivingMailServer. In some mail systems (such as the sendmail program), SendingMailServer and ReceivingMailServer functionality is handled by the same program. Other systems (such as qmail) break the functionality into multiple programs. For example, the qmail-smptd program acts as a ReceivingMailServer, the qmail-lspawn/qmail-local program handles delivery to the user, and the qmail-rspawn/qmail-remote program acts as a SendingMailServer.

To see how the responsibilities for a full mail system can be separated into multiple processes ("Do a Little Job Well and You May Be Called Upon Often"), look at Figure 16-4, which is an outline for a design for a complete system.*

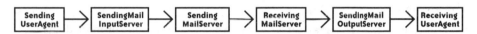

FIGURE 16-4. Processes for delivering mail

Each process plays a role in delivering mail ("Separate of Concerns to Make Smaller Concerns"):

SendingUserAgent

This user agent (e.g., Outlook, Eudora, etc.) creates mail and sends it to a SendingMailInputServer.†

SendingMailInputServer

The server is responsible for verifying that SendingUserAgent has permission to send mail to it and that the **sending_user** in the Envelope represents an EmailAddress for which the SendingUserAgent has permission to send mail.

The server transforms the mail into a MailDTO. It calls MailExaminers to check for spam. If the message is determined to be spam, it can refuse to deliver the message and notify the SendingUserAgent of this decision along with the MailReport. Alternatively, it can send the message, but notify the sender with a message that includes the MailReport. Messages to be sent are placed on a SendingMailQueue along with an Envelope.

---

* An additional process—a relay—can be part of the flow. A relay acts as a ReceivingMailServer and a SendingMailServer. Relaying mail, except from trusted SendingMailServers, is strongly discouraged by antispam guidelines.

† The SendingMailInputServer might require the same SMTP port (port 25) as a ReceivingMailServer to receive mail from SendingUserAgents. Only one process on a host can listen on a particular port. If both processes require the SMTP port, placing each server on a different host avoids this conflict.

MailExaminers

In addition to the checks performed for ReceivingMailServers, specific MailExaminers could also:

- Check for mail limitations by the user

- Check for mail for conformity to header requirements

- Check that the "From:" header comes from a domain for which the host is a SendingMailServer

SendingMailServer

- Takes the messages in the SendingMailQueue and contacts the ReceivingMailServer for each recipient's domain.

- Transfers the message using SMTP, as described earlier in this chapter.

- If the ReceivingMailServer refuses to accept responsibility for delivery (transient or permanent failure), it sends back a message to the *SendingUser*.

ReceivingMailServer

- Contacted by the SendingMailServer to receive messages for one or more domains, as shown in this chapter.

- If a mail message has been accepted for one or more recipients, it places the message in the ReceivingMailQueue along with the Envelope and the MailReport.

ReceivingMailOutputServer

- Reads the ReceivingMailQueue and delivers each message to the recipient's mailboxes.

- Alters the recipients in the Envelope based on address aliases.

- Distributes to individual identity mailboxes according to the Envelope.

- Checks individual user configurations to see what form is desired for delivery of the MailReport (e.g., appended to the end of the message, added as header lines, or ignored).

ReceivingUserAgent

- This user agent (e.g., Outlook, Eudora, etc.) retrieves mail from a mailbox and displays it to the user.

CHAPTER SEVENTEEN

Epilogue

SAM'S **CD** RENTAL SYSTEM DEMONSTRATED PREFACTORING GUIDELINES IN A SPECIFIC SITUATION. There is always a tradeoff in expressing ideas in specifics. The use of ideas in other contexts might not be apparent. The specific versus general dichotomy is demonstrated in the subject matter of Sam's system. The design of Sam's system was specific; the applicability of the design can be more general.

Some guidelines might appear too general for your specific situation, since this book has intentionally avoided language- or environment-specific issues. Take those guidelines as a starting point. Develop guidelines from them that are more specific to the languages and frameworks you use.

Prefactoring is not just about static guidelines. It also is about learning from your own experience. Keeping a journal of why adherence to or disregard for a guideline worked or did not work in a particular situation will help you develop your own variations and additions.

You can add to your list of guidelines by reading books such as those mentioned in the text, or by reading almost anything by Fred Brooks, Gerry Weinberg, David Parnas, and Edsger W Dijkstra.

I welcome the opportunity to hear from you regarding any guidelines that you develop.

Guidelines and Principles

THIS APPENDIX OUTLINES THE GUIDELINES LISTED IN THIS BOOK, as well as the chapters they appear in.

Guidelines

The following subsections list the guidelines that are introduced in this book. Some guidelines are repeated in multiple chapters, as they can be applied in multiple contexts.

Big Picture

Don't Reinvent the Wheel
Look for existing solutions to problems before creating new solutions (Chapter 2).

Think About the Big Picture
Decisions within a system should be congruent with the big picture (Chapter 3).

Document Your Assumptions and Your Decisions
Keep a journal for retrospectives (Chapter 3).

Don't Repeat Yourself (DRY)
Every piece of knowledge must have a single, unambiguous, authoritative representation within a system (Chapter 3).

Plan Globally, Develop Locally
  Incremental implementations should fit into a global plan (Chapter 4).

Extreme Abstraction

Splitters Can Be Lumped More Easily Than Lumpers Can Be Split
  It is easier to combine two concepts than it is to separate them (Chapter 2).

Clump Data So That There Is Less to Think About
  Clumping data cuts down on the number of concepts that have to be kept in mind (Chapter 2).

When You're Abstract, Be Abstract All the Way
  Do not describe data items using primitive data types (Chapter 2).

Strings Are More Than Just a String
  Treat String as a primitive data type. Describe attributes with abstract data types, instead of as Strings (Chapter 2).

Never Let a Constant Slip into Code
  Use a symbolic name for all values (Chapter 2).

To Text or Not to Text
  Use text between programs, not within programs (Chapter 5).

If It Has Collection Operations, Make It a Collection
  Collections separate object usage from object storage and hide implementation of aggregate operations (Chapter 5).

Don't Change What It Is
  Create new terms rather than trying to apply new meanings to current terms (Chapter 12)

Extreme Separation

Adapt a Prefactoring Attitude
  Eliminate duplication before it occurs (Chapter 3).

Don't Overclassify
  Separate concepts into different classes based on behavior, not on data (Chapter 5).

Place Methods in Classes Based on What They Need
  If a method does not require instance data, it should not be a member of the class. Conversely, if all the method requires is the instance data, it should be a member of the class (Chapter 6).

Honor the Class Maxims
  Make loosely coupled cohesive classes (Chapter 6).

Do a Little Job Well and You May Be Called Upon Often
  Methods and classes that perform specific jobs can be reused more often (Chapter 6).

Separate Policy from Implementation
  Keeping the *what* separated from the *how* makes the *what* more readable and maintainable (Chapter 6).

Separate Concerns to Make Smaller Concerns

Split responsibilities among multiple methods and multiple classes to simplify each method and class (Chapter 7).

Test or Production; That Is the Question

Place all test-only methods in a test interface (Chapter 8).

Build Flexibility for Testing

Plan for flexibility in your design to allow for ease of testing (Chapter 8).

Decouple with Associations

Association classes decouple the two classes being associated (Chapter 9).

Split Interfaces

Split a single interface into multiple interfaces if multiple clients use different portions of the interface (Chapter 10).

Do a Little and Pass the Buck

Add proxies to interfaces to add functionality (Chapter 11).

Business Rules Are a Business unto Themselves

Keep business rules separate from other logic (Chapter 13).

Extreme Readability

A Rose by Any Other Name Is Not a Rose

Create a clearly defined name for each concept in a system (Chapter 2).

Prototypes Are Worth a Thousand Words

A picture of an interface, such as a screen, can be more powerful than just a description (Chapter 2).

Communicate with Your Code

Your code should communicate its purpose and intent (Chapter 3).

Explicitness Beats Implicitness

Being explicit reduces misinterpretation (Chapter 3).

Declaration over Execution

Declarative-style programming can provide flexibility without code changes (Chapter 5).

Use the Same Layout to Get the Same Layout

Use templates or scripts for classes and methods to create consistent logic (Chapter 10).

The Easiest Code to Debug Is That Which Is Not Written

Never write functionality that already exists in usable form (Chapter 11).

Use the Client's Language

Use the client's language in your code to make it easier to compare the logic in the code to the logic of the client (Chapter 13).

Interfaces

Create Interface Contracts
Design with well-defined interfaces and enforce the contracts for those interfaces (Chapter 3).

Validate, Validate, Validate
At each interface, validate that the input matches the contract (Chapter 3).

Test the Interface, Not the Implementation
Use the contract of the interface to develop the functional tests, not the implementation behind it (Chapter 10).

Adopt and Adapt
Create the interface you desire and adapt the implementation to it (Chapter 11).

Don't Let the Cold Air In
With interfaces exposed to the outside world, ensure that input validation and logging occurs (Chapter 14).

Error Handling

Decide on a Strategy to Deal with Deviations and Errors
Determine for your system what are deviations and what are errors, and how to deal with both (Chapter 3).

Report Meaningful User Messages
Error messages should be reported in the context of what the user can do about the error, instead of in terms of what the underlying error is (Chapter 3).

Never Be Silent
If a method encounters an error, it should report it, not remain silent (Chapter 6).

Consider Failure an Expectation, Not an Exception
Plan how operations should respond to failures (Chapter 13).

General Issues

Don't Speed Until You Know Where You Are Going
Make the system right, before you make it fast (Chapter 3).

The Spreadsheet Conundrum
Recognize when you are making the row/column decision (Chapter 3).

Consistency Is Simplicity
A consistent approach to style and solutions can make code easier to maintain (Chapter 3).

If It Can't Be Tested, Don't Require It
Every functionality requirement, whether formally or informally stated, should have a test created for it. If you cannot test a requirement, there is no way to determine whether you have met it (Chapter 4).

Plan for Testing
   Developing test strategies in advance can lead to a better design (Chapter 4).

Figure Out How to Migrate Before You Migrate
   Considering the migration path might help you discover additional considerations in other areas of the design (Chapter 7).

Know Who It Is
   Determine uniqueness criteria for objects that should be unique (Chapter 7).

Perform a Retrospective After Each Release
   Examining your design and how you created it can help in the next release (Chapter 8).

Nothing Is Perfect
   There is usually a better solution, but you can stop with good enough (Chapter 8).

See What Condition Your Condition Is In
   Use state-based analysis to examine object behavior (Chapter 9).

Get Something Working
   Create something basic before adding refinements (Chapter 10).

Plan Your Logging Strategy
   Determine where and how you are going to log (Chapter 11).

More Is Sometimes Less
   Use a prewritten module with more features than you currently need and adapt it to your current needs (Chapter 11).

Be Ready to Import and Export
   Data should be available for use outside the system via a well-defined data interface (Chapter 12).

Avoid Premature Generalization
   Solve the specific problem before making the solution general (Chapter 14).

Security

If You Forget Security, You're Not Secure
   Security should not be an afterthought. Consider it during all phases of development (Chapter 4).

Consider Privacy
   Systems need to be designed with privacy in mind (Chapter 13).

General Objects

Avoid Premature Inheritance
   Inheritance needs time to evolve (Chapter 5).

Think Interfaces, Not Inheritance
   Interfaces provide more fluidity in the relationships between classes (Chapter 6).

Overloading Functions Can Become Overloading
   By using unique names, functions can be more self-describing (Chapter 6).

When in Doubt, Indirect
Indirection, using either methods or data, adds flexibility (Chapter 11).

Guidelines in Alphabetical Order

Here are the guidelines in alphabetical order with the page number on which they appear.

"A Rose by Any Other Name Is Not a Rose" on page 13

"Adapt a Prefactoring Attitude" on page 33

"Adopt and Adapt" on page 128

"Avoid Premature Generalization" on page 160

"Avoid Premature Inheritance" on page 64

"Be Ready to Import and Export" on page 143

"Build Flexibility for Testing" on page 101

"Business Rules Are a Business unto Themselves" on page 152

"Clump Data so That There Is Less to Think About" on page 16

"Communicate with Your Code" on page 28

"Consider Failure an Expectation, Not an Exception" on page 148

"Consider Privacy" on page 153

"Consistency Is Simplicity" on page 32

"Create Interface Contracts" on page 26

"Decide on a Strategy to Deal with Deviations and Errors" on page 36

"Declaration over Execution" on page 63

"Decouple with Associations" on page 110

"Do a Little and Pass the Buck" on page 130

"Do a Little Job Well and You May Be Called upon Often" on page 80

"Document Your Assumptions and Your Decisions" on page 34

"Don't Change What It Is" on page 141

"Don't Let the Cold Air in" on page 159

"Don't Overclassify" on page 62

"Don't Reinvent the Wheel" on page 11

"Don't Repeat Yourself (DRY)" on page 33

"Don't Speed Until You Know Where You Are Going" on page 40

"Exceptional Guideline" on page 3

"Explicitness Beats Implicitness" on page 29

"Figure Out How to Migrate Before You Migrate" on page 92

"Get Something Working" on page 123

"If It Can't Be Tested, Don't Require It" on page 53

"If It Has Collection Operations, Make It a Collection" on page 68

"If You Forget Security, You're Not Secure" on page 58

"Honor the Class Maxims" on page 71

"Know Who It Is" on page 94

"More Is Sometimes Less" on page 132

"Most Strings Are more than just a String" on page 19

"Never Be Silent" on page 73

"Never Let a Constant Slip into Code" on page 20

"Nothing Is Perfect" on page 104

"Overloading Functions Can Become Overloading" on page 82

"Perform a Retrospective After Each Release" on page 96

"Place Methods in Classes Based on What They Need" on page 75

"Plan for Testing" on page 55

"Plan Globally, Develop Locally" on page 51

"Plan Your Logging Strategy" on page 136

"Prototypes Are Worth a Thousand Words" on page 22

"Report Meaningful User Messages" on page 38

"See What Condition Your Condition Is in" on page 112

"Separate Concerns to Make Smaller Concerns" on page 86

"Separate Policy from Implementation" on page 81

"Split Interfaces" on page 122

"Splitters Can Be Lumped More Easily than Lumpers Can Be Split" on page 15

"Test or Production: That Is the Question" on page 100

"Test the Interface, Not the Implementation" on page 121

"The Easiest Code to Debug Is That Which Is Not Written" on page 131

"The Spreadsheet Conundrum" on page 41

"Think About the Big Picture" on page 24

"Think Interfaces, Not Inheritance" on page 77

"To Text or Not to Text" on page 66

"Use the Client's Language" on page 151

"Use the Same Layout to Get the Same Layout" on page 124

"Validate, Validate, Validate" on page 27

"When in Doubt, Indirect" on page 134

"When You're Abstract, Be Abstract All the Way" on page 17

Software Design Principles

Software design principles underlie the guidelines presented in this book. These principles embrace some common underlying themes including abstraction and separation of concerns. Some of these principles are directly reflected in the guidelines and others are implicit. Here are some generally accepted principles that are embodied in the guidelines:

Well-Defined Interfaces

A well-defined interface is like a great user's manual. The user knows exactly how to perform desired operations and what the result will be. An interface includes the operations that it performs for the user, as well as any access control that designates which users can perform an operation. The *Liskov Substitution Principle*[*] denotes that any implementation of an interface should respect the definition of that interface.

---

[*] Barbara Liskov, *Data Abstraction and Hierarchy*, SIGPLAN Notices, 23,5 (May, 1988). See *http://c2.com/cgi/wiki?LiskovSubstitutionPrinciple*.

Decomposition and Modularity

Systems should be decomposed into modular components. Components should be designed to be reusable, if possible.

Prioritized Requirements

All requirements cannot be implemented at the same time. Requirements need to be prioritized by the client to determine what should be implemented first.

Abstraction

Abstraction deals with the essential characteristics of a system and the components of the system. Data and control are represented by abstract descriptions, not by specific implementations. The concentration is on the *what* and not the *how*. Implementation details, such as the language in which a system will be written, or the platform on which it runs, are not considered. Thus, abstractions are more stable than implementations.

Information Hiding

Information hiding is a means for achieving abstraction. Well-defined interfaces expose functionality, but not implementation. Algorithms, I/O formats, and data representation are not exposed outside the interface.

Extensibility

The *Open/Closed Principle*, as stated by Bertrand Meyer (*Object-Oriented Software Construction*, [Prentice Hall, 2000]), says that components should be open so that they are available for extension, yet closed so that they are usable by other components. This principle is typically demonstrated with inheritance. A base class is closed, but it is open to extension by inheritance.

Hierarchy

There are levels in systems, such as inheritance hierarchies or layers of abstraction.

Separation of Concerns

Modules are split up into components that have separate orthogonal concerns.

Packaging

Components that change together should be packaged together.

Source Code

HERE ARE THE CLASS DESCRIPTIONS FOR THE FIRST VERSION OF SAM'S CD RENTAL PROGRAM that is described in Chapter 8. The entire source is shown for a few of the classes. The full source code is available at *http://www.oreilly.com/catalog/prefactoring*.

com.samscdrental.configuration Package

This package contains the central source for configuration information.

Configuration.java

```
public class Configuration
    {
    static public Configuration getInstance( )
    public DataAccessConfiguration getDataAccessConfiguration( )
    public ReportConfiguration getReportConfiguration( )
    }
```

DataAccessConfiguration.java

```
public class DataAccessConfiguration
    {
    public String dataFilename;
    }
```

ReportConfiguration.java

```
public class ReportConfiguration
    {
    public String printFilename;
    }
```

com.samscdrental.controller Package

This package contains the three operation classes.

MaintenanceOperations.java

```
public class MaintenanceOperations
    {
    static public MaintenanceOperations getInstance( )
    public void collectionsInitialize(
        String customerFilename, String cdDiscFilename,
        String cdReleaseFilename ) throws ImportFormatDeviation,
        ImportFileDeviation
    }
```

RentalOperations.java

```
public class RentalOperations
    {
    static public RentalOperations getInstance( )
    public void checkinCDDisc( PhysicalID aPhysicalID ) throws CheckInDeviation,
        LateReturnDeviation
    public boolean isCDDiscRented( PhysicalID aPhysicalID ) throws
        StatusDeviation
    public RentalContractDTO checkoutCDDisc( PhysicalID aPhysicalID,
         CustomerID aCustomerID ) throws
        CheckOutDeviation
    public void dispose( )
    }
```

ReportOperations.java

```
public class ReportOperations
    {
    static public ReportOperations getInstance( )
    public CDDiscInventoryReportPlainTextFormat
        makeCDDiscInventoryReportPlainTextFormat( )
    public CDDiscInventoryDTO makeCDDiscInventoryDTO( )
    }
```

com.samscdrental.dataaccess Package

This package contains the classes that access the data for the system.

CDDiscDataAccess.java

```
public class CDDiscDataAccess
    implements java.io.Serializable
    {
    public void add( CDDisc aCDDisc )
    public void remove( CDDisc aCDDisc )
    public CDDisc[] findByCDRelease( CDRelease aCDRelease )
```

```
    public CDDisc findByPhysicalID( PhysicalID aPhysicalID )
    public void removeAll_TestingOnly( )
    public CDDisc[] findAll( )
    }
```

CDReleaseDataAccess.java

```
public class CDReleaseDataAccess
    implements java.io.Serializable
    {
    public void add( CDRelease aCDRelease )
    public void remove( CDRelease aCDRelease )
    public CDRelease findByUPCCode( UPCCode aUPCCode )
    public void removeAll_TestingOnly( )
    }
```

CustomerDataAccess.java

```
public class CustomerDataAccess
    implements java.io.Serializable
    {
    public void add( Customer aCustomer )
    public void remove( Customer aCustomer )
    public Customer findByCustomerID( CustomerID aCustomerID )
    public void removeAll_TestingOnly( )
    }
```

DataAccessHelper.java

```
public class DataAccessHelper
    {
    public static Object readObjectFromOpenStream( Class expectedClass,
        ObjectInputStream input )
    public static void writeObjectToOpenStream( Object anObject,
    ObjectOutputStream output )
    }
```

StoreDataAccess.java

```
public class StoreDataAccess
    {
    public CDDiscDataAccess theCDDiscDataAccess
        = new CDDiscDataAccess( );
    public CustomerDataAccess theCustomerDataAccess
        = new CustomerDataAccess( );
    public CDReleaseDataAccess theCDReleaseDataAccess
        = new CDReleaseDataAccess( );
    public static StoreDataAccess getInstance( )
    public static StoreDataAccess makeNew( )
    public void dispose( )
    }
```

com.samscdrental.display.adt Package

These are the two display widgets that correspond to the abstract data type (ADT) classes.

CustomerIDTextField.java

```
public class CustomerIDTextField
    extends JTextField
```

```
    {
    public CustomerIDTextField( )
    public CustomerID getCustomerID( ) throws CustomerIDFormatDeviation
    }
```

PhysicalIDTextField.java

```
public class PhysicalIDTextField
    extends JTextField
    {
    public PhysicalIDTextField( )
    public PhysicalID getPhysicalID( ) throws PhysicalIDFormatDeviation
    }
```

com.samscdrental.display Package

These are the graphical user interface (GUI) display classes.

CheckinDialog.java

```
public class CheckinDialog
    extends JDialog
    {
    void DoneButton_actionPerformed( ActionEvent e )
    void CancelButton_actionPerformed( ActionEvent e )
    // Other GUI related methods
    }
```

CheckoutDialog.java

```
public class CheckoutDialog
    extends JDialog
    {
    void DoneButton_actionPerformed( ActionEvent e )
    void CancelButton_actionPerformed( ActionEvent e )
    // Other GUI related methods
    }
```

DisplayHelper.java

```
public class DisplayHelper
    {
    public static void displayError( Component component, String text )
    public static void displayMessage( String text )
    }
```

Main.java

```
public class Main
    {
    public static void main( String[] args )
    }
```

MainFrame.java

```
public class MainFrame
    extends JFrame
    {
```

```
void checkoutButton_actionPerformed( ActionEvent e )
void checkinButton_actionPerformed( ActionEvent e )
// Other GUI related methods
}
```

com.samscdrental.failures Package

These are all the deviations and errors that occur during processing. All of the deviations are derived from Deviation.

Deviation.java

```
public class Deviation
    extends Exception
    {
    public Deviation( String explanation )
    }
```

CDCategoryFormatDeviation.java

```
public class CDCategoryFormatDeviation
    extends Deviation
    {
    public CDCategoryFormatDeviation( String explanation )
    }
```

Other Deviations

```
CheckInDeviation.java

CheckOutDeviation.java

CustomerIDFormatDeviation.java

DollarFormatDeviation.java

ImportFileDeviation.java

ImportFormatDeviation.java

LateReturnDeviation.java

NameFormatDeviation.java

ParseLineDeviation.java

PhysicalIDFormatDeviation.java

PrinterFailureDeviation.java

StatusDeviation.java

UPCCodeFormatDeviation.java
```

SeriousErrorException.java

```
public class SeriousErrorException
    extends RuntimeException
    {
    public SeriousErrorException( )
    public SeriousErrorException( String explanation, Exception aException )
    }
```

com.samscdrental.helper Package

This contains a single helper class for strings.

StringHelper.java

```
public class StringHelper
    {
    public static boolean containsOnlyAlphanumerics( String aString )
    public static boolean containsOnlyNumerics( String aString )
    public static boolean containsNoControls( String aString )
    }
```

com.samscdrental.importexport Package

These classes import text files into the data access collections.

AddFromFileInterface.java

```
public interface AddFromFileInterface
    {
    void addToCollection( String line ) throws ParseLineDeviation;
    }
```

CDDiscDataAccessImportExport.java

```
public class CDDiscDataAccessImportExport
    {
    public CDDiscDataAccessImportExport( CDDiscDataAccess aCDDiscCollection )
    public void addCDDiscsFromFile( String filename ) throws
        ImportFormatDeviation, ImportFileDeviation
    }
```

CDDiscImportExport.java

```
public class CDDiscImportExport
    {
    public static CDDisc parseLine( String line ) throws ParseLineDeviation
    }
```

CDReleaseDataAccessImportExport.java

```
public class CDReleaseDataAccessImportExport
    {
    public CDReleaseDataAccessImportExport(
        CDReleaseDataAccess aCDReleaseStateCollection )
    public void addCDReleasesFromFile( String filename ) throws
        ImportFormatDeviation, ImportFileDeviation
    }
```

CDReleaseImportExport.java

```
public class CDReleaseImportExport
    {
    public static CDRelease parseLine( String line ) throws ParseLineDeviation
    }
```

CustomerDataAccessExport.java

```
public class CustomerDataAccessExport
```

```
    {
    public CustomerDataAccesstExport( CustomerDataAccess
        aCustomerStateCollection )
    public void addCustomersFromFile( String filename ) throws
        ImportFormatDeviation, ImportFileDeviation
    }
```

CustomerImportExport.java

```
public class CustomerImportExport
    {
    public static Customer parseLine( String line ) throws ParseLineDeviation
    }
```

DataAccessImportExportHelper.java

```
public class DataAccessImportExportHelper
    {
    public void addCDDiscsFromFile( String filename,
            String nameForErrors, AddFromFileInterface addFromFile )
            throws ImportFormatDeviation, ImportFileDeviation
    }
```

com.samscdrental.migration Package

This contains the main program for importing text files.

MigrateMain.java

```
public class MigrateMain
    {
    public static void main( String[] args )
    }
```

com.samscdrental.model.adt Package

The ADTs are in this package.

CustomerID.java

```
public class CustomerID
    implements java.io.Serializable
    {
    public CustomerID( )
    public CustomerID( String aString ) throws CustomerIDFormatDeviation
    public void fromString( String aString ) throws CustomerIDFormatDeviation
    public static CustomerID parseString( String aString ) throws
        CustomerIDFormatDeviation
    boolean isInvalid( )
    public String toString( )
    public boolean equals( CustomerID aCustomerID )
    public boolean equals( Object obj )
    }
```

Dollar.java

```
public class Dollar
    implements java.io.Serializable
    {
```

```
        public Dollar( )
        public Dollar( double value )
        public void fromString( String aString ) throws DollarFormatDeviation
        public static Dollar parseString( String aString ) throws
            DollarFormatDeviation
        public boolean equals( Dollar aDollar )
        void fromDouble( double value )
        public String toString( )
        public boolean equals( Object obj )
        }
```

Name.java

```
    public class Name
        implements java.io.Serializable
        {
        public Name( )
        public Name( String aString ) throws NameFormatDeviation
        boolean isInvalid( )
        public static Name parseString( String aString ) throws
            NameFormatDeviation
        public boolean equals( Name aName )
        public String toString( )
        public boolean equals( Object obj )
        }
```

PhysicalID.java

```
    public class PhysicalID
        implements java.io.Serializable
        {
        public PhysicalID( )
        public PhysicalID( String aString ) throws PhysicalIDFormatDeviation
        boolean isInvalid( )
        public static PhysicalID parseString( String aString ) throws
            PhysicalIDFormatDeviation
        public boolean equals( PhysicalID aPhysicalID )
        public String toString( )
        public boolean equals( Object obj )
        }
```

Timestamp.java

```
    public class Timestamp
        implements java.io.Serializable
        {
        public Timestamp( )
            // Will be initialized to the current time
        public int differenceInDays( Timestamp aTimestamp )
        public Timestamp addDays( int days )
        public String toString( )
        public boolean equals( Timestamp aTimestamp )
        public boolean equals( Object obj )
        }
```

UPCCode.java

```
    public class UPCCode
        implements java.io.Serializable
        {
```

```
public UPCCode( )
public static UPCCode parseString( String aString ) throws
    UPCCodeFormatDeviation
public UPCCode( String aString ) throws UPCCodeFormatDeviation
public boolean equals( UPCCode aUPCCode )
public String toString( )
public boolean equals( Object obj )
}
```

com.samscdrental.model.dto Package

These are the Data Transfer Objects (DTOs) used in creating reports.

CDDiscInventoryDTO.java

```
public class CDDiscInventoryDTO
    {
    public CDDiscInventoryItem[] theCDDiscInventoryItems;
    }
```

CDDiscInventoryItem.java

```
public class CDDiscInventoryItem
    {
    public PhysicalID theCDDiscPhysicalID;
    public boolean isCDDiscRented;
    public CustomerID theCustomerID;
    }
```

OverdueRentalDTO.java

```
public class OverdueRentalDTO
    {
    public Timestamp theRentalStartTime;
    public Timestamp theRentalDueTime;
    public Timestamp theRentalEndTime;
    public Dollar theOverdueFee;
    public CustomerID theCustomerID;
    public Name theCustomerName;
    public Name theCDReleaseTitle;
    public PhysicalID theCDDiscPhysicalID;
    }
```

RentalContractDTO.java

```
public class RentalContractDTO
    {
    public Timestamp theRentalStartTime;
    public Timestamp theRentalDueTime;
    public Name theCustomerName;
    public Name theCDReleaseTitle;
    public PhysicalID theCDDiscPhysicalID;
    public Dollar theRentalFee;
    }
```

com.samscdrental.model Package

The classes in the model are in this package. The code is shown for CDDisc.

CDCategory.java

```
public class CDCategory
    implements java.io.Serializable
    {
    public CDCategory( )
    public CDCategory( int value )
    public String toString( )
    public static CDCategory parseString( String aString ) throws
        CDCategoryFormatDeviation
    public boolean equals( CDCategory aCDCategory )
    public boolean equals( Object obj )
    }
```

CDCategoryValues.java

```
public class CDCategoryValues
    {
    int getBaseRentalPeriodDays( CDCategory cdCategory )
    Dollar getRentalFee( CDCategory cdCategory )
    }
```

CDDisc.java

```
public class CDDisc
    implements java.io.Serializable
    {
    public CDDisc( CDRelease aCDRelease, PhysicalID aPhysicalID )
    public Rental getRental( )
    public CDRelease getCdRelease( )
    public PhysicalID getPhysicalID( )
    public boolean isRented( )
    public RentalContractDTO startRental( Customer aCustomer ) throws
        CheckOutDeviation
    public void endRental( ) throws CheckInDeviation, LateReturnDeviation
    }
```

CDRelease.java

```
public class CDRelease
    implements java.io.Serializable
    {
    public CDCategory getCdCategory( )
    public Name getTitle( )
    public UPCCode getUPCCode( )
    public CDRelease( CDCategory aCDCategory, Name aTitle, UPCCode aUPCCode )
    int getBaseRentalPeriodDays( )
    Dollar getRentalFee( )
    }
```

Customer.java

```
public class Customer
    implements java.io.Serializable
    {
```

```
public CustomerID getCustomerID( )
public Name getName( )
public Customer( Name aName, CustomerID aCustomerID )
}
```

Rental.java

```
public class Rental
    implements java.io.Serializable
    {
    public Rental( Customer aCustomer, int baseRentalPeriodDays,
        Dollar rentalFee )
    public boolean isOverdue( )
    public void checkIn( )
    public boolean isLateReturn( )
    public void setStartTime( Timestamp startTime )
    public Customer getCustomer( )
    public Timestamp getStartTime( )
    public Timestamp getEndTime( )
    public Dollar getRentalFee( )
    public int getBaseRentalPeriodDays( )
    public Timestamp getDueTime( )
    }
```

com.samscdrental.reports Package

The reports are in this package.

CDDiscInventoryMain.java

```
public class CDDiscInventoryMain
    {
    public static void main( String[] args )
    }
```

CDDiscInventoryReportPlainTextFormat.java

```
public class CDDiscInventoryReportPlainTextFormat
    implements ReportPlainTextFormat
    {
    public CDDiscInventoryReportPlainTextFormat( )
    public String getReportString( )
    public CDDiscInventoryReportPlainTextFormat( CDDiscInventoryDTO
        aCDDiscInventoryDTO )
    }
```

ContractReportPlainTextFormat.java

```
public class ContractReportPlainTextFormat
    implements ReportPlainTextFormat
    {
    public String getReportString( )
    public ContractReportPlainTextFormat( RentalContractDTO rentalContractDTO )
    }
```

OverdueRentalReportPlainTextFormat.java

```
public class OverdueRentalReportPlainTextFormat
    implements ReportPlainTextFormat
    {
```

```
    public String getReportString( )
    public OverdueRentalReportPlainTextFormat( OverdueRentalDTO
        aOverdueRentalContractDTO )
    }
```

ReportPlainTextFormat.java

```
public interface ReportPlainTextFormat
    {
    String getReportString( );
    }
```

Reports.java

```
public class Reports
    {
    public static void printReport( ReportPlainTextFormat
        aReportPlainTextFormat ) throws
        PrinterFailureDeviation
    public static ContractReportPlainTextFormat createContractReport(
        RentalContractDTO aRentalContractDTO )
    }
```

com.samscdrental.tests Package

The tests for the RentalOperations are in this package.

CheckinCheckoutTests.java

```
public class CheckinCheckoutTests
    extends TestCase
    {
    public CheckinCheckoutTests( )
    public CheckinCheckoutTests( String name )
    public void testNormalOperation( ) throws Exception
    public void testLateReturn( ) throws Exception
    public void testBadPhysicalID( ) throws Exception
    public void testBadCustomerID( ) throws Exception
    public void testNonExistentPhysicalID( ) throws Exception
    public void testNonExistentCustomerID( ) throws Exception
    public void testAlreadyRented( ) throws Exception
    public void testReturnNotRented( ) throws Exception
    public static Test suite( )
    public static void main( String[] args )
    protected void setUp( ) throws Exception
    protected void tearDown( ) throws Exception
    }
```

TestOnlyOperations.java

```
public class TestOnlyOperations
    {
    static TestOnlyOperations getInstance( )
    void collectionsClear( )
    void setStartTimeForRentalBackSomeDays( PhysicalID aPhysicalID,
        int days )
    }
```

INDEX

A

abstraction, 16
  classes, 70
  introduction, 2
  (see also ADTs)
abstraction guidelines, 196
Address class, Sam's system, 15, 18, 126
ADTs (abstract data types), 16
  CRCs and, 49
  descriptions, 16
agile development, 6
analysis, 46
analysis paralysis, 47
antispam case study (see email)
AOP (Aspect-Oriented Programming)
  join points, 131
  pointcuts, 131
assertions, 38
association classes, 109
  coupling and, 110
attacks, SQL injection, 26
attributes, association classes, 109
avoiding reinvention, 11

B

big picture, 23
  guidelines, 195
binary state, objects, 111
business rules, discounts, 151

C

called methods, 25
case studies
  antispam efforts, 175–192
  printserver, 163–173
catalog search use case, 115
catalog searches
  interface design, 117
  interface development, 119
  interface splitting, 121
  interface testing, 120
  limit setting, 123

categories, classes and, 59
CDCatalogItem( ) class, Sam's system, 119
CDCatalogItemCollection interface, 119
CDCatalogItemInfo class, Sam's system, 119
CDCategory class, Sam's system, 66
CDDisc class, Sam's system, 67, 70
CDDiscCollection class, Sam's system, 68
CDRelease class, Sam's system, 49, 51, 60, 61
  methods, 64
checked exceptions, 36
classes
  abstractions and, 70
  association, 109
  categories and, 59
  cohesive, 70
    coupling, 70
  combining, 19
  configuration classes, 98
  coupling
    association classes, 110
    unintended, 104
  inheritance, 63–65
  inheritance-oriented, hierarchy, 60
  objects, 61
  operation classes, 97
  (see also Sam's system)
clients
  needs list, 8
  use cases, 8–10
    abstractions, 45
clumping, 15
code
  communication and, 27–31
  consistency, 31
  copying, 32
  declarative-style programming, 62
  examples, using, xiv
  executable-style programming, 62
  explicitness, 28
  implicitness, 28
  readability, 3
  repeating, 33
  spellcheck, 30

code (*continued*)
    table driven, 62
    templates, 32
    (see also source code)
cohesive classes, 70
    coupling, 70
collections, 67
com.samscdrental.configuration package
        source code, 203
com.samscdrental.controller package source
        code, 204
com.samscdrental.dataaccess package source
        code, 204
com.samscdrental.display package source
        code, 206
com.samscdrental.display.adt package source
        code, 205
com.samscdrental.failures package source
        code, 207
com.samscdrental.helper package source
        code, 208
com.samscdrental.importexport package
        source code, 208
com.samscdrental.migration package source
        code, 209
com.samscdrental.model package source
        code, 212
com.samscdrental.model.adt package source
        code, 209
com.samscdrental.model.dto package source
        code, 211
com.samscdrental.reports package source
        code, 213
com.samscdrental.tests package source
        code, 214
commands, 185
common coupling, classes, 70
communication, code and, 27–31
concept, 118
concerns, separation of, 86
configuration classes, 98
consistency in code, 31
constant values, 20
contains, 101
context, 4
conventions, deviations, 101
copying code, 32
could, 119
coupling classes
    association classes, 110
    unintended, 104
coupling cohesive classes, 70
CRC (Class-Responsibility-
        Collaboration), 48
CRC cards, 48

credit cards
    invoicing and, 145
    multiple vendors, 147
    processing, 145
    security, 152
    testing, 148
crosscutting concerns, 131
CSS (Cascading Style Sheets), indirection
        and, 135
currency flexibility, web sales and, 159
Customer class, Sam's system, 50, 88, 161
customer discounts, business rules and, 151
CustomerCollection class, Sam's system, 91

D

data
    loading current for migration, 91
    spreadsheets, 41–43
data types, 18
    enumerated, language dependent, 66
debugging, 99
declaration, execution and, 62
declarative-style programming, 62
delegation, inheritance alternative, 64
descriptions, ADT, 16
design, 46
    global planning, 51
    initial design, 48–50
    interface, catalog search, 117
    local design, 51
    software design principles, 201
design paralysis, 48
design patterns, definition, ix
deviations, 34, 37
diagrams, object state, 110
discounts, business rules and, 151
displaying reports, 90
documentation, 34
Dollar class, Sam's system, 17
DRY (Don't Repeat Yourself), 33

E

element, 29
elements, text, 29
email
    antispam case study, 175
    mail servers, 175
        ReceivingMailServer, 179–186
        state diagram, 178
    ReceivedMailExaminer, 186–191
    SMTP (Simple Mail Transfer
        Protocol), 176–178
    spam checking, 179
    user agent, 175
enumerated data types, language
        dependent, 66

EnvisionWare, printserver example, 164–173
error handling guidelines, 198
errors, 34
    failure distance, 36
    fatal errors, 35
    messages, 37
    nonfatal, 35
exceptions
    checked, 36
    recoverable, 37
    unchecked, 36
executable-style programming, 62
execution, declaration and, 62
expansion to multiple locations, 155–162
experience, 5
explicitness, code, 28
exporting reports, 142
extreme abstraction guidelines, 196
extreme readability guidelines, 197
extreme separation guidelines, 196

F

Factory pattern, indirection and, 132
failure distance, 36
fatal errors, 35
files, import errors, 102
flexibility in testing, 100
fractals, testing and, 54
frameworks, inheritance and, 77
functionality testing, 52–56
functions, overloading, 81

G

general guidelines, 198
general object guidelines, 199
global planning, 51
    incremental implementation and, 51
groups, 67
    collections, 67
guidelines, 3
    abstraction, 196
    alphabetical listing, 200
    big picture, 195
    error handling, 198
    extreme abstraction, 196
    extreme readability, 197
    extreme separation, 196
    general issues, 198
    general objects, 199
    interfaces, 198
    readability, 197
    security, 199
    separation, 196

H

has, 101
HTML (Hypertext Markup Language)
    reports and, 138

I

IDE (integrated development environment)
    interface implementation, 32
    working with, 43
ilities, 10
implementation, 97
    incremental, global plan and, 51
    interfaces and, 136
    methods, 80
implicitness, code, 28
importing files, errors, 102
incremental implementation, global plan
    and, 51
indirection, 132
    CSS and, 135
    Factory pattern and, 132
inheritance, 63–65
    CDRelease class, Sam's system, 64
    delegation as alternative, 64
    frameworks and, 77
    polymorphism and, 75
    switch statements and, 63
    unnecessary, 64
inheritance-oriented classes, hierarchy, 60
initial design, 48–50
    CRC cards, 48
interfaces, 24
    CDCatalogItemCollection, 119
    contracts, 24–26
    design, catalog search, 117
    development, catalog search, 119
    guidelines, 198
    implementation and, 136
    invoicing, 147
    operational interface, 97
    paradigm mismatch, 136
    polymorphism and, 75
    ReceivedMailExaminer, 187
    splitting, catalog search, 121
    testing, catalog search, 120
    web service, 158
    Zip Codes, 126
    ZipCodeVerificationService, 127
Invoice class, Sam's system, 146
invoicing, 145
    interfaces, 147
    privacy and, 152
    testing, 148
    unpaid, 146
is, 131

J

join points, AOP, 131

L

language, web sales and, 161
libraries, Zip Codes, 130
loading current data for migration, 91
local design, 51
logger library, Zip Codes, 130
logging
    printserver example, 171
    Zip Codes and, 135
loose coupling, classes, 70
lumpers and splitters, 13, 102

M

mail servers, 175
    ReceivingMailServer, 179
        command processing, 185
        MailDTO class, 183
        process method, 183
        Response class, 182
    state diagram, 178
MailDTO class, ReceivingMailServer, 183
MailExaminers, 188
MailReport, ReceivedMailExaminer, 188
meaningful names, 29
messages
    deviations, 37
    errors, 37
    printserver example, 165
method, 73
methods
    called methods, 25
    CDRelease class, Sam's system, 64
    implementation methods, 80
    names, 81
        overloading, 81
    objects and, 72
    policy methods, 80
    values, validation, 26
MFS (minimum feature set), 46
migration
    loading current data, 91
    planning, 92
    problem anticipation, 92
    uniqueness of data and, 93
misuse cases, 52
MM changes, 107
Model-View-Controller pattern, 86
Money class, Sam's system, 159
multiple locations, 155–162
MultipleRental class, Sam's system, 142

N

Name class, Sam's system, 18
names, 11–13
    lumpers, 13
    meaningful, 29
    Methods, 81
    methods, Overloading, 81
    splitters, 13
    system, 29
    values, 20
needs of client, 8
    use cases, 8–10
nonfatal errors, 35

O

objects
    groups, 67
    guidelines, 199
    methods and, 72
    polymorphism, 75
    state, 110
        binary, 111
        diagrams, 110
        multiple, 111
        switching, 113
    Three Laws of Objects, 71
occur, 101
of, 102
operation classes, 97
overloading functions, 81

P

payment, web sales and, 159
personal style, 4
pointcuts, AOP, 131
policy methods, 80
polymorphism, 75
    inheritance and, 75
    interfaces and, 75
practice, theory and, 103
preconditions, 25
prefactoring
    introduction, 1
    mentality, adopting, 103
prefactoring attitude, 32
principles of software design, 201
privacy, rental records and, 152
process
    analysis, 46
    analysis paralysis, 47
    design, 46
    design paralysis, 48
process method, ReceivingMailServer, 183
production, testing and, 99

project journal, retrospective and, 96
prototypes, 20
Proxy pattern, 79, 129

Q

quality testing, 56

R

readability guidelines, 197
readability of code, 3
ReceivedMailExaminer, 186
    interface alternatives, 187
    MailExaminers, 188
    MailReport, 188
    responsibility assignment, 187
ReceivingMailServer, 179
    command processing, 185
    MailDTO class, 183
    process method, 183
    Response class, 182
recoverable exceptions, 37
refactoring, definition, ix
reinvention avoidance, 11
Rental class, Sam's system, 70, 89
rental contract
    calculation, 87
    creating, 89
RentalContractDTO class, Sam's system, 88
RentalEvent class, Sam's system, 67
RentalHistory class, Sam's system, 67
RentalOperations class, Sam's system, 121
repeating code, 33
ReportPlainTextFormat class, Sam's
    system, 89
reports, 51, 137
    displaying, 90
    exports, 142
    HTML and, 138
    multiple, 139
    spreadsheet conundrum and, 138
    types, 138
requirements, MFS (minimum feature
    set), 46
Response class, ReceivingMailServer, 182
responsibility assignment,
    ReceivedMailExaminer, 187
results, spreadsheets, 41–43
retrospective, 96

S

Sam's system
    Address class, 15, 18, 126
    CDCatalogItem class, 119
    CDCatalogItemCollection interface, 119
    CDCatalogItemInfo class, 119
    CDCategory class, 66
    CDDisc class, 67, 70
    CDDiscCollection class, 68
    CDRelease class, 49, 51, 60, 61
        methods, 64
    Customer class, 50, 88, 161
    CustomerCollection class, 91
    Dollar class, 17
    Invoice class, 146
    Money class, 159
    MultipleRental class, 142
    Name class, 18
    Rental class, 70, 89
    RentalContractDTO class, 88
    RentalEvent class, 67
    RentalHistory, 67
    RentalOperations class, 121
    ReportPlainTextFormat class, 89
    Store class, 157
    StoreCollection class, 157
    StringHelper class, 74
    ZipCodeVerificationService interface, 127
    ZipCodeVerificationServiceFactory
        class, 132
    ZipCodeVerificationTracker class, 129
searches, catalog search
    interface design, 117
    interface development, 119
    interface splitting, 121
    interface testing, 120
    limit setting, 123
searches, catalog search use case, 115
security, 57
    credit cards, 152
    guidelines, 199
separation guidelines, 196
separation of concerns, 2, 86
separation, printserver example, 172
SMTP (Simple Mail Transfer Protocol), 176–
    178
software design principles, 201
source code
    com.samscdrental.configuration
        package, 203
    com.samscdrental.controller package, 204
    com.samscdrental.dataaccess
        package, 204
    com.samscdrental.display package, 206
    com.samscdrental.display.adt
        package, 205
    com.samscdrental.failures package, 207
    com.samscdrental.helper package, 208
    com.samscdrental.importexport
        package, 208
    com.samscdrental.migration package, 209

source code (*continued*)
    com.samscdrental.model package, 212
    com.samscdrental.model.adt
      package, 209
    com.samscdrental.model.dto
      package, 211
    com.samscdrental.reports package, 213
    com.samscdrental.tests package, 214
spam checking, email, 179
specific jobs, 78
speed, problems with, 39
spellchecking code, 30
splitters and lumpers, 13, 102
splitting interface, catalog search, 121
spreadsheet conundrum, reports and, 138
spreadsheets, 41–43
SQL (Structured Query Language),
    injection, 26
state diagram, mail server, 178
state, objects, 110
    binary, 111
    diagrams, 110
    multiple, 111
    switching, 113
Store class, Sam's system, 157
StoreCollection class, Sam's system, 157
StringHelper class, Sam's system, 74
strings, 18
switch statements, inheritance and, 63
symbolic names, values, 20

T

table-driven code, 62
templates, code, 32
testing
    CDCatalogItemCollection interface, 120
    credit cards, 148
    feedback, 55
    flexibility and, 100
    fractals and, 54
    functionality, 52–56
    interfaces, catalog search and, 120
    invoicing, 148
    library example, 54
    printserver example, 170
    production and, 99
    quality, 56
    strategy development, 55

text, 65
    elements, 29
the, 98
theory, practice and, 103
Three Laws of Objects, 71
tight coupling, classes, 70
tools
    IDEs, 43
    multiple, 44

U

UML (Unified Modeling Language),
    diagram, 48
unchecked exceptions, 36
uniqueness, data and, 93
unpaid invoices, 146
UpdateData( ) method (MFC library), 29
use cases, 8–10
    abstractions, 45
    catalog search, 115
    misuse cases, 52
user agent, email, 175

V

validation, 26
    values, 26
values
    constant, 20
    names, symbolic, 20
    validation, 26
verification, Zip Code, 129

W

web interface, 157
    currency, 159
    language, 161

Z

Zip Code verification, 125
    third-party provider, 129
ZipCodeVerificationService interface, Sam's
    system, 127
ZipCodeVerificationServiceFactory class,
    Sam's system, 132
ZipCodeVerificationTracker class, Sam's
    system, 129

ABOUT THE AUTHOR

KEN PUGH has extensive experience in the area of software analysis and design. He has worked on systems ranging from goat serum process control to financial analysis to noise recording to satellite tracking. His previous books were on C and Unix, and he is a former columnist for the *C/C++ Users Journal*. He has taught programming courses for Wellesley College and the University of Hawaii, as well as numerous corporate courses, and he frequently presents at national conferences. As an independent consultant for over 20 years, he has served clients from London to Sydney. As an expert witness, he has provided testimony in both civil suits and criminal cases.

When not computing, he enjoys snowboarding, windsurfing, biking, and hiking the Appalachian Trail.

COLOPHON

OUR LOOK IS THE RESULT of reader comments, our own experimentation, and feedback from distribution channels. Distinctive covers complement our distinctive approach to technical topics, breathing personality and life into potentially dry subjects.

Sarah Sherman was the production editor and proofreader, and Audrey Doyle was the copyeditor for *Prefactoring*. Mary Anne Weeks Mayo and Claire Cloutier provided quality control. Lydia Onofrei provided production assistance. Johnna VanHoose Dinse wrote the index.

MendeDesign designed and created the cover artwork of this book. Karen Montgomery produced the cover layout with Adobe InDesign CS using the Akzidenz Grotesk and Orator fonts.

Marcia Friedman designed the interior layout. Melanie Wang designed the template; Phyllis McKee adapted the template. The book was converted by Keith Fahlgren to FrameMaker 5.5.6 with a format conversion tool created by Erik Ray, Jason McIntosh, Neil Walls, and Mike Sierra that uses Perl and XML technologies. The text font is Adobe's Meridien; the heading font is ITC Bailey. The illustrations that appear in the book were produced by Robert Romano, Jessamyn Read, and Lesley Borash using Macromedia FreeHand MX and Adobe Photoshop CS.

Better than e-books

Buy *Prefactoring* and access the digital
edition FREE on Safari for 45 days.

Go to www.oreilly.com/go/safarienabled
and type in coupon code 6IJI-FZNK-WH51-FLKQ-DQJJ

Search
thousands of
top tech books

Download
whole chapters

Cut and Paste
code examples

Find
answers fast

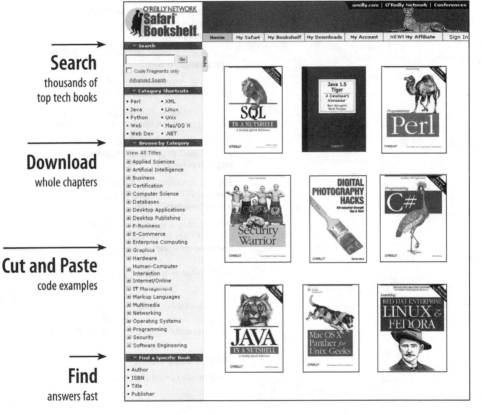

Search Safari! The premier electronic reference
library for programmers and IT professionals.

Keep in touch with O'Reilly

Download examples from our books

To find example files from a book, go to: *www.oreilly.com/catalog* select the book, and follow the "Examples" link.

Register your O'Reilly books

Register your book at *register.oreilly.com* Why register your books? Once you've registered your O'Reilly books you can:

- Win O'Reilly books, T-shirts or discount coupons in our monthly drawing.
- Get special offers available only to registered O'Reilly customers.
- Get catalogs announcing new books (US and UK only).
- Get email notification of new editions of the O'Reilly books you own.

Join our email lists

Sign up to get topic-specific email announcements of new books and conferences, special offers, and O'Reilly Network technology newsletters at:

elists.oreilly.com

It's easy to customize your free elists subscription so you'll get exactly the O'Reilly news you want.

Get the latest news, tips, and tools

www.oreilly.com

- "Top 100 Sites on the Web"—PC Magazine
- CIO Magazine's Web Business 50 Awards

Our web site contains a library of comprehensive product information (including book excerpts and tables of contents), downloadable software, background articles, interviews with technology leaders, links to relevant sites, book cover art, and more.

Work for O'Reilly

Check out our web site for current employment opportunities:

jobs.oreilly.com

Contact us

O'Reilly Media, Inc.
1005 Gravenstein Hwy North
Sebastopol, CA 95472 USA
Tel: 707-827-7000 or 800-998-9938
    (6am to 5pm PST)
Fax: 707-829-0104

Contact us by email

For answers to problems regarding your order or our products:
order@oreilly.com

To request a copy of our latest catalog:
catalog@oreilly.com

For book content technical questions or corrections: **booktech@oreilly.com**

For educational, library, government, and corporate sales: **corporate@oreilly.com**

To submit new book proposals to our editors and product managers:
proposals@oreilly.com

For information about our international distributors or translation queries:
international@oreilly.com

For information about academic use of O'Reilly books:
adoption@oreilly.com
or visit:
academic.oreilly.com

For a list of our distributors outside of North America check out:
international.oreilly.com/distributors.html

Order a book online

www.oreilly.com/order_new

Our books are available at most retail and online bookstores.
To order direct: 1-800-998-9938 • *order@oreilly.com* • *www.oreilly.com*
Online editions of most O'Reilly titles are available by subscription at *safari.oreilly.com*